Welty
A Life in Literature

Welty
A Life in Literature

Edited by
Albert J. Devlin

UNIVERSITY PRESS OF MISSISSIPPI
Jackson & London

IN MEMORIAM
Peyton Williams,
1916–1987

The paper in this book meets the guideline for permanence and durability of the Committee on Production Guidelines for Book Longevity of the Council on Library Resources.

Photographs on pages 180–82 courtesy of Mississippi Department of Archives and History, Eudora Welty Collection

Library of Congress Cataloging-in-Publication Data

Welty : a life in literature.

   Bibliography: p.
   Includes index.
   1. Welty, Eudora, 1909–   —Criticism and interpretation.   I. Devlin, Albert J.
PS3545.E6Z94   1988   813′.52   87-14267
ISBN 0-87805-315-8 (alk. paper)

Contents

Introduction

Our intention in presenting this collection to Eudora Welty is to mark the fiftieth anniversary of her first publication, "Death of a Traveling Salesman" (1936), and to celebrate her distinguished achievement of five decades in American letters.

Several years ago, Miss Welty recalled the occasion of her "first appearance in print." (See the *Georgia Review*, Winter 1979.) Her friend Hubert Creekmore had identified *Manuscript* as a "little" magazine to which Welty might submit "Death of a Traveling Salesman"—her "first submitted story anywhere." Probably Creekmore knew that John Rood and Mary Lawhead, the editors of *Manuscript* in Athens, Ohio, were especially regardful of new, young, and relatively unknown writers. In any event, Eudora Welty has suppressed, with characteristic modesty, the high enthusiasm that marked the editorial letter of acceptance. On March 19, 1936, John Rood and his wife Mary Lawhead wrote to thank Eudora Welty for "one of the best stories that has come to our attention," and to recognize "a new author who shows a great deal more than promise." "Everything else read like nothing on earth," Mary Lawhead concluded, after reading of Welty's impoverished hill folk and their troubled visitor—R. J. Bowman. The editors would break normal publishing sequence and make an immediate place for "Death of a Traveling Salesman" in the June number of *Manuscript*. Their sense of urgency, however, was no greater than Harold Strauss's. He had read "Death of a Traveling

Salesman" in manuscript form and wrote on May 13, 1936, on behalf of Covici Publishers, to assure Welty of its breadth and dimension: her first published story "seemed to contain within it the seeds of a broad social perspective."

Nearly forty years later, Eudora Welty seemed to recognize the flowering of that image. Of her many awards, she has particular regard for the Gold Medal for Fiction (1972). "It was for a body of work," rather than for "some one effort," she notes of her recognition by the National Institute of Arts and Letters. It is precisely the magnitude and authority of this life in literature that we celebrate and, at least implicitly, advance as an exemplum for all writers. In very few recent American writers have talent, intensity, and temperament found the same productive relation. The first readers of "Death of a Traveling Salesman" sensed, I think, how full and abiding Eudora Welty's career would be, and thus anticipated the many audiences that she would delight. They anticipated the recognition that her peers would soon confer. Perhaps no group so talented and diverse as Robert Penn Warren, Katherine Anne Porter, and Elizabeth Bowen could be expected to reach consensus, save in admiring their colleague from Jackson, Mississippi. She too (in her own words) was "a serious writer," who "wanted from the first to be a professional." Welty's first readers also anticipated the several generations of student readers and all the paraphernalia of anthologies, assignments, and formal explication. More than a few of these young readers have put down "Powerhouse," or "Livvie," or more probably "A Worn Path," the most frequently anthologized of Welty's stories, and felt something akin to Mary Lawhead's surprise: "Everything else read like nothing on earth." Finally, in their most impressive reach of imagination, Welty's first readers may have anticipated the success of *One Writer's Beginnings*. Published in 1984 by Harvard University Press, Welty's memoir—delivered as the Massey Lectures in the History of American Civilization—found an audience as broad and democratic as her patiently elaborated vision. These readers understood that in defining the artistic vocation, Eudora Welty had placed its rigor and responsibility, and surely its origins as well, deeply within the human family of shared aspirations. Although diverse in taste and temperament, these audiences are one, and they include the critics, scholars, and bibliographers who have contributed to the present volume.

The essays in *Welty: A Life in Literature* practice a variety of methods, but their authors are bound together, and to Welty's earlier readers as well, by the pleasure that her writing has afforded them all. When told of this solidarity by the editor, Miss Welty replied in firm measure and cadence: "I'm glad to hear that word, 'pleasure.'" To those who know and deeply value her achievement, no other response could be expected of a writer who loves her readers at least as much as they love her—although the relationship is not without its perils—and no critical or scholarly study of Welty could long sustain itself if its strategies, methodologies, maneuvers did not admit the radiance of her writing and the pleasure that it affords.

The following essays do not mark each title in Welty's extensive list—now nearly a dozen volumes of fiction, criticism, photography, and personal reflection. Time and circumstance work to draw attention to one text rather than another, to identify those concerns, problems, or interests that characterize readers of the present moment. The better editorial practice, I think, is to represent these attachments, for they may help to show what is most vital in Welty's work. In the following essays—composed, with two exceptions, for this collection—formal and mythic criticism continues to offer fresh access to *A Curtain of Green*, *The Wide Net*, and *Delta Wedding*. Bibliographical study shows Eudora Welty to be keenly attuned to the nuances of meaning as she revises *The Optimist's Daughter*, deepening, clarifying, making more precise a novel of inestimable personal feeling. Welty's close attention to the world, to her wholly unavoidable sources, is studied in relation to an early story, "At The

Landing," to the remarkable photography of *One Time, One Place*, and to her recent memoir, *One Writer's Beginnings*. The same work promotes study of Eudora Welty in relation to Elizabeth Bowen, the Anglo-Irish writer who remains formative for Welty. Reader-response, feminist criticism—with emphasis upon *The Golden Apples*—and philosophic inquiry into Welty's modernity help to bring her work into firmer and more systematic contact with contemporary critical theory. An essay of personal reminiscence by Ruth Vande Kieft—with a forceful aside to Welty's critics—places Welty and her texts in nearly seamless relation. The checklists of Noel Polk (reprinted from the *Mississippi Quarterly*, Fall 1973) and Pearl McHaney are comprehensive in listing primary Welty materials. They offer as well a selective guide to Welty criticism and scholarship from the beginnings through 1986. The editor is particularly grateful for the efforts of Noel Polk and Pearl McHaney in support of this volume.

Many require thanks for their help in preparing this collection. No one, though, was more supportive than Peyton Williams, Jr., editor of the *Mississippi Quarterly*, where these essays first appeared (Fall 1986) in a special Welty issue. He gave advice and assistance that was always wise and timely. His death on April 16, 1987, is the sad occasion for the dedication of this volume. The contributors have all been generous of their time and talents: their time in answering correspondence, meeting deadlines, and attending to all of the details of publication; their talents in honestly engaging the work of Eudora Welty. Professor Timothy Materer, chair of English at the University of Missouri, has been supportive throughout the project, as has Professor Haskell Hinnant, interim chair. Mary Weaks, my research assistant at UMC, has performed many unsung tasks. I wish to thank her for this as well as for past assistance.

Seetha Srinivasan and Hunter Cole of the University Press of Mississippi generously assisted in arranging the Welty interview conducted on September 22, 1986. For Peggy Prenshaw and for me, this was a rare afternoon, and we thank Miss Welty for receiving us. The atmosphere of her home confirms the humane and unpretentious tone of her fiction. There is, of course, no adequate way of thanking Eudora Welty for her calm and sustained life in literature—except, perhaps, by taking on the dignity that she has ascribed to all of us.

Albert J. Devlin
Columbia, Missouri
May 1, 1987

ALBERT J. DEVLIN

AND

PEGGY WHITMAN PRENSHAW

A Conversation with Eudora Welty

Jackson, Mississippi, 22 September 1986

AJD: Peggy and I want to start by thanking you for what is obviously a kind gesture. We're very appreciative.

EW: Well, thank you. I'm honored by the issue you're getting out. I just didn't know how I could help. You said earlier that you were pleased with the contributions.

AJD: Very much so. They're intense and varied, I think, and yet they have a point where they all meet. It's the evidence of the great pleasure the contributors take in your writing.

EW: I'm glad to hear that word, "pleasure."

AJD: Pleasure just shines through. Some of the essays are rather closely argued, and perhaps at times we try to say highfalutin things, but there's a deep pleasure, so strongly felt, in all of them.

EW: That's very reassuring.

AJD: I wanted to tell you that.

EW: I'm glad you did at this point, too, because it makes me feel more comfortable. [laughter]

AJD: Miss Welty, this interview was a wonderful excuse for me to reread several authors and stories that I know you love, and which I do too. In reading I found myself very much aware of your presence, both in my mind and in the text too, it seemed. It was a comforting and yet challenging presence.

EW: What stories were you reading?

3

AJD: Oh, I was reading, for example, Katherine Mansfield's "Prelude," and *To the Lighthouse*.

EW: You felt my presence? That's extraordinary. That's wonderful of you to say. Do you mean, you could understand how I responded to them?

AJD: Not only how you responded, I felt your values and your perceptions, and your authority as well. Perhaps that's how real literary community is founded or formed today. Individuals meeting in texts like that.

EW: You remember what Henry Green said—I know it, I've quoted it myself—about prose. "Prose is a long—

AJD: "—intimacy"

EW: "—intimacy between strangers. It uses terms that neither knows." I would like to quote it exactly, but that's the sort of thing you were saying. That it's a connection, a communication that doesn't depend on knowing the same people or speaking the same idiom or anything like that. I was thrilled when I read that passage. It's like what you're saying, only I didn't at first recognize how it was meant.

PWP: In writing an essay for this issue, on *One Writer's Beginnings* and Elizabeth Bowen's *Seven Winters and Afterthoughts* and *Pictures and Conversations*, I also read *Collected Impressions* and *Bowen's Court*. As I read, I saw much in Bowen of what I felt would have appealed to you, would have excited you, especially the wonderful visual, material quality.

EW: She was a marvelous lady, a responsive person, you know, to mood and place, and she was so happy, so delighted by things in life. And very apprehensive too. It was an Irishness, a sense of your surroundings, very sensitive to what you can feel all the time.

PWP: You met her first in Ireland or in England?

EW: I met her in Ireland first. At Bowen's Court.

PWP: What was Bowen's Court like? What was it like to visit there?

EW: I met Elizabeth during my first trip to Europe, which was Holy Year, as I remember. I sailed late in the fall of 1949. This was on a Guggenheim and I was trying to make it last. I was in France and Italy for much of the time, but I decided I *had* to go and see England and Ireland. I had always wanted to see Ireland, though I didn't know anyone there. I went over on the ferry, first to Dun Laoghaire, and then I just walked around Dublin, looking at all the places I'd read about. It was just heavenly. I'd go out in the country and walk on these little roads and get under the hedge when it rained. I just wanted to see it for myself, just to be there. I loved Dublin. And then I thought—someone had told me in Paris that they'd seen Elizabeth Bowen at a party and Elizabeth had said something about my work. She was reviewing then a lot. And so whoever it was told her that I had been in Paris lately, and she said, "Oh, I wish I had met her." Well, I had never in my life looked up anybody that I didn't know. But it kept tempting me, like a fantasy almost. I thought that Bowen's Court was in Dublin; I didn't know it was a long way off. I wrote Elizabeth a note and told her that if it were possible, I would like to pay a call on her during the next week or so. And then she telephoned me at my hotel and told me that she was in County Cork and for me to come down that weekend. This turned out to be very typical of her. So I went down and she had me met in a car at Cork and we drove to Bowen's Court. It was my first sight of the South of Ireland, the real South. Later on I saw that still further south there were palm trees and fuchsia hedges and pink and blue plastered houses that made you think of Savannah or New Orleans. It's almost tropical. At any rate, Elizabeth is a *Southerner.* She said that wherever she went, in the whole world almost, the Southerners were always different from the Northerners. She always felt the congeniality.

PWP: She had lived in Ireland when she was young, but she left when her father was so ill.

EW: Those were the "seven winters" of her book. Then she went to school in England. When I saw Bowen's Court, she had moved back into it, and as she could, she was restoring all of the rooms. Some were partly done and some were not. I had this wonderful room, it was on the second floor. You know what the house looked like—huge, stone, three story, perfectly straightforward.

PWP: Utterly rectangular and balanced on either side.

EW: Yes, Georgian, with a porch and steps out front where everyone sat in the summer afternoons. As far as you could see was the demesne. And a group of elms out there on the lawn. Elizabeth said that when she was growing up, they used to call this the lamb's drawing room, because the little lambs would come there and browse in the afternoon.

PWP: Isn't that the setting she uses in *Last September?*

EW: Yes, she does. It was so lovely to be in that house, and I immediately fell into the way things were done. Elizabeth worked in the morning, which is what I like to do, and at about eleven o'clock you could come downstairs if you wanted to and have a sherry, and then go back to work. Then you met at lunch, I mean to talk, and the whole afternoon was spent riding around, and the long twilights coming back. There was usually company at dinner time. And evenings, just a few people, or maybe more, easy and—We liked to play games. Eddy Sackville-West was visiting her once when I was there and we all played "Happy Families," a children's card game—it's just like "Going Fishing" where you try to get all of a family in your hand by asking, "May I have?" except that it's done with Victorian decorum. The cards are designed with Dickens-like illustrations and names like Mr. Bones, the butcher, and Mrs. Bones, the butcher's wife, and Miss Bones, the butcher's daughter, and Master Bones, the butcher's boy, all with huge heads and little bodies. What you do is say, "May I have Mrs. Bones, the butcher's wife?" and I say, "*Sorry*, she isn't at home." So you've missed your turn. There are more thanks and a whole lot of politeness. [laughter] I would get the giggles to see Elizabeth and Eddy being so unfailingly *courteous* to each other. So we'd sit around the fire in the evenings, drinking whiskey and playing "Happy Families."

PWP: I read several times Bowen's "Notes on Writing a Novel," and it struck me that there's a certain sympathy between her views and some of the things that you've done and talked about, for example, place in fiction.

EW: I learned from her. I think she had the best analytical mind of a writer, about writing, that I've ever come across. She had a marvelous mind, you know, all aside from imagination and the sensibilities you need to write fiction. I know they felt that in Oxford, where she and her husband lived for a time. She was such marvelous company in the evening for these Oxford people. She was not in the *least* academic, but their minds could play together.

AJD: I'm sure you remember the fine introduction that she wrote for the Vintage collection [1956] of Katherine Mansfield's stories.

EW: Oh, yes, and it was so needed, wasn't it? Katherine Mansfield was going unappreciated.

AJD: One passage in particular reveals that "marvelous mind" for me. Bowen writes of Katherine Mansfield reaching her maturity as a writer shortly before her death. She goes on to say that "it is with maturity that the really searching ordeal of the writer begins. Maturity, remember, must last a long time—" Isn't that wonderful?

EW: That's marvelous. No escaping it once you've got it.

AJD: "—and it must not be confused with single perfec-

> tions, such as she had accomplished without yet
> having solved her abiding problems."

EW: Isn't that marvelous? It's just the very seed of things,
      isn't it? The very core.

AJD: So often, I think, your own criticism works on much
      the same high level of perception. I especially admire
      the Cather and Porter essays—they're extraordinary,
      and they certainly belie for me the overly modest
      statements that you've made at times about your
      criticism.

EW: I'm glad to hear you say it, but if you think so, the
      reason is that I won't even try something about
      which I don't feel a great empathy. I turn down so
      many things because I can't feel close to them.

AJD: Well, isn't that a good lesson in itself for critics?

EW: It's the only way I feel halfway equipped. I *can't*—
      I'm not much good at destructive things. One person
      I tried to destroy once. But the thing that you feel
      you love about your work is overpowering, and that's
      what teaches you, I mean me, that's the way I learn.
      It's my ability, imagined ability maybe, to enter in
      by imagination. I find criticism very, very hard to
      do.

AJD: I know that you find it hard to think about your own
      work.

EW: I don't think of it analytically. I can't because the
      process of writing a story is different, taking the
      opposite direction.

AJD: I'm fascinated by what seems to happen to your
      work in *Delta Wedding*. For me it's your most valuable
      book.

EW: I wonder why—I mean in my case—if that's true.

AJD: I sensed that you had addressed those "abiding prob-
      lems" that Bowen mentions, whatever they may be,
      and in a very decisive way.

EW: I would have been lucky if I had, because the way I
      happened to write *Delta Wedding* was almost acciden-
      tal. I was writing short stories, and I sent the story

"Delta Cousins" to Diarmuid Russell, my agent, who was very astute. He read it and said this is chapter 2 of a novel. It challenged me when he said that, and then I had a good friend, John Robinson— this was war time, you know—who was in the Air Force overseas. He came from the Delta and had introduced me to it. So as I wrote *Delta Wedding*, I sent it to him chapter by chapter. I just made it up as I went; part of it was to entertain him, and part of it was to try to do something Diarmuid thought I could do. [laughter] It was the most ill-planned or unplanned of books. I was just writing about what a family is like, trying to put them down in a place where they could just spread themselves—that's also why I set *Delta Wedding* in that special time the twenties. It's what I've always done, I guess, the whole time.

PWP: I don't think I've ever heard you read from *Delta Wedding*.

EW: I haven't ever read from the novels—this is reading for a living, I mean. This means reading short stories, of which there is just a handful that I can use.

AJD: What strikes me about *Delta Wedding*, Miss Welty, is that in Ellen Fairchild you discovered or shaped someone who is unlike any character in your earlier stories.

EW: That's certainly true.

AJD: She's a richly imaginative character and she's in part at least the outsider.

EW: That's true. I think that was probably my first conception of that figure in my work, when you come to think of it. I realize I have used outsiders in fiction from time to time since; it gives you a point of view, a place to walk in. It gives you the outside view of what you're writing about. And I have to have that.

AJD: There's a wonderful moment at the dance—after the wedding which takes place in about a line—when Ellen sees each of her children individually, and then sees them together, inseparable, "in a turn" of India's skirt. Ellen's imagination seems to be bringing together powerful forces in your world. It's a thrilling moment, and it seems unlike earlier ones in your fiction.

EW: I'm glad I did that, I'm glad I could. And I thank you for telling me this. You know what you try to do, but not what you—

AJD: Was Ellen Fairchild a difficult character to show?

EW: She was easy, in fact she was the only one. I was writing about people I didn't know, I didn't know Delta people, only the surrounding of this one family. But I'd been up there sometimes—this was in the old days with cotton and all that when the Delta really was a different world—I'd been up there to visit this friend's family, while he was away. They had lots of old diaries that they let me read, which gave me a feeling of the background of the Delta. You know what a *short* history it's had. It was the wilderness till just about yesterday. And I hadn't realized any of these things. When I wrote the story "Delta Cousins," it was what I had gathered over the years about the kind of mood that abided there and the kind of people that made the Delta families. But I had to have a character that was not of the Delta, that I could kind of latch onto. It was Ellen showing *me*. That's my feeling about her, as I say. I used several outsiders, young ones, and in a way the hero's an outsider, George. But I didn't reduce them, I didn't call them outsiders or anything like that.

AJD: They certainly weren't outside your novel.

EW: No, but you have to compose the inside out of all that world's different colors and moods and varieties of viewpoint. I loved writing about all those children.

AJD: I thought you did. The games you gave them were so boisterous.

PWP: And that novel is so full of voices, but it also has the poetical and mystical side. I guess that all of the family, except for Ellen, are the busy talkers. She brings the reflective and meditative side.

EW: The only one that does. I loved the names I got for the people too. Some of them I had heard but my characters weren't at all like the people. I loved India—that's a Southern thing to give people such exotic names.

PWP: I have a cousin named China.

EW: Exactly. I knew a girl named India, a lady named India. But of course, not this girl. And I like Bluet; I knew a girl named Bluet one time. And a Battle. They all seemed to me very Delta names. Do you think so?

PWP: Oh, I think so.

EW: That was so much fun, you know, finding the thing that you needed to help you along. I was happy about the names.

PWP: The first time I saw any of the typescripts, when they became available at the archives in Jackson, it was exciting to discover that you had changed the names of characters sometimes.

EW: When I first began writing I didn't realize the importance of names. I would just name characters anything. And then I realized how much it mattered, for cadence, and, for example, how families name their children in a kind of pattern, you know, everybody's name beginning with a B.

PWP: By the alphabet.

EW: Well, you've got to get people to sound like brothers and sisters. The same parents. By the way, there are *still* wonderful names to be found in the Mississippi newspapers. The other day I was reading in the *Jackson Daily News* the list of people arrested for drunk driving. There was this man whose name was Quovadis something. "Quovadis, whither goest thou?" [laughter] It's just wonderful. They'd once heard of somebody else named Quovadis, I'm sure.

It surfaces from no telling what kind of history.

PWP: I wanted to ask about your visit to Cambridge, when you gave the "Place in Fiction" lecture.

EW: Can you imagine?

PWP: Well, yes. It's an extraordinary essay and many readers like me have certainly learned from it.

EW: I worked a year on that. It was three lectures to begin with, I combined them to make the published essay. I think it was the first time I'd been invited to lecture anywhere. How could I turn down a free trip to England, with a year to work on it? Did either of you ever take part in one of those exchanges? They brought American teachers over to talk to British teachers of American subjects. The six-week session was held in the University, though the University didn't do anything but provide a place and entertainment. Cambridge was a lovely host. I was the only one who was not a teacher. No, Jack Fisher, who was editor of *Harper's*, also went. This was the year of the McCarthy hearings and the first question any Britisher asked the lecturer, no matter what your subject, was "What do you think about McCarthy?" The University program lasted five years. I was the first woman invited. And I was the first woman ever to cross the threshold into the hall at Peterhouse College, where they had a special dinner. Women weren't allowed there. They were so dear the way they told me: they said, "Miss Welty, you are invited to come to this, but we must tell you that we debated for a long time about whether or not we should ask you. No woman has ever crossed the threshold, including Queen Victoria, who *demanded* to and was refused." And I thought, well now, what would be the correct thing for me to do, they having given me this leave? And then I thought, I'm going to do it. They've already decided that I can, and I think to back out would sort of demean the *greatness*, the *momentousness*, of this invitation. Besides, I was curious.

AJD: Isn't it interesting that Cambridge intellectual life, which in large part officially excluded Virginia Woolf, is now so often remembered by us through her reflections?

EW: Absolutely. Just extraordinary. Forster was still alive at the time, by the way, when I was over there, living in Kings College, and he invited me to lunch. He was writing *Marianne Thornton*. I love that book. And Dadie Rylands was still alive. All these people that show up in Woolf's diary.

PWP: You have spoken of Katherine Anne Porter as having a gift for—or of valuing the gift of—making people feel at ease. Elizabeth Bowen and you, too, in spite of having a writer's solitary life, have spent much of yourself with people.

EW: I enjoy people, and I think there's a great difference in that respect between Katherine Anne and Elizabeth. Katherine Anne might enjoy having a circle around her, but there she really remained within herself. Elizabeth was the opposite; she was an intaker. She just took everything in. She was curious and fascinated by most people she met, and she really wanted to know. She had a wonderful curiosity, too, but it was more outgoing. She was very sharply aware and very cognizant of what was going on. She quickly got the feel in a room. She could come in and she would know that there may have been two people at odds just about ten minutes before—she could get the feel of everything. And she was always in command. That sounds as if she were authoritative. I mean, she was in command of herself. She had the best time; she loved gaiety and dancing and she loved a party. Loved to give one. She loved to go to the movies. Over and over and over. She thought that the cinema and fiction were much alike, which was instructive to me. I think that's true, too, don't you? I went with her one time in New York to see *Breathless*. She just loved that movie. I went with her and Howard Moss. Elizabeth had already seen it, of course, several times. She could drop off to sleep in the movies, as she often did, and wake up and point, "That's his brother." Howard said, "Elizabeth is *wired* to the screen." [laughter] Not much escaped her that was going on, even while she was asleep. She traveled a great deal, she knew this country well. She's been here three or four times, I guess. She liked being in the South. I always enjoyed coming together.

PWP: I have heard a friend mention that you and Elizabeth made a trip to Longwood and saw a ghost.

EW: We did see a ghost. I found this out weeks later, after I was back in Jackson. And Elizabeth was a little disconcerted because she believed in ghosts, but never had seen one. Do you want me to tell you? Well, this was not the tourist season in Natchez. I wouldn't have taken her down there then. This was right around Hallowe'en. I remember a huge moon came up and Elizabeth said, "That's the biggest moon I ever saw in my life." I took her to see Longwood because I thought that would amuse her. We got out of the car on a Sunday morning and walked up through the woods. I knew she loved strange houses, I knew she'd be fascinated by it. We were walking around it and this man came out of the woods from beyond and said, "Would you like to see the house? I can take you over it if you'd like to," and Elizabeth said, "Very much." So we went in the house and he said, "Would you care for a drink?" [laughter] It was about ten o'clock Sunday morning and we said "Thanks, no, not now." So he took us all over the house—a very garrulous old man. He explained that the reason he knew the house so well was that he had lived in it as a caretaker for all these years. After I got back to Jackson, I was talking to a friend about seeing Longwood and I said, "The caretaker took us over." She said, "Oh, he couldn't have, he was killed in an automobile accident about three months ago." Some months ago. She said he was driving down that little winding road that runs to Longwood and was hit by something coming the other way, and killed, and that now there was nobody in the house. There *was* somebody at the house.

PWP: Do you take it to have been a ghost?

EW: I don't know. I told Elizabeth it was due to her—she didn't too much like that.

AJD: I know that you've tried your hand at one ghost story ["The Purple Hat"], and maybe others would qualify too. It is hard, do you think, for a writer to get the supernatural into a story?

EW: I don't think it would be hard to get it in. It's probably harder to employ it correctly so that the reader will accept the thing. I have a very strong feeling about there being something—I don't mean ghosts or bogeymen, not that kind of thing, but the sense of a personality. I think those things can hang about a house, for instance. I don't see any reason not to think so if you should feel that. It doesn't bother me, that is.

AJD: Can you help me with a passage in *Losing Battles?*

EW: If I can.

AJD: It's that meditation of Vaughn's.

EW: The one time I get into somebody's mind.

AJD: He seems perplexed throughout that passage, and then Granny's invitation seals his perplexity and sends him to the barn. I'm not sure how to understand, or how to react to, the nature or cosmos of that passage. Vaughn is listening with ears that "stick out like funnels"—I think that's your image—but is it the intention of that nature to speak to him? Is it a nature that wants to communicate itself?

EW: I don't know, but I think it's his nature to want to. He thinks there's something else besides the voices he's heard all day. He feels that everything may have a voice. But he's *in* the world, he's in this strange, blue-lit night, and he feels—what I was trying to say—that there's so much more than what he's been listening to all day. I don't know whether I conveyed that. He is the introspective one; he's questioned so many things that the others don't, and he's also young enough not yet to have got that armor over him. I think I just tried to express an awareness that there was something over and beyond the circle of the family that was still capable of being understood. It was just my one chance—I never meant to have anybody at the reunion betray introspection all the way through. I wanted to show everything by action and speech, but when I got to that part, and when it was night and everything had been so strained, I succumbed.

PWP: Vaughn was the perfect one to choose.

EW: The only one.

AJD: Miss Welty, do you by any chance remember Virginia Woolf's little essay, "On Being Ill"?

EW: I'm trying to think—I haven't read it recently.

AJD: She describes illness as a time of reflection when we become "irresponsible and disinterested" in our ordinary lives, and can see, "perhaps for the first time for years," the extraordinary performance of the sky—its "endless activity" and plunging experiments with color. And then she goes on to say, "Divinely beautiful it is also divinely heartless. Immeasurable resources are used for some purpose which has nothing to do with human pleasure or human profit." Does this help to explain Vaughn's perplexity and the apparent distance between him and the marvelous performance of the sky? You say he could neither "stop" nor "out-ride" the great "wheel of the sky."

EW: I don't think so. I think he feels very close to what's going on. He sees the acrobatics of the falling star, like the feats he's been hearing about all day. No, I think he is a little frightened, but I think he accepts all that just the way he's accepted everything he's heard all day. I mean, it's all part of the world and part of life, part of living. I know he had no philosophical attitude. When Virginia Woolf wrote that essay she may have been going through strange phases—you know, when the birds spoke Greek, and the world was very much apart from her in her illness. Maybe there were different phases and stages of that feeling that she had, which would be likely with such a consciously learning mind. But, of course, Vaughn didn't have anything like that, just the sensitivity.

PWP: That moment for Vaughn is the same sort of experience, a moment of deepening insight, that Laura has in *Delta Wedding* at the conclusion.

EW: They're probably all about nine years old.

PWP: I think that's a special age, about nine years old, just coming out of childhood. There are those beginning sparks.

EW: I think so too. I thought so at the time, didn't you, that nine was wonderful. I used to write N-I-N-E, nine, nine, nine, all the time, as if it were something magical.

PWP: I was always so eager to be a little older. I was always short a year or two, I thought, of happiness—if I could only be eleven, when I was nine.

EW: That's right, you're always reaching ahead—"In two years I'll be a teenager." [laughter] That's a very frightening statement.

PWP: Recently, I had occasion to reread some historical romances that I had loved when I was about eleven or twelve years old. Also, I was reading Elizabeth Bowen's *Collected Impressions*, anticipating our conversation today. She's quite stern in her view that one should never go back and read the books one has read as a child. She talks about Dickens, saying she could never go back and read Dickens, that he was "used up" for her.

EW: I heard her talking about Dickens here in this room. It was the time she met my mother. They had Dickens in common because they both loved reading him in childhood. I had to confess that when I was little I was so perverse that when my mother said you have to read Dickens—"I read Dickens when I was your age"—I wouldn't read him. I said I guess I'll have to go on and do it, and both of them said it's too late. [laughter] It's too late now. You have to read Dickens when you're very young, they agreed on that. That's when he's a master. Elizabeth thinks that he's a wonderful writer, but that the time when he really breathes something in you that you never forget is when you're young.

AJD: Peggy and I were talking earlier about a story of yours that you're not too fond of, "The Burning." I think Peggy agrees, in part at least, with you.

PWP: No, I said I thought I understood the objections you had to the story, the reservations that you had.

EW: I think I stuck my neck out.

AJD: I like the story very much.

EW: You do? Well, I haven't gone back to read it, but I had a feeling—this comes from the questions people ask me in letters—that I didn't do at all what I wanted to. I think it's too elaborate, too impressionistic.

AJD: I felt freedom in the gaps in the story. I thought they were purposive, they invited me.

EW: That interests me. I think I'll go back and read it. I was ashamed to because I thought I would see everywhere I fell down.

AJD: You said in an earlier interview—you'll probably rue this—that you wrote historically and you shouldn't have done that.

EW: That's true, because I don't like to write things that I could not have experienced—I mean, a life that I haven't experienced in the world where those things happen. I don't like to write historical stories, though I did a couple of other times.

AJD: I guess you did in part in *Delta Wedding* by filling in the middle distance with ancestors and Civil War stories.

EW: Yes, that's true, but as they were handed down; they weren't going on during the story. The reader and writer weren't present in it in the way they are in "The Burning." I used Aaron Burr in "First Love," but I made the story told through a deaf-and-dumb boy because I didn't know what Aaron Burr would have said, since he was a real person. So I had to make it understood by the deaf boy, who then could say what he thought. I never could understand how people could write historical novels with real people speaking. I would feel very inhibited. Don't you feel that you would always be aware of the great chasm?

AJD: Isn't that what a certain kind of writer tries to do, though, to dare that chasm, to bridge it?

EW: I know it is, but it's something I'm not equipped to do, I couldn't do.

PWP: You did "Circe," though, wonderfully.

EW: Yes, but "Circe" is not really historical. I had so much fun writing that story. That was on my first trip to Europe. I never thought I was going to write anything. I was looking. I didn't write anything till I got home. We were passing Sicily and all of those other islands where Circe was supposed to be. And I thought, "What would it be like to be condemned to live forever?" To see everybody that you love die and not be able to feel anything about mortality or the preciousness of the moment. That must have been what she felt.

AJD: I thought that "The Burning" was also a daring kind of experiment. For lots of reasons, I think it's still hard to write about that plantation world and the effect of civil war upon it. There's a residue of ideology and partisan romance that's ready to intrude on a writer, but I thought you warded that off and found the human core.

EW: Well, thank you. That's the only way I would have entered into a story about which I knew so little, as I would almost any other story of a murder or a suicide that came about through a hopeless situation. You know, I don't like reading anything about the Civil War, that's the truth. I hate the Civil War. I hate it. I never have read *Gone with the Wind*. I'm totally ignorant about the Civil War. I mean, I had people on both sides, being half-Yankee and half-Southern. [laughter] But I just hate it, all those hideous battles and the terrible loss.

PWP: We're only just now beginning to get beyond it in Mississippi.

EW: I know that. It's something that Elizabeth Bowen understood too, because she said in Ireland scenes of Cromwell's destruction, the burned churches and abbeys, are still standing, and people look at them all day long. They can be in your yard. And it's the same way in the South. You still have the physical memories of things that happened on your property, in your homeplace. That's one reason why it's so hard to forget.

PWP: I remember in John Crowe Ransom's "Antique Harvesters" one of the characters says, "On this spot stood heroes and drenched it with their only blood."

EW: Yes, and they say of the Archbishop of Canterbury, "Right here is where he was murdered." Blood stains in Canterbury. No, it's just too much.

AJD: May I ask a related question that begins on a personal note of sorts? I became interested in politics in the early 1960s, and I found both President Kennedy and the Civil Rights legislation of '64 and '65 to be inspiring. Maybe I deceived myself, but I felt a sense of unity then and also a national purpose. Today I have no idea where we are, either nationally or more individually. You've seen this over a longer period of time, do you have a sense of perplexity too?

EW: I do, I feel that the perplexity is all over the nation. I don't feel that the answer is *this* anymore. And I also loved John F. Kennedy; I thought something wonderful was going to happen in the world when he was elected. And that really vanished with his assassination and with the thing that happened after that. When I was growing up here, politics was everywhere, but there was not any kind of glorification of politics in my family on either of my parents' sides. There were Mississippians like Bilbo and Vardaman who were almost unbelievable. And that is the kind of thing that a lot of people who were on the wrong side of Civil Rights hark back to: "What we need is somebody like . . .!" So that's where their ideals led them, an idiotic return to something that was not any good in the first place. Well, that's not anything to place too much confidence in. I can't talk. Such a tremendous— I do feel that private relationships between blacks and whites have always been the steadying thing. I believe in private human relations anyway, for understanding. And I've always had faith that they would resolve problems. And I think by and large that that eventually has happened here in Jackson. It was last Christmas, or maybe the Christmas before, that the President of Tougaloo College had a wonderful troupe of mimes and medieval music players who came and did all the early Church music. I went with some friends from Millsaps. And it was an interesting thing to see because Tougaloo, you know, had always been very congenial with Millsaps—teachers would go back and forth and we always went to each others' lyceums—but during the worst of the Civil Rights times Tougaloo barred its doors, severed relations. Then last year the President said to a very large half and half, black and white, audience, "This is a free evening, it's Tougaloo's Christmas gift to Jackson." That was so spontaneous. Have you ever been in that college? It started out as a kind of Northern missionary project and it was needed. It was a private school to educate black students. In the old auditorium there are pews brass plated with names from New England, donors' names like Alcott and Peabody. They had given these pews to the college and now they were inhabited all alike by the black and white citizens of Jackson. It was something spontaneous and solid and *convincing*. Of course it was Christmas, but I still found it convincing. Because I am a writer people come up and speak to me sometimes in the Jitney or the library. Many are black and they may say, "I'm a teacher and I've read all of your works," and so on. And then we have conversations, straightforward conversations about what I've written. I think they feel they can trust me when I write stories about black people, many black people.

PWP: My black students have read your short stories. Many of them, of course, come from the Jackson area. They have read them in high school.

EW: Of course, the stories go back in time, such a long time, for them.

PWP: Most of these students, in fact, have no memory of the 1960s. And there are not many stories being told now about the '60s, much less before.

EW: You know what Patti Black said when she put on the Civil Rights exhibition in the Old Capitol. The whole history of what happened on the home scene was there in photographs and newsprint. And classes of students were taken to look at it. Patti said she would go and listen to the children, and a lot of them didn't even know anything about segregation, had no family memory or race memory of it.

PWP: Some don't believe it.

EW: Here was this evidence, and the children didn't know what it was. They were pretty bored, too. So strange. Patti said, "But they should know it! It's so important to know what happened, both white and black. To know what we did."

PWP: My students read Richard Wright's *Black Boy*, and many question it—black and white alike. They don't believe such times happened. They take it to be gross exaggeration.

EW: I put some of the blame for that on the fact that we've become so dependent on television. People believe what they see on the screen, which has happened today. And they have no sense of a perspective of time, of things growing and changing and becoming something. It's never brought to mind. Never brought to their attention. It worries me that there's not going to be any memory someday. People will have these things stored up on a computer if they need to use them. [laughter] Another thing that is related is the way we travel now. You know, from airport to airport, with no sense of the country that you're flying over and no sense of the difference between one place and another. Just airports, the same *strip* along the road. You know, I was thinking this morning of a birthday party I went to the other night in my family. I said to the honoree, who was thirty-nine, [laughter] "I remember the day you were born because I was in San Francisco then, and I got a telegram from your parents." I always remember that exactly. And Mittie, my sister-in-law, said, "Do you know, people don't know what *telegrams* are anymore." Nothing in a telegram was ever tranquil, the most dramatic messages, sad and happy, always came in telegrams. I thought about writing an article titled, "Daddy, What Was a Telegram?" [laughter] It would show a lot. The arrival of messages used to be important. There was suspense, drama, in everything.

PWP: Even the way the movies depicted the receipt of telegrams, that was always high drama.

EW: They came on a bicycle and rang your doorbell. If it was a death message, there were three stars on the envelope to prepare the recipient.

PWP: Oh, I didn't know that.

EW: Well, that's what they told us they did. So that you wouldn't tear it open, expecting something good, only to find: "Susie died." Three Stars. [laughter] The telegraph carrier wore a uniform and was supposed to wait if there was a death message, just to be sure that the family *took* it all right. They felt a certain sense of responsibility. You didn't get telegrams from strangers that said, "Congratulations, you have just won a free trip to the Virgin Islands! All you have to do is . . ." You know, one of those ads that mimics a telegram. Honest telegrams were *serious*. In fiction you're trying to convey living life, but so many of the old daily trappings now are meaningless to readers. In many respects you have a new vocabulary that you have to write with. I think we have to do it.

AJD: Were you trying to find a new vocabulary in *One Writer's Beginnings?*

EW: That was unlike anything else I'd ever written. My mind was entirely on what I was trying to convey, but I never have written about myself as myself. Non-fiction to begin with is hard for me. But I'm glad I did it—I at least learned what the writing of it taught me.

AJD: Terms like memoir, autobiography, or non-fiction seem so inadequate to describe the feel of that book. It's so intensely imagined.

EW: I think it sort of created itself when I was writing it because I wrote much, much more than I used. It was three lectures, and there's more there than in the book. I didn't think it was fair to assume that people attending a lecture had necessarily read my books. I was so frightened when I went. I did it because Dan Aaron invited me to do the Massey lectures. I told him I could not possibly lecture to graduate students at Harvard. "I'm not an academic. I don't know anything they don't know better." He said, "You know one thing, and that's what in your life you think made you become a writer." And I started

thinking about it and it rather interested me. Everything began to come in. I've got a pretty good memory, at least so far, and I thought of, remembered, so
many things that I just didn't know where to take
hold of them. Then I hit on a construction I could
make, the simplest one. And then everything was
magnetized; the things that didn't magnetize I threw
out. But it was so much fun putting my life together,
so much enlightenment. I advise everybody to do it.

AJD: We began, Miss Welty, by talking about a special
kind of literary community that's founded in stories,
one that brings strangers together before dispersing
them for the rest of their lives. The values of that
community are not inconsiderable. I seem to be
making a speech, but that's really one half of a question. The other half concerns a call that we hear
increasingly in our political forums. Secretary of
Education Bennett lectured last week in Columbia,
and he called for Americans to recover the virtues of
a moral citizenship, which he roots in a Judeo-Chris-
tian heritage. On the one hand is a literary culture
which is terribly private, even anonymous, on the
other, this national entity, whatever it is. Do you
have any faith or hope that the two are continuous,
that they meet at some point?

EW: No. I don't think literature—I'm talking about fiction now—I don't think it can exhort. Or it loses
every bit of its reality and value. I think it speaks to
what is more deeply within, that is, the personal,
and conveys its meaning that way. And then one
hopes that a person made alert or aroused to be more
sensitive to other human beings would go on to look
at things on a larger scale by himself. I wouldn't like
to read a work of fiction that I thought had an
ulterior motive, to persuade me politically. I auto-
matically react the other way. Is that just perversity?
I think things should be written to persuade, but
openly as a column or an editorial or a speech. But
perfectly on the up and up. That's because I under-

stand as a person, not as a motto. This is not to say that I condescend to such writing or think of it as less important. It's just that I don't think the two meet, except accidentally in something in the composition of the reader. But there are no rules. Anybody can exhort us that wants to. And I don't think anybody should be censored or held down. But a lot of people are open to inhibiting others. Smearing people, shutting people up. Killing all the people who have AIDS, you know, just get rid of those who give us trouble. It's scary the things that you read that are written in cold blood in the paper.

PWP: It does seem that we're embarked on a new era of dogmatism.

EW: I think so too, and it scares me, it really does, but I can't let that apply to what I do with fiction. Which does not mean that I don't often in stories use such a character as a fictional creation who speaks for himself *in* the story. He shows a reader what he is, out of his own mouth. I'm not advocating, but I'm *presenting* it as honestly as I can. My stories tried to do that sometimes in the days of the [Civil Rights] troubles. I may not be answering your question.

AJD: It was probably more a reflection than a question. It seems that our intellectual and cultural life attempts to create intensely personal virtues, almost as Bloomsbury did, as Virginia Woolf, if I'm not reaching too far afield.

EW: Yes, I know, but you see what that led to. I guess the thing I don't really like is any kind of group existing for its own sake. I could never have belonged to anything like Bloomsbury. There wasn't any danger! Everything aside—qualifications aside—I just wouldn't have flourished as a writer in a closely interknit group like that, all talking to each other. I'm just interested in people as individuals and caring for individuals so much.

RUTH M. VANDE KIEFT

Eudora Welty:
Visited and Revisited

What I hope my title will suggest is visits, both metaphorical and literal, to both the writer and her work, which I shall describe for what they can reveal about each. I might have used "Visions and Revisions" or "Search and Research" as my subtitle, though neither speaks clearly to the occasion, which is a double celebration.

The golden anniversary of Eudora Welty's first publication, "Death of a Traveling Salesman," is also a silver anniversary, for a quarter century has passed since my critical study of her fiction (*Eudora Welty*, Twayne, 1962) appeared, and the revised and updated edition of that book, an effort of several years, is due to appear in March 1987. The two achievements cannot be compared as gold is to silver, in terms of their comparative value. A truer metaphor would make of my work an alloy—not because I regard it as "base metal" wholly unworthy of her fiction, but rather as "a metal mixed with a more valuable metal to give durability or some other desired quality." The desired quality is understanding and appreciation. The stories will endure without my or anyone else's mediation to the end of their communicating all the golden truth and beauty Eudora Welty has wrought through the alchemy of her imagination. But there may be fewer to perceive and appropriate it, making its destiny, even in a world miraculously preserved from disaster, as precarious as that of "gold to aery thinness beat" on pages of illuminated manuscript, locked in museum and

27

library cases and viewed only by a few cognoscenti and custodians of artistic treasures. I think all true readers know that value not perceived and enjoyed is the nearest thing to value lost and wasted.

In what follows I shall be personal in a way that may appear self-indulgent. I hope it will become apparent that my object is not to broadcast myself or seem to bask in reflected glory, but rather to share the subjects and causes of my celebration. I make no claim to some unique knowledge of Eudora Welty, nor to have or even aspire to the final word on her fiction. The most I lay claim to is a singleness and ardor of devotion to the writer and her work which has steadily grown through the years, and a zeal for their welfare, for the stories' finding their way into the hearts of responsive readers.

It was strange, and prophetic, that although I lived in the South for three and a half years and graduated from a Southern woman's college, my first introduction to Eudora Welty's fiction was not as a reader, but as an instructor of English at a Northern woman's college. A few farsighted, discriminating colleagues at Wellesley had selected the Modern Library edition of Eudora Welty's *Collected Stories* (then the first two volumes only) to teach in an introductory literature course, along with Shakespeare's sonnets, Donne, James *(Portrait of a Lady)*, Ibsen, and Yeats. The stature of the authors, the dedication of the students ("good," bright young women though rather anxious readers), the critical brilliance and commitment to teaching of my colleagues— "close readers" who loved literature and believed it meant something complex, subtle, and beautiful that could be put into words appropriately complex, vigorous, and clear— lent a certain strenuousness to our class discussions and informal literary talk; but it was a serious and fruitful activity in which this relatively unknown contemporary writer seemed in no way diminished by tests of comparison, while her stories challenged our combined talent, moved and delighted us as readers.

I think I must always have had the "right eyes" for looking

at Eudora Welty's work (to borrow Rilke's phrase for his viewing of Cezanne's paintings), though at first I did not know why; and I had some difficulty articulating even *what* I saw there, still less why the stories so intrigued and pleased me. This has been a slow process of discovery, still continuing in my present writing, though I can now trace the disclosures in terms of affinities of temperament and experience, a "confluence" of spirit and process of life development as her reader, critic, and friend, much as in *One Writer's Beginnings* she traces the significance of events in her early life to her development as a fiction writer. In my earliest impressions of her stories, four things were central. Primary was the *mystery* I found there, and with it, the awareness that the revelation in them was paradoxical—part disclosure, part concealment. The stories were charged with the burden, or joy, of something hidden that cried out to be expressed, as impossible to be repressed. In every stage of its "growing up"—from the child's delight in its cherished secrets, its devouring curiosity and thirst for "grown-up" knowledge and experience; to the adolescent's romantic hope and dream of finding in love the answer (ah!) to life's "sweet mystery"; to the mature adult's awareness of the enigma that confronts him as loved ones misunderstand and often unintentionally hurt each other, as nature keeps her green curtains closed and fate pours blow after blow upon our naked heads—it was mystery that blessed and cursed human existence, in her stories as in life. The stories were bright but elusive, baffling and sometimes terrifying, leading to disclosures as often joyful as sorrowful, but still inscrutable. Robert Heilman spoke of "the penumbra of mystery—a mystery to be accepted, not solved—always bordering the clean light of Welty's characters and scenes": that seemed a fine summation of what I saw there.

Closely related to this quality of mystery was the "doubleness" of Eudora Welty's vision. Love and separateness (a pervasive theme discovered by Robert Penn Warren) were two sides of the same coin. Victim and conquerer were one, for "did it matter which poor, avid life took the gaze and which gave it?" (this is a cat's stalking vision in "Music from Spain"). "The excursion is the same when you go looking for your sorrow as when you go looking for your joy" (this is Doc in "The Wide Net"). "Virgie never saw it differently, never doubted that all the opposites on earth were close together, love close to hate, living to dying; but of them all, hope and despair were the closest blood—unrecognizable one from the other sometimes, making moments double upon themselves, and in the doubling double again, amending but never taking back" ("The Wanderers"). Every impulse of the heart proclaimed that also to be true. And in Eudora Welty's fiction it was a vision everywhere fleshed out in the persons, events, places necessary to give it solidity.

Then there was the variety—God's plenty, at least one story for every reader, every mood; experimentation in point of view, freshness, spontaneity. This variety eminently suited her stories to the classroom, where consideration of her use of the genre, her fictional technique, her subtle control and flexibility of tone, clarity of language, lovely surfaces and textures, fidelity to speech idiom, provided a wealth of possibilities for introducing students to the art of fiction. As part of this variety I count Eudora Welty's effectiveness in tragedy and comedy, satire, fantasy, sometimes "pure," sometimes "mixed" (or "streaked," as I like to think of it). In this respect she is like the greatest modern writers, such as Chekhov or Beckett, masters of "mixed" forms.

Finally I cherished the stories because behind them I intuited a writer whom I could *trust*. "Never trust the artist. Trust the tale," Lawrence famously advised in his *Studies in Classic American Literature*. "The proper function of a critic is to save the tale from the artist who created it." He was like a superior hound sniffing through the forest of our national literature for the freedom he thought our writers were denying by acts of subterfuge. *Blood-consciousness* he craved, and we have had to heed his advice in reading his own fiction. But that advice must fall on deaf ears, I think, to a reader of Eudora Welty's fiction. For teller and tale are here so seamless in their integrity that a critic's best office to her fiction can only be that of keeping the analysis as close to her as possible in artistic spirit and intention, true to each story's perceived fidelity to human experience, and thus returning it to her, giving beauty back to beauty's giver, with the self as an assimilated part of the gift.

Communication has been her goal from the first, even though her methods of achieving it have not been the easy or obvious ones. It is still her purpose, constantly stressed throughout the years and recently repeated to a wide television audience on NBC's *1986* in an interview with Roger Mudd: "I hope the characters will reveal themselves so that the reader will think what I think." To which Roger Mudd added a further truth of her intention, "You hope you're speaking for all human beings."

We have come a long way since Lawrence gave his advice, and now many critics trust the tale no more than the teller—its very language, the kind of wholeness the teller tried to give it from truth wooed, won, pressed into words. The divorce is more thoroughgoing than that between and among tellers, tales, and reader-critics. But I was fortunate to come upon Eudora Welty's stories at a time when "the text" was trusted and the writer trusted language, when signifier and signified were not divided, and the complexity of language was part of its interest and beauty, giving pleasure to interpretation. The words were not trapped in their several closed systems or contexts, so many pigment oils locked in their cool little tubes. Seized from a rich variety of vernacular and literary sources, the words, the colors, had already been squeezed out onto her artist's palette and put up there on her canvas, *in the world*, the transformations wrought by her imagination for all to see. The light broke through, on them, from them.

I turned to writing about Eudora Welty's fiction in order to understand it better for myself, and then to share that understanding, that pleasure, with my students, friends, and other readers. In writing, I instinctively took, for my critical tools, "instruments of air" (a phrase she used in

"Circe" to suggest a peculiarly human way of analyzing), as I sought to probe meaning in her fiction. As I wrote I was always aware that the writer whose work so intrigued and delighted me was very much alive and at work. So I summoned my courage and wrote to her, expressing my admiration of her work, and enclosing an article, as yet unpublished, to demonstrate what I was up to. She read "The Mysteries of Eudora Welty" and answered graciously in a letter full of assurances. I was astonished and grateful, and had more than enough encouragement to go on with my work. I wrote in answer to simple questions of meaning and fictional technique: "What's going on here?" I quoted freely, and tried to keep my own language suitable to breathing in the atmosphere of hers in her fiction, trying to make it clear but subtle and complex, avoiding a ponderous critical vocabulary. It was a labor of love, as one reviewer of my book noted, though I hope that did not make me seem blind.

My "revisits" to Eudora Welty's fiction have been continuous through the years, for scarcely one has gone by without my teaching a few of her stories. It was in answer to the need for a short paperback collection with an introduction, designed chiefly for classroom use, that I edited and introduced *Thirteen Stories by Eudora Welty* in 1965. The selection of the stories was a collaborative effort. I drew up the original list of stories in an effort to show both their quality and variety, and submitted it to Eudora Welty. She complained about the number of "old war horses," as she put it, and suggested a quite different list of stories she wanted to see included, most of them relatively unknown. I argued that these much-anthologized stories were not old war horses to young students just beginning to read great fiction, and were perennially fresh to old war-horse readers; she graciously took my advice, in the main, though a couple of her choices, such as "Lily Daw and the Three Ladies," were included. Her then editor at Harcourt, Brace, Daniel Wickenden, refined the list with an eye to such practical considerations as the length of the stories: thus "Moon Lake" from *The Golden Apples* was preferred to the longer

"June Recital." Of the two salesmen stories, I selected "The Hitch-Hikers" rather than "Death of a Traveling Salesman," not because it is more beautiful, but it is far more complex, an excellent story for classroom use and paper assignments. Never at any point have I written about Eudora Welty's fiction without having the mediating function of the critic clearly in mind, not only in relation to students, but to my peers and all fellow readers as well.

My first visits with Eudora Welty took place in the spring of 1961 at the Algonquin Hotel, where she always stayed when she was in New York, and still does, enjoying both its privacy and protection of its guests, and the comings and goings of theatre people and other contemporary figures in the arts. From the first, the unique blending in her manner of dignity, shyness, reserve, with a welcoming simplicity, warmth, and candor, made the atmosphere easy for the development of friendship and trust. From those first meetings two major impressions stand out clearly. One was of her at one point murmuring, with an admiring tone and expression as we sat in the lobby over drinks, "Look, there's Brendan Behan." I turned to see the stout little red-faced Irish playwright enter the elevator, banked round by taller companions, who burst into laughter as the doors closed upon some fresh merriment he was making. I later thought of Powerhouse, "a person of joy," of her adoring love of entertainers—the monkey man, the Spanish guitarist—her pleasure in writing tributes to them. The other solid impression was of her recoil from thinly disguised autobiographical fiction, particularly when it exposed family secrets, resulting in painful and permanent alienations. "My sister hasn't spoken to me since," a Yaddo writer I told her about had said to me. She did not, *would not*, do it. As firm as she was about her own privacy, she was doubly fierce for others'—even distant others. She was, and is, as insistent upon fiction's being the product of imagination as she is on the need for its own particular kind of truth—the truth given it by the necessities of place, the natural world, the indigenous idiom, and the universality of basic human feelings. She "protected" all kinds of people who would never have dreamed they needed "any such of a thing," who might have gloried in exposure had they known she had caused them to "appear," however unattractively, in her fiction. Above all, she has protected her loved ones, since imagination works on all "real" persons to transform them into fictional characters. On such strong convictions was trust founded, and built, though I would never have guessed it to be different, from all I had learned from her fiction.

In succeeding years there were several visits with Eudora, among the happiest of which were at my New York apartment, and at her appearances, when I was fortunate enough to be included on a panel discussion of her work, to introduce her at a reading, or to be part of a celebration. Each appearance seemed, in fact, to be a celebration. Student audiences were especially receptive. At Oberlin, every line of "Why I Live at the P.O." was greeted with gleeful explosions; at Harvard, when she read the William E. Massey lectures that led to *One Writer's Beginnings*, the students waited for hours, clamored to get in the hall, crowded the aisles and windows, edged the small stage, feet dangling, strained forward to hear every word her soft voice uttered. They were enchanted, enthralled; they gave their hearts to her.

My first visit to Eudora at her home in Jackson was extraordinary. It was to be Eudora's seventieth birthday, 1979, though no special celebration had been planned. Since she was born on April 13, the date sometimes falls on Friday the thirteenth, and this one happened, additionally, to be a "Good" (or "black") Friday.

I left New York on Wednesday. The plan was to stay with Eudora for a couple of days, be shown some nearby "haunts" by her on Thursday, and on Friday, to be joined by my friend Virginia Rock for some prowling around the state in a rented car, ending up in New Orleans.

There was bad weather on the flight from Atlanta to Jackson, late and bumpy, and tornado warnings, dark skies, and heavy winds greeted me at Jackson. A fellow passenger delivered me to Eudora's door, and once I had arrived, I settled into the excitement of being Eudora's guest. She served me a delicious ham dinner on her mother's laurel-patterned china, with her mother's family silver. We had an exotic dessert brought in by a neighbor: the cook had christened it "Raspberry Rapture." I was impressed that the guest room, the one I was to stay in, had been her mother's—a charming room, dazzlingly clean, with white curtains and bedspread, a four-poster bed, a dresser, a drop-leaf desk, and bedside table with a reading lamp. On the walls were a couple of small crayon sketches of beach scenes from a notebook, Eudora told me, of "AE's," the Irish poet and artist, father of her literary agent and friend, Diarmuid Russell. On the dresser was propped a glossy photograph of Eudora and three friends standing in front of a beauty parlor that looked like Leota's in "Petrified Man." Our evening visit was brief and rather anxious, because weather reports were ominous.

A spectacular night followed. A hurricane was moving in from the Mississippi Gulf coast, spawning tornadoes as it passed over Jackson, 150 miles inland, with increasing velocity, unleashing vast quantities of wind and rain, thunder and lightning. It was impossible to sleep, and I didn't even try, but lay back wide-eyed or sat upright in bed, amazed, or posted myself at the rain-streaked windows waiting for the brief, lurid revelations the lightning brought of wildly tossing bushes and tree branches outside. Although usually anxious in heavy storms, particularly in the threat of tornadoes, I was strangely fearless, and felt protected and secure. I had framed myself inside two of Eudora's stories: "The Winds" (in which a little girl named Josie, under her parents' tender care, endures an imaginative growing-up experience during an equinoctial storm), and *The Optimist's Daughter* (in which a greater ordeal is suffered by the mature heroine, Laurel Hand—but survived). It was not remotely possible that harm could come to me with Eudora hovering upstairs, doubtless alert, on guard, and I in her mother's fragrantly clean, white bedroom, safely ensconced in the stories.

But as the rains came, kept coming in the heaviest downpours I had ever experienced, I became aware of a trickling sound somewhere near. I opened the closet door and discovered that water was leaking in from a corner in the ceiling. A brief survey disclosed that three items were in a fair way to being swamped: on the shelves directly below the leak, a pile of neatly folded white curtains; and another deep black pile of academic hoods with colorful velvet and satin trimmings; and on the floor, a large cardboard box filled with photographs. I promptly removed these items from the closet and placed them on the bedroom floor. The symbolism of the trinity of things rescued, their juxtaposition, seemed full of meaning. I did not look at the photographs, but I judged they would be the most valuable of the three, and the clean, white, airy curtains seemed a rebuke to the pomp and circumstance of black academic hoods. Though tangible evidence of the honors and awards that had been heaped on Eudora, they seemed less valuable, in that room, than the curtains: perhaps, if these were old, they had once been laundered and ironed by her mother. A mood of nostalgia and of childlike heroism filled me as I thought of saving the symbolic endangered items and protecting the closet and room from this small and insistent but governable stream of the wild symbolic flood invading the house. I fetched a tray from the kitchen to catch the water, emptied it once or twice, and thus endured the night in a state of mind half romantic, half practical. Danger was an imagined thing; death and destruction were safely outside or packed away in fiction, or in the past, like the symbolic photographs in the cardboard box.

When I emerged from my room, Eudora, who, it turned out, had also been up all night following the storm's progress on the radio, had already been down for her breakfast and gone back upstairs. I heard more water running: she was drawing her bath!

The gray light of morning exposed my foolishness as, with a dismayed and woeful Eudora, I surveyed the damage. The lawns, gardens and streets, sopping wet with a million rivulets and standing pools of water, were badly littered by fallen branches and twigs. The azaleas and camellia bushes in front of the house were bent low, their blossoms soaked, bedraggled, ruined. But the great water oak in front of the house had been spared. ("One is taken and the other left": the Presbyterians', across the street on their college campus, had been taken.) And the pines, five or six left of all the dozen or so original forest pines among which the house had been completed in 1925—felled over the years by these violent Mississippi storms—these trees too had been spared. Eudora was grateful for that. She was appalled by the leak, by the nuisance to me, my sleepless night. She resisted my strong impulse, which I quickly acted upon, to gather up as many of the fallen twigs and branches as I could, I'm sure because it did not seem a suitable thing for her guest to be doing, any more than was emptying a closet in the dead of night and collecting water in a kitchen tray. She failed to see any romance, or anything at all heroic or thrilling, in that long night. She claimed the photographs were not valuable, but I did not believe her. Not *old*, perhaps, but not valuable? Everything in the house was valuable!

I know I was sobered, but in retrospect, I believe that nothing short of actual injury to a person could have repressed my childishly high spirits. At table I tried to divert Eudora by amusing her. I compared the house to Venice— beautiful, historied, and doomed—slowly sinking into the sea. Eudora did not seem to enjoy this analogy. I reached for my copy of the *New York Review of Books*, and read aloud an excerpt from a review of Flannery O'Connor's letters, *The Habit of Being*, in which Flannery writes to the Fitzgeralds,

Regina is getting very literary. "Who is this Kafka?" she says. "People ask me." A German Jew, I says, I think. He wrote a book about a man that turns into a roach. "Well, I can't tell people *that*," she says. "Who is this Evalin Wow?"

I laughed as I spelled the name aloud.

Eudora did not find the excerpt at all funny. "People are always saying Flannery didn't get along with her mother," she complained. I looked up, puzzled and surprised. "Oh, but she *did*," I protested. "They got on very well. The letters show that, the reviewer understands that too. She *loved* her mother." "Well, she *did*," said Eudora emphatically, and that ended the matter.

These were failures in tone—all mine—I who thought myself to be practiced in reading Eudora Welty's tone in her fiction. But I had failed to realize that there is a time and a season for everything under the sun, and this was no time for romantic attitudes or frivolous attempts at comedy. And I learned, further, that with Eudora Welty there was *never* a time to tell stories and make jokes which are, or even appear to be, at the expense of anyone's parents. I think her own strongest and most admirable piety is the filial one: *One Writer's Beginnings* shows that. It was one I shared, and that formed a bond between us. Touched off by the storm's devastation, memories of other storms, her parents' determined efforts to stave off disaster, their protection and prevention—perhaps she did not understand why Flannery O'Connor had written those words about her mother, any more than either she or I could have addressed our parents by their first names, as Flannery did, apparently from an early age. I learned that the actual and the fictional should not be confused, that a shocking event and a sober occasion should be given their due.

The destructive power of the storm became evident as the waters rose. The heavy rainfall caused the Pearl River to back up into all the little creeks and tributaries surrounding Jackson, overflowing quietly by late Saturday, flooding all of the low ground of Jackson and its vicinity (though not the comparatively high ground in Eudora's section of town), and cutting off the city. There could be no thought of an excursion the day after the storm, though Eudora showed me some of the sights in Jackson. The flood rose and crested, and many Jacksonians had to abandon their homes to the muddy water. Millions of dollars of property damage resulted, and the catastrophe was featured on national news. It was strange to see pictures of rescue operations on television in the motel where Virginia Rock and I were now staying—crowded, by Sunday morning, with people who had been evacuated from their homes. Fortunately, there were no fatalities or major injuries.

Easter day, calm and bright, was filled with anomalous scenes. Just down the hill from where stood the old Episcopal church we attended (next to the Lamar Life Insurance Company, Mr. Welty's firm), the flood waters were spread, smooth and placid, reflecting perfect images of city buildings. At the services, the male contingent of the choir was completely missing, as were most of the other men in the congregation—off on rescue missions.

One result of the flood, for Virginia and me as tourists, was oddly beneficent, for there were few people wherever we went. The roads, especially the Parkway along the Natchez Trace, were deserted, automobile access prohibited since the city was almost entirely cut off. A lonesome tranquility descended as we investigated old Indian burial mounds or sat in daisies beside the highway. We walked along the old Trace, dappled in warm sunlight and shade, twelve or more feet down in the forest floor, its banks making walls so beautiful in their mixed colors and textures that I turned my camera lens straight into one for an "impressionistic" photograph. Time lapsed into an eternal present in which animals, traders, riverboatmen, bandits, settlers, circuit riders, Indians, men on horseback or on foot, and lovers of every era, traveled along the Trace— scene of so many of Eudora Welty's stories. Never can a literary pilgrimage have been as successful, darkly clouded though it was by Jackson's tragedy and the grief and loss Eudora felt for her beloved home town and its folk.

"Welcome always, and come back to a better flavor next time—without the tornado and without the flood!" So Eudora inscribed my copy of *The Jackson Cookbook*, which I purchased in Natchez on that visit, just under her introduction, titled "The Flavor of Jackson." I did return three years later in 1982—on a visit I thought of as "search and research." I was on sabbatical leave, and had a small grant to work on a comparative study of Eudora Welty and Flannery O'Connor. I planned to divide my time (about ten weeks) evenly between Jackson and Milledgeville, Georgia, to immerse myself in the Eudora Welty collection at the Mississippi Department of Archives and History, and Flannery O'Connor Memorial Room Collection at Georgia College in Milledgeville.

In both places I found the "search" more deeply rewarding than the "research," though often in ways serendipitous rather than planned, and for more reasons than my finding it so much more pleasant to spend beautiful spring days full of blossoms and balmy weather (translated as I was from the hard Northern winter) outdoors rather than inside libraries. I continued to find *places and persons* more absorbing than anything new the libraries contained. In Jackson there was Eudora, and in Milledgeville, there was Sally Fitzgerald, the next best thing to meeting Flannery in the flesh, though she was everywhere a palpable presence, especially in her own words, and on the O'Connor farm, Andalusia. Not that the collections weren't fascinating—above all, the manuscripts in both collections; and in the Mississippi Archives, hundreds of Eudora's early photographs, letters telling the story of her earliest publications, including "Death of a Traveling Salesman"; an exhaustive newspaper clipping file; interesting Educational Television films; secondary sources. But I didn't spend too many days in the library. Ensconced in the "Admirable Benbow" (my epithet for the motel) with my cat, I took short excursions around Jackson, discovering such things, in a town called Raymond, as what a "stile" is. Virgie, of course, sits on one at the end of *The Golden Apples*. I found "The Little Store," now a restaurant, and more importantly, the Welty house at 741 North Congress Street, freshly painted a creamy beige with white trim, looking warm yellow under the chartreuse of nascent leaves back-lighted by the sun. There were tenants—offices of a most pleasant young woman practising as an industrial psychologist, and a real-estate firm—but I was allowed to have a look around, and especially enjoyed the sight of Eudora's room, on the front of the second story across from her parents', with a bay window. I could imagine her curled up there, reading, or gazing across the street at the school, or looking intently on a passerby, or the moon or the stars, her imagination always busy with something or other. On the sleeping porch, where the Welty children slept nearly year round, I found two young women who worked for the real-estate firm, still in disarray because of their recent move into the house. Standing in the doorway, I waved my arms and told them about "The Winds," the first scene of which had taken place on that very porch during an equinoctial storm. They listened curiously, and probably thought me a bit cracked, though they said I "must be a very good teacher."

Since my search was for the writer herself, the times with Eudora, whether short visits or an excursion, were most valuable to me. She took me to Mendenhall, a town thirty miles south of Jackson, and a small hotel near the railroad tracks, famous as "the home of the revolving tables." There, seated with sixteen people around a large round table, we helped ourselves to a great variety of Southern foods, which turned slowly before us on a great lazy Susan—delicious, and constantly replenished from the kitchen. The pro-prietor was immensely proud of his guest, by now familiar, and she responded to him warmly, with her single gracious manner and the natural dignity that springs from reserve rather than pride and self-consciousness.

One exploratory evening took us, with Peggy Prenshaw, out to dinner at a French restaurant located on the ex-pressway leading north of Jackson, indistinguishable from many other comparable strips of suburban highway in the United States. Eudora had never been there. The restaurant turned out to be fairly glamorous, though without a "period" or style, its chief decorative feature being a wall of mirrors, which of course repeated everything into infinity and thus lent the room a kind of unearned spaciousness.

Once seated, Eudora looked around and observed, "It reminds me of a ship." This was exactly right, for the room, though pleasant, was part of a floating modern culture no more local, or even national, than its inauthentic cuisine. Eudora is not "at sea" anywhere and talked kindly, as always, to two young waiters who recognized and were proud and delighted to be serving her—one Jacksonian and one New Yorker. Her presence, I realized, rescues both places and persons from anonymity, since it is the quality of her attention that causes particularity to emerge, and harmony among all sorts and conditions of men and women.

On that visit Eudora told me much of what she relates with such generosity and candor about her parents in *One Writer's Beginnings*. It emerged that both of our parents had endured the loss of a child before we were born, which had caused my mother to name me her "comfort child." To be much loved and responsive to that love, to be reared in a home where the strictest veracity was assumed and practised as well as kindness to others, to be both shy and adventuresome, to be imaginative, an avid reader with an active fantasy life, to take risks—these, I discovered, were some of the chief sources of the confluence of feeling which had drawn me to her work.

Yet another was that of our feelings and attitudes about social and political issues, particularly race relationships. Our homes had been free of the blight of racial prejudice, and we both felt a natural liking of black people, she, of course, with a longer and richer experience of them than I had had. The photographs and introduction to *One Time, One Place* show her admiration of the courage of black people, their capacity for love and loyalty, their gifts of imagination, their power to create fantasy, to enjoy life, even against the greatest odds. In my mixed Northern and Southern experiences and sympathies, I shared with Eudora, in a strong personal way, the national wound of which the Civil War had been both cause and symptom. The war between brothers—Northern and Southern, black and white—is a terrible thing. As a fiction writer she has worked indirectly to heal that wound by fighting for the human right to be a private, mysterious, dignified, and unrepeatable self. That is what "The Demonstrators" is about, and I think it is the best story from a white person's perspective to have come out of the Civil Rights Era. The eye of the story, Dr. Strickland's, could be that of another good doctor, Chekhov, set down in small-town Mississippi in the 1960's.

Being with Eudora, I found slowly and in diffusion, as though observing an effect almost without a cause, since it is so rare in persons not given over to a religious faith, sheer *goodness*. Purity of heart. Artistic integrity. Humility. A capacity for shedding fame like a garment. A comic sense without a trace of malice. I felt blessed to know her *together with* her work, but became aware that of the two inestimable treasures, it was the person I cherished more.

The process of coming to know a great writer and her work is part of the life-long process of self-discovery. As a further step taken in my search for Eudora Welty, I became aware not only of the confluence of our lives but the divergences between them. A few of these were disclosed to me in an evening of epiphanies, and all but soundlessly.

It happened that two series of programs we both were keen on were running in sequence on Educational Television that spring, and one evening we watched them together. The first was Lord Attenborough's brilliant, original nature series, and the second was *Brideshead Revisited*. When I arrived for our viewing, I found Eudora somewhat apprehensive, for the announced program was to be devoted to carnivores.

As anyone knows who has graduated from Walt Disney nature films to the best among current offerings in this genre, viewers with tender sensibilities are no longer spared the sight of nature "red in tooth and claw." Lord Attenborough spared us nothing in that episode (though the failure of color on Eudora's television set did spare us at least the shocking color of blood), and I watched closely as the big cats attacked, tore into and devoured the beautiful gazelles and zebras, usually the young or weaklings of the herd. Through all of this, I noticed that Eudora kept her eyes mostly averted from the screen, and said nothing.

Why did I feel compelled to watch while she did not? It is not, I think, that she was the more squeamish or I the less tender-hearted, nor is it because she does not confront pain in nature, what it can do to human beings through sickness and accident. But she does not expend her spirit in trying to part the curtain of green, as does her fictional character, the young widow Mrs. Larkin in that title story of her first collection, to see what metaphysical or mystical meanings may be disclosed from plunging her own life into nature. Death stops Eudora Welty: her speculation, her quest for meaning—not her memory, her enduring love. My own need is to see what goes on behind the curtain of green, starting with the pain and fear of animals, for I have a strong sense of some mysterious damage done to man and nature together. I am surely an animal, myself a carnivore (though I allow others to do my killing for me), harboring in my bosom a small tiger who instinctively pulls in his claws when I caress him and bares both teeth and claws when I play with him, or when he plays with, and perhaps fatally wounds, a chipmunk.

My father was a Dutch Calvinist minister, as pure in doctrine as in his morally uncontaminated life, for he was neither proud nor self-righteous, but sweet and humble, not unlike Jonathan Edwards. Eudora was buffered a full generation on both sides of her family from the harsher doctrines of American Protestantism, as from Bible-belt fundamentalism. Whether this accounts for the difference between us, I do not know. She seems to believe in "primal joy"—"the kind you were born and began with"—as though it were an Original Blessing: surely a better thing to believe in than the Fall, which is an Original Curse resulting from an Original Sin.

We barely had time to recover from the ordeal of Lord Attenborough's carnivores when *Brideshead Revisited* inflicted another, and worse, upon us. It was the episode in which

Julia Flyte flees out to the fountain in tears, having been shocked and wounded by her brother Brideshead's reducing of her and Charles Ryder's love to a formula, "living in sin." There in the dusk Charles embraces and tries to comfort her by attacking the formula and its petty use, the cruelty of its user—to no avail. Julia's Catholic conscience agonizes with the phrase *"Living in sin,* with sin, for sin, every hour, every day, year in, year out . . ."; teases it into every nuance of implication, piles up its heavy load of guilt and suffering:

> ". . . mummy dying with my sin eating at her, more cruelly than her own deadly illness. . . . Christ dying with it, nailed hand and foot, hanging over the bed in the night nursery; . . . hanging in the dark church; . . . hanging at noon, high among the crowds and soldiers; no comfort except a sponge of vinegar and the kind words of a thief; hanging for ever; . . . never the cool sepulcher . . . never the shelter of the cave or of the castle walls. . . . Nothing but bare stone and dust and the smouldering dumps. Thrown away, scrapped, rotting down; the old man with lupus and the forked stick who limps out at nightfall to turn the rubbish. . . . Nameless and dead, like the baby wrapped up and took away before I had seen her."

The scene was brilliantly acted and ravaged the feelings as Lord Attenborough's carnivores never had. Inner eyes could not be averted from Julia's torn and broken spirit.

No word passed between us. There was only a helpless, smothered sound of pain and protest from Eudora as she fetched perhaps the deepest sigh I had ever heard. I knew that she rejected the rigid doctrine that would make Julia's love guilty, linked with and cause of the whole world's suffering; that would deny these lovers their long-delayed human joy of fulfillment. And in that moment I felt only and exactly as she did. But I understood, too, what was implicit in Waugh's vision, which becomes more clear after Julia and Charles have witnessed Lord Marchmain's death-bed repentance: "I saw today there was one thing unforgivable," Julia says, "the bad thing I was on the point of doing, that I'm not quite bad enough to do; to set up a rival good to God's."

But what is "God's good" and how can our suffering hearts know it, bring our wills and actions in conformity to it? Can it be trusted to a human religious institution? To ask such questions is to attempt to part not only the curtain of green, but the invisible curtain between natural and supernatural, flesh and spirit, time and eternity. I must do this, tirelessly, and Eudora does not—perhaps because she finds it futile, not productive of the open, tolerant humanistic values she espouses; not productive, at least, of her kind of fiction. "I have been told, both in approval and in accusation, that I seem to love all my characters," she says in her preface to her *Collected Stories*. "What I do in writing of any character is to try to enter into the mind, heart, and skin of a human being who is not myself." If there is no evil or cruelty in a writer's heart, how, by an act of imagination, can she find it in another's heart? Or perhaps, knowing so much, she refuses to judge, or blame. To understand all is to forgive all. . . .

So far my search for Eudora Welty led me on that visit. To her charitable humanistic vision, her stopping with human mysteries without venturing beyond, her rich comedy of affirmation.

Two years later I was to learn how widely my own devotion was shared, how greatly she had enriched others' lives as well as my own. I flew to Jackson for Eudora's seventy-fifth birthday celebration. *One Writer's Beginnings* had recently appeared and was enjoying an enormous success. She had invited the whole world into her life and her creative imagination. She had completely captured the attention and hearts of her fellow Mississippians, along with a great many other Americans, several of whom testified, as I had done, to a confluence of experience with hers. The rotunda of the old State Capitol, now the Historical Museum, was full of photographs of her and her family, most of them taken by her father, and printed in the exhibit catalogue titled simply *Eudora*. There was a great gathering of fellow writers, family and friends, teachers and students, scholars and critics, townsfolk. There were academic lectures and symposiums, readings, and receptions at Millsaps College, sponsor of this combined birthday celebration and literary conference, and a lavish champagne supper at the home of Mrs. Warren Reimers. Eudora was tirelessly gracious in receiving the congratulations of her well-wishers and admirers.

After all these events Eudora gave a party for a few friends from near and far at her home and then at a small Greek restaurant, Bill's Greek Tavern. The proprietor, who boasted a limited and uncertain English, a beautiful young Mississippi wife, and two even more beautiful little daughters in white party frocks, was effusive with cries of "God bless America! God bless Eudora Welty!" An eight-course Greek dinner was served, a belly dancer flew in with castanets (accompanied by an accordion player), "Happy Birthday" inscribed across her belly, and undulated briefly before the small booths into which we had squeezed ourselves, our stomachs bursting with food, drink, and mirth. A birthday cake appeared, in the shape of a book lying open, ready for Eudora's cutting, with "One Writer's Beginnings" and "God Bless Eudora Welty!" inscribed in icing on its chocolate pages. At my own table, Charlotte Capers and Reynolds Price launched into a hilarious tale which lasted through four courses and left all of us weak with laughter. How much *fun* there is in and around Eudora, though her friends tend to be a bit noisier than she, as there is restraint in her joy even as in her grief. How unlike my first visit this one was!—truly a time for rejoicing.

And the memory of it served me well, because the following week found me at my mother's bedside while she lay near death from an overdose of chemotherapy. I spent the whole of that Good Friday in the hospital close by her, and many another in the weeks and months to follow before she died. "It's when you know you've done all you *can!*" Eudora's low voice on the telephone would implore and comfort, urgent with her concern, her shared knowledge of my afflicted daughter's heart. She was a friend for all seasons.

Our lives go on, our love and our memories, and I am beginning to feel a survivor, like Eudora. The friend and mentor to whom I dedicated my book on her work, Austin Warren, died in August of this year; the revision will again be dedicated to him, this time with the dates of his birth and death, 1899–1986. He is one of those critics who could speak with the voice of authority.

For the past several years I have been working on a new edition of *Eudora Welty*, enjoying fresh "visions" as part of the task of revision. I found no need to make radical changes in my general approach to the fiction: it had served its purpose, and seemed durable; had I made radical changes, the book would not have been "of a piece." However, I did try to get rid of all traces of what might appear to have been simple equations: this, in the text, equals that, in the explication. It never does. Then, I also realized that I had given disproportionate attention to certain stories I admired less than others simply because they had seemed "harder nuts to crack" and I had wanted to try my hand at them. I saved space by condensing discussions I saw to be over-wrought or useless, and was able to add fresh insights on more interesting stories, thus making a few implicit value judgments. I omitted altogether the final chapter in which I had attempted to "place" Eudora Welty among modern fiction writers, particularly Southern. It no longer seemed necessary, seemed almost presumptuous: time had "placed" her, she had "placed" herself, and her position was very high.

The revision of *Eudora Welty* has also been an "updating," with all the work published since *The Bride of the Innisfallen* to be considered. This was inviting, difficult but never daunting, a largely enjoyable task. It involved me in one complete "revision." I had "missed" *Losing Battles* on my first, too anxious and careful reading, partly because I labored under the pressure of having to write two very different kinds of reviews of the novel, and succeeded at neither. I think also that my Northern urban self resisted the garrulity of Southern country folk, as though their speech had been the sound of country music—is *Losing Battles* not the noisiest book in the world? But all that changed when I surrendered to it, developed the right "mental set," which is not a "set" at all but a state of alert relaxation, adjustment to the hectic-leisurely pace of the novel, a readiness for sudden shifts in tone, from comic to absurd to tragic. I discovered why Eudora Welty, against her short-story writer's will and inclination, watched it grow, made it grow, because she fell in love with her hero, Jack Renfro, could not resist the Banner folk who rose in her imagination and clamored for her attention, made her laugh out loud as she listened to their talk and watched their antics. The zest of the author in this creation is amazing and infectious; it provides the necessary "staying power" that the novel requires for full appreciation.

The Optimist's Daughter seemed to me essentially a threnody of the greatest beauty, though, as always, "streaked" with comedy and satire. The book is perfectly constructed, and seems to carry the reader to the deepest places in the author's mind and heart, all light and all mystery together. The novel confirmed more fully than anything she has yet written the distinctions she makes between life and art. She gave to Becky McKelva the same mountain place and family from which her mother had come, and yet the character was in so many important ways unlike her mother—to whom the book is dedicated—and in none more than in the husband she'd married, completely different from her father, even in the complex reasons for his being an "optimist." *One Writer's Beginnings* was to reveal those parents in "portraits." There she was to explain how she invents characters, never writes "by invasion into the life of a real person." Instinctively she avoids writing about people to whom she feels close, since "those known to you in ways too deep, too overflowing, ever to be plumbed outside love—do not yield to, could never fit into, the demands of a story." She works her way toward "dramatic counterparts" of persons and experiences in real life. One could say that Eudora Welty is a "literalist of the imagination," to use Marianne Moore's phrase. She puts imaginary people in real gardens with real toads in them.

One Writer's Beginnings seemed to me a paean of praise. It revealed to me the importance of the lyrical to *all* of Eudora Welty's fiction, something I was impressed by in my rereading of the stories in *The Bride of the Innisfallen*. Bringing to her stories something of the emotional, aesthetic, and even logical expectations that we bring to the experience of music, song, poetry, I believe, results in the best reading of them. This begins with awareness of the celebrative impulse which she says is the source of her fiction—the desire "to praise, to love, to call up into view." The reader should be prepared for something "more felt than seen ahead like prophecy," to borrow Robert Frost's words about poetry, a certain "wildness of logic" to be found in lyrical works—the surprise and delight of choices made from an abundance of possibilities supplied by imagination. Lyricism affects form, language, subjects, themes, tone, and sound in Eudora Welty's fiction, and it is evident from the first in her autobiography.

She opens with a kind of prose poem, epigraph, or musical prelude, which appears by itself on the first page, italicized. It tells about how as a child she "tunes in" to her parents' lovely way of making their own habitual morning tasks light by whistling and humming the waltz from "The Merry Widow," up and down, back and forth, her father upstairs shaving, her mother downstairs frying the bacon. The child listens upstairs while she buttons her shoes, rhythmically drawing the buttonhook in and out in time to the antiphonal love exchange; the tune is fluid on the musical "stairs"; it ends as the little girl stands ready to run "clattering down" them. The child's containment, through listening, of an overflowing pleasure in what's heard; her sense of inclusion, expectancy, confidence in loving approval to follow as she "show[s] them [her] shoes," and the promise of the new day to be lived excitedly within the shelter of parental love—all these feelings are packed into the small button-shoed listener who is to become the writer and lift her own song, decades later, in praise of the beloved parents. The lyrical prelude, utterly simple and pure in language, becomes not only a tribute, but also an invocation to the muses of her fiction.

From all her work, she selects the character of the German-speaking music teacher in "June Recital" as the one in whose *making* she achieved the essence of her own fictional voice. The life and identity of this music teacher in no way resembled her own, and yet she realized that "Miss Eckhart came from me. . . . What I have put into her is my passion for my own life work, my own art. Exposing yourself to risk is a truth Miss Eckhart and I had in common. What animates and possesses me is what drives Miss Eckhart, the love of her art and the love of giving it, the desire to give it until there is no more left." In *creating* this character she found her "most inward and deeply feeling self." Characteristically, the narrator views Miss Eckhart's passion from a distance, the emotional remove of the child Cassie, an observer, who feels, in response to the music teacher's wild sonata playing during a sudden morning storm, that "something had burst out, unwanted, exciting, from the wrong person's life." Cassie looks for an escape. Only the mature Virgie Rainey begins to comprehend her old teacher after the remove of time. She had offered Virgie "*the* Beethoven"—the great Romantic composer who had absorbed the hero and the victim and had *that* passion to give. The Beethoven who seems closer in feeling to the author's in "June Recital," as to Cassie's, is the composer of "Für Elise"—that tender, affecting tune in a minor key, written by the master for a child.

The work of mediation continues. Is there not some way for the teacher-critic also to engage that "inward and deeply feeling self," the passion Eudora Welty put into Miss Eckhart, in discussion of her fiction, whether in critical articles or in the classroom? Because the pattern continues, of growing rifts between critic-teachers and literary texts (and their authors), and between teachers and students, with graduate students (often beginning teachers) caught somewhere in the middle of things, struggling to find a critical vocabulary, a way of thinking and talking about the fiction which will seem inventive, profound, and new.

Naturally enough, they take their cues from the reigning critical ideologies, and their most powerful and eminent exponents, which are largely post-Saussurean, abstract and theoretical, employing the language of scientific analysis (philosophical, linguistic, psychological, sociological), or new combinations of vocabularies (as in reader-response theory or feminist criticism). The work of art seems then to lose its integrity, to become a construct which is subject to deconstruction in largely abstract language. This may lead to a complete disjunction between the feelings of the critic and the writer, at least Eudora Welty's kind of writer. It often seems to me that certain kinds of critics have been erecting heavy, elaborate scaffolding around the work of art addressed—as though she were Miss Liberty in need of repairs. Undue attention seems to fall on the ingenuity of the scaffolding, the skill and athleticism of the critic, and the obvious is overlooked, which is what Miss Liberty is all about. What she means is visible in the thrust of her whole body upward and forward, her lifted heel showing under the back of her robe, her energy in its folds along her back. What she means is apparent from her severe, serene brow under the heavy parted hair and crown, her deeply set eyes gazing with stern sweetness over the harbor, her eyes seeming to devour the expanse of sky and sea in searching out the places from where the needy are coming. Miss Liberty's meaning is revealed in a gesture—that of holding the torch high and steadily—and in a noble expression on her face. Her meaning is freedom.

If I had to venture a single word for what Eudora Welty's fiction is all about, it would be *praise*. "Rühmen, das ists!" cries Rilke in the seventh of his Sonnets to Orpheus. "To praise is the whole thing!"

We cannot, as critics, always be praising; and furthermore, an illuminating piece of criticism, disclosing perhaps even to the author something new and undoubtedly present in the work, is an indirect form of praise, a tribute to an author's rich and varied achievement. Yet it seems patronizing to seize the work entirely from the author's hands and build a competing structure around it. Fiction writers who play games with readers are fair game for such treatment, but Eudora Welty does not play such games, and has made her larger hopes and intentions clear.

I think critics also have a duty to be clear, to resist ponderous critical vocabularies and heavy logistical structures which dissipate all feeling, all grace of style, along with the energy of a vigorous mind at work on a text. Good criticism is not obfuscating, an ordeal in the reading, but a source of illumination and pleasure.

Teachers have a different set of responsibilities. In some contexts they may be compared to performing artists—actors, singers, dancers who make the work of Shakespeare, Verdi, or Balanchine at least available to young people unprepared for art experiences more complex than those of rock music and television sit-coms. Before such students can be drawn into the delights of full enjoyment, some very humble tasks must be seen to, explanations made, entrenched attitudes challenged. We must remain flexible and patient, I think, and stay close to the text, reading it with the sound of her voice, which is in the text, in our ears, withholding the kind of critical theories we may expound in articles, allowing Eudora Welty's words to *create* the appropriate responses in students. Fortunately, her comedy seems to travel well in time and place, perhaps because most students today come prepared with at least one quality of mind and temperament my anxious, symbol-hunting Wellesley students did not possess years ago. They even have a word for it: "laid-back." Not at all a bad attitude for "Why I Live at the P. O." or "A Piece of News."

The word that keeps rising to her lips of praise is *blessed*: the epithet conveys the sense of a gift twice bestowed, as the word used in modern biblical translations, *happy*, does not. For everything she has been to us as a writer and friend, why should we not celebrate her as blessed?

Words Between Strangers: On Welty, Her Style, and Her Audience

Eudora Welty often speaks of her storytelling in terms that suggest it is a strategy for dealing with separateness.[1] She identifies the source of her work as "attentiveness and *care* for the world . . . and a wish to connect with it,"[2] and she tells us that her "continuing passion" is "to part a curtain . . . that falls between people."[3] But paradoxically, while Welty expresses her desire for "connection," she nonetheless prefers what she calls obstruction as the means to this end. "The fine story writers seem to be . . . obstructionists," she notes in "The Reading and Writing of Short Stories,"[4] and she finds the "quondam obstruction"—the sheer curtain that veils the meaning of a work—to be "the source of the deepest pleasure we receive from a writer."[5] I find this paradoxical combination of her thematic concern for "connection" and her preference for technical obstruction surprising and provocative, even though Welty's commentators have long discussed it and even though obstruction is commonplace in contemporary fiction.[6] Welty's stated purpose—she writes of successful fiction as "love accomplished"[7]—seems to be contradicted by a reader's experience of the technique she often chooses: a richly articulate style that holds back initially as if she were reluctant to give her fiction to her audience.

One result of this tension between message and technique

is fiction before which—as Ruth Vande Kieft has re-marked—"the welcome mat [is] clearly out . . . while the sign on the gate post [reads] 'Keep Out.'"[8] This is not the case with all, but with many of Welty's fictions: "Powerhouse," "The Wide Net," *The Golden Apples,* the stories of *The Bride of the Innisfallen* and others. These are fictions which may delight readers of various levels of so-phistication and training and yet leave them intrigued, feel-ing as if perhaps they have missed something in their under-standing. And these are fictions that, once they have de-lighted and puzzled, invite us to ask questions about Welty's style. Some of these questions are larger than how she uses point of view, plot, genre. We might ask, for example, precisely how love and obstruction can become the terms of one artistic equation and what role Welty's style plays in her relationship with her audience—or in other words, how much and exactly what Welty expects of her reader.

The question that occurs to me as I pursue this sort of speculation is whether Welty's style is at times a strategy for winning the struggle that can occur between writer and reader when a text is read, interpreted, and in some sense completed. The hotly debated critical question of who con-trols the meaning of a text—writer or reader—seems rele-vant here. Important reader-response critics such as Stanley Fish, Norman Holland, Wolfgang Iser and Jonathan Culler, among many others, have each illuminated the reading pro-cess as they see it. Fish and Holland, in their efforts to describe the reader's too-often ignored role in the creation of meaning, have assigned the primary position in this process to the reader and have granted him a remarkable degree of autonomy from the text. Stanley Fish, for example, has denied that a text has meaning independent of the reader's relationship to it. He asserts that a text is not "a thing-in-itself, but an *event,* something that *happens* . . . with the participation of the reader," and that the constraints that determine meaning do not "inhere in language but in situa-tions,"[9] that is, in a reader's situations. And Norman Hol-land has proposed that interpretation is the imposition of the reader's particular "identity theme,"[10] the characteristic pattern of understanding that has more to do with the reader's psychology and obsessive interests than with the text itself. These theories that give the reader control over meaning might reasonably unsettle any writer who has worked to polish and perfect a text, and yet they suggest an undeniable circumstance, that texts, as they are consumed and interpreted, do shade off into ideas that exist in readers' minds. Only there is a book completed.

In contrast to Fish and Holland's theories, Wolfgang Iser's formulation of the reading process admits the reader's role, and yet describes a less autonomous, but perhaps ideal reader who is out-going in his textual encounters and therefore careful to respond to the text itself. Iser paints what seems to me the portrait not of every reader in every reading encounter but of what a sensitive reader strives to be. Iser sees reading as a fluid process of self-correction that involves reaction, rereading, and revision as the reader provides a sequence of changing conceptual frameworks for the fiction. "We look forward, we look back, we decide, we change our decisions, we form expectations, we are shocked by their nonfulfillment, we question, we muse, we accept, we reject."[11] Meaning is built gradually: "smaller units progressively merge into bigger ones so that meaning gathers meaning in a kind of snowballing process."[12] Understanding of a text is a carefully constructed product of considerable interaction. Interpretations vary as each reader selects meaning from the potential text and completes it uniquely in response to sensitivities shaped by his education, his social, psychological, and philosophical backgrounds, and his historical place. But meaning does not rest wholly in the imagination of the reader; it resides in the coming together of the reader and the text. The process of reading a text provides the author's blueprint for making meaning with it; the reader builds meaning in part by responding to literary expectations which the text evokes.

In Jonathan Culler's terms, the text bids the reader to draw on his "literary competence." This competence, which is a knowledge of implicit but well-recognized literary conventions, allows a reader to recognize a story pattern, plot type, or genre, to identify a technique of point of view or an allusion and, on the basis of expectations cued by the text, to predict a kind of meaning to be made. In a successful reading, these conventions are the shared knowledge of the author and reader. Otherwise we have the case of the inexperienced student reader of "The Wide Net" who is perplexed when William Wallace, searching for the remains of his wife Hazel, wanders into the pleasures of a golden day. This none too hypothetical reader, perhaps unfamiliar with the conventions of the heroic epic, cannot predict that the wandering of a hero may prove to be his track, the path by which he will arrive where he is going. In Culler's view, conventional literary expectations make reading and writing possible. These

> the author can write against, certainly, . . . may attempt to subvert, but [they are] none the less the context within which his activity takes place, as surely as the failure to keep a promise is made possible by the institution of promising. Choices between words, between sentences, between different modes of presentation, will be made on the basis of their effects; and the notion of effect presupposes modes of reading which are not random or haphazard. Even if an author does not think of readers, he is himself a reader of his own work and will not be satisfied with it unless he can read it as producing effects.[13]

Here, Culler is able to grant the reader his place in the literary process while affirming that the author's text guides his expectations.

My own reaction to the work of these four critics is to recognize that they have highlighted an obvious but somehow long-neglected variable in the meaning-making process: readers and their responses. Yet when Fish and Holland picture the reader's process as largely independent of an author's control, I cannot help feeling that their correcting visions are misleading, although their strong emphasis on the reader's role is certainly predictable when the goal is to establish his place. One result of their influential discourse has been to make literary discussion of the author and his intentions unfashionable. But because I view reading as an encounter with minds and worlds, times and cultures distinct from my own, I find myself wanting to reverse this trend away from the author who is other.[14] One particular value of the reader-response critical model, if we put it into such reverse, would be to bring attention unexpectedly back to the writer. In other words, reader-response theory, having raised the issues of who controls meaning and of how it is negotiated by author and reader, both invites us and enables us to ask how an author attempts to direct his readers' somewhat unpredictable responses. For this reason, Iser's and Culler's work is more useful to me as I consider reading as an encounter, taking place sometimes over long distances of time and space, yet yielding an interaction and perhaps even an intimacy. In reading, as in a conversation, two minds can meet. And the one who speaks first, the author, tries to establish expectations to which a reader can predictably respond, albeit somewhat differently from every other reader. Together, through their shared knowledge of literary convention, over their different and mutual interests as well as their historical and cultural perspectives, the author and reader produce the individual literary performance.

The reader-response debate may seem far afield from Welty's own critical vocabulary, but it is relevant to a consideration of her style. A writer such as Welty, who I will argue hopes above all to be met in her fiction, might reasonably be concerned that the shared literary performance of author and reader should not ignore the guidelines that her written text imposes. Welty's concern with the question of who controls meaning in the reading process is clearest in her essay "How I Write," which was first published in 1955 and later revised for inclusion in *The Eye of the Story* (1978). In the first published version, Welty discussed the faults of a type of reader who sees the writing of a story as only "his own process in reverse":

> The analyst, should the story come under his eye, may miss
> the gentle shock and this pleasure too, for he's picked up the
> story at once by the heels (as if it had swallowed a button) and
> is examining the writing as his own process in reverse, as
> though a story (or any system of feeling) could be more
> accessible to understanding for being hung upside down.[15]

Apparently, Welty was giving careful thought to the writing
and reading processes, to their difference and to their relationship, years before the reader-response critics became
vocal in the 1970's. I take Welty as my subject here because
she has explicitly shown her awareness of the reading process and the risks that an author faces when giving fiction
over to a reader, but also because I believe she has developed
a stylistic trait that is her personal strategy for guiding her
reader towards meaning. My goal is to identify this particular trait while defining all that Welty hopes for from the
writer-reader relation, its hazards notwithstanding. Ultimately, I would like to suggest why when asked by Joanna
Maclay in 1980 "how [her] notion of the potential reader"
affected what she did "to make [her] meaning clear," Welty
answered by quoting a line of Henry Green's: "Prose should
be a long intimacy between strangers."[16]

My argument is that Welty's style demonstrates, and in
its way seems designed to demonstrate, the primacy of the
text in the reading process. Her fiction repeatedly elicits
expectations that it promptly defies. Yet the mistaken expectations that a reader develops as he follows the experience provided by her language are a part of her directions to
the text's meaning. The effect is to invite the reader to
return to the story again and again, to urge him to read it
closely and attentively. Areas of obstruction—for example,
unusual uses of point of view, of plot, genre, and allusion—
are themselves clues in Welty's fiction; and once a reader has
identified which of his expectations are frustrated, he is
usually on his way to understanding the fiction at hand,
having found its center. Seen in this light, Welty's use of
obstruction could be a technique for shaping a responsive
reader through her control of the textual experience. By

composing texts that require attentiveness and yield best to rereading, she might invite a reader to practice self-correction and to follow more closely her lead through the reading process. How she achieves this by manipulating the reader's expectations (of the sort that Iser and Culler stress) will, I hope, become clear in this essay.

Evidence of Welty's interest in the encounter of author and audience, and in the potential struggle between them for control of meaning, is available in several of her fictions that inherently explore problems in audience reception (for example, "Keela, the Outcast Indian Maiden," 1941, or *Losing Battles*, 1970). One of the earliest of these and, in my view, one of her more "obstructed" short stories is "Powerhouse," an opaque parable (in Welty's words) about "the traveling artist . . . in the alien world"[17] that portrays his interaction with audiences of varying degrees of receptivity. At second glance this story can reveal Welty's perception of the fragility and achievement of the writer-reader relationship, as well as the technical process by which she herself manages and creates that encounter. For the sake of what this story reveals about these issues, I take it as my point of reference and departure.

When we first meet him, Powerhouse is performing for a white audience that has come to marvel at a grotesque "Negro man," to see not the artist behind the mask but the mask they have urged onto him. To them, the black jazz musician looks "Asiatic, monkey, Jewish, Babylonian, Peruvian, fanatic, devil" (p. 131).[18] Powerhouse, stomping and smooching, improvises, however, with the stereotypes that his audience attributes to "people on a stage—and people of a darker race" (p. 131). In his performances, he tries to work this imposed identity until it becomes a medium for expressing his private self. But this particular audience on this particularly rainy night in Alligator, Mississippi, is not ready to receive the man behind his mask. Instead of sympathetically receiving his performance, instead of sharing his effort and his eventual achievement, they "feel ashamed for" the jazzman who seems to them to give everything (p.

133), and who, holding nothing in reserve, seems to expose himself before their unsympathetic eyes. They are curious, enthusiastic, but not in tune with him.

Attempting to give himself to these alienating spectators, Powerhouse feels displaced and begins to retreat behind the mask that reflects his audience's expectations for a "vast and obscene jazzman" (p. 131). He plays "Pagan Love Song," a sad song that he touches and that touches him back, confirming his estranged mood. Like Welty herself, Powerhouse is an artist who needs to place himself by recognizing his emotions, and to touch home with them in his work. And so he plunges into a depth of self by inventing the suicide of his wife, Gypsy, a story that he tells at first with his "wandering fingers," that is, in a musical exchange perhaps accompanied by stage whispers. The story he improvises creates a reason for his blues: a fictional telegram signed "Uranus Knockwood" that announces the news "Your wife is dead" (pp. 133–134).

Powerhouse's audience for this narrative performance is—in addition to the reader—the band itself, whose members vary in their capacities for sympathy and receptivity. They are implicitly different models of the reader. The far section of the band is "all studious, wearing glasses, every one," and "don't count." These technicians are figuratively and literally too far away to hear the jazzman's story. "Only those playing around Powerhouse are the real ones" (p. 132), the co-creating audience of Valentine, Little Brother, and perhaps Scoot. Of this group, Valentine and Little Brother readily receive, participate in, and protect Powerhouse's invention; Valentine immediately picks up the theme that Powerhouse establishes and begins to improvise on it: " 'You say you got a telegram' " (p. 134). But Scoot, who is a "disbelieving maniac," is not so cooperative; he asks a series of challenging, although participating, questions: " 'Gypsy? Why how come her to die, didn't you just phone her up in the night last night long distance?' "(p. 133). Such questions are inappropriate because they take the fiction literally, and so resist Powerhouse's fiction-making project and his purposes. They are combative as well and force Powerhouse to move his story in new directions; they challenge his control of the performance instead of inviting him to proceed with it. For a time, however, Scoot's questions serve Powerhouse well enough. For although Scoot asks Powerhouse to justify his creation rather than to expand it, his questions nevertheless give Powerhouse the opportunity to elaborate; the drummer's bantering questions establish the beat to create against, a function appropriate to his musical instrument.

Leaving the dance hall at intermission with his three accompanists, Powerhouse—now between sets in Negrotown's World Cafe—finds a large audience ready to respond to him as he develops the theme of Gypsy's death in a solely narrative performance that discloses themes of loneliness, disappointment, anger, and defiance. Powerhouse asks first to hear Bessie Smith's "Empty Bed Blues," but the juke box plays instead "Sent For You Yesterday and Here You Come Today," and Powerhouse imagines Gypsy wanting him. She listens for his footsteps and hears those of a stranger passing by. Powerhouse does not come. And she, defiant in her separateness, angrily kills herself by busting her brains all over the world.

> "Listen how it is. My wife gets missing me. Gypsy. She goes to the window. She looks out and sees you know what. Street. Sign saying Hotel. People walking. Somebody looks up. Old man. She looks down, out the window. Well? . . . *Ssssst! Plooey!* What do she do? Jump out and bust her brains all over the world." (p. 137)

Splattering Gypsy in a fantasy that investigates solitude, separateness, and death but is not itself sorrowful, the improvisation transforms Powerhouse's mood of lonely anxiety. As his mood changes, he elaborates on that comic, mythic nemesis, Uranus Knockwood, the father of all misfortune, the man who "takes our wives when we are gone," and who finds Gypsy when she dies:

> "That no-good pussyfooted crooning creeper, that creeper that follow around after me, coming up like weeds behind me,

following around after me everything I do and messing
around on the trail I leave. Bets my numbers, sings my songs,
gets close to my agent like a Betsy-bug; when I going out he
just coming in. I got him now! I got my eye on him." (p. 137–
138)

For Powerhouse, Knockwood personifies affliction; he is the
troublesome carrier of misfortune who brings disappointment, failure, and anxiety.

During this performance, Valentine and Little Brother
encourage and protect Powerhouse's creation. Gradually, a
larger audience has formed around the small group and its
collaborative members recognize Knockwood immediately.
"'Middle-size man.' 'Wears a hat.' 'That's him.' Everybody
in the room moans with pleasure" (p. 138). Powerhouse's
creation of Knockwood—the man who brings the Blues—
becomes for this sympathetic audience a means of chasing
those blues away. A waitress, in full sympathy with
Powerhouse, calls out, "'I hates that Mr. Knockwoods'" (p.
139). And she is also the one who asks him, "'All that the
truth?'" Her admiring question, like Scoot's belligerent
inquiries, once more raises the problem of the truth of
fiction. The musician, performing for this flirtatious,
provoking "Little-Bit" (p. 137), at first offers to show his
telegram. He is halted for a moment by the protective cry of
Little Brother, who does not want the energy building for
the next set to be lost, and who fears that if Powerhouse
reveals his art, he may sacrifice its power. But Powerhouse,
who is now playing primarily for the waitress, explains it
anyhow:

> "No, babe, it ain't the truth. . . . Truth is something worse, I
> ain't said what, yet. It's something hasn't come to me, but I
> ain't saying it won't. And when it does, then want me to tell
> you?" (p. 139)

The truth that has not yet come to Powerhouse is something
worse and something better than the story of Gypsy's
death. That truth is on its way; it is the transfiguration that

his story generates once it is successfully received and completed by this audience.

Powerhouse has told a story about loneliness and with it
he has produced a sense of belonging. This familiar pattern
of the blues performance is analyzed by Ralph Ellison in his
essay "Richard Wright's Blues": it fingers a wound, and yet
through the joy of expressing, surviving, and successfully
sharing a painful emotion with a sympathetic audience,
transforms it into something nearly or clearly celebratory.[19]
And so Powerhouse, singing the blues, has transcended his
isolation and "come out the other side" (p. 140). Heading
back to the dance, he creates a telegram of reply that puts
the four of them "in a wonderful humor." He will wire the
offending Knockwood: " 'What in the hell you talking
about? Don't make any difference: I gotcha.' " Members of
the small group agree, " 'You got him now' "(p. 140), and feel
that transformation, the surge of power generated by the
fiction. They see that Powerhouse has investigated a death
no one believes in—though all know it to be real and haunt-
ing—and somehow located through it his own life and
strength. With his story, he has mastered his experience; he
has transformed his disconcerting present into a future of
his choice and created joy by fabricating a tragedy. The
truth of his tale is the emotion that it has reflected and
transformed.

As Powerhouse prepares to re-enter the white dance hall,
Scoot, in crazy obtuseness, asks if Powerhouse isn't going to
call home and learn how Gypsy really is. Then "there is a
measure of silence." Scoot, "one crazy drummer that's going
to get his neck broken some day" (p. 140), endangers the
success of Powerhouse's art by failing to receive it. But
because Powerhouse has the audience he needs in Valentine
and Little Brother, Scoot's belligerence will not harm the
evening's culminating musical performance.

In the final section of the story, we see that Powerhouse's
successful narrative performance has recharged his
creativity. Back in the dance hall and in the audience, we

watch Powerhouse approach his piano as if "he saw it for the first time in his life." Then he

> tested it for strength, hit it down in the bass, played an octave
> with his elbow, lifted the top, looked inside, and leaned
> against it with all his might. He sat down and played it for a
> few minutes with outrageous force and got it under his
> power—a bass deep and coarse as a sea net—then produced
> something glimmering and fragile, and smiled. (pp. 140–141)

In this scene Powerhouse moves from his theme "I got a telegram my wife is dead" to the number "Somebody Loves Me." He has cast off his loneliness for a certainty that someone loves him—a certainty based on his interaction with the audience at the World Cafe—and he calls and shouts, "'I wonder who?'" Grimacing, he challenges his white audience with the line "Maybe . . . Maybe . . . Maybe it's you!" (p. 141).[20] And with this furious invitation, he also addresses the reader. In a blunt confrontation between author and audience, Powerhouse and Welty may seem to merge, to ask, "What kind of reader are you?" Are you like the white audience, alien, gawking at an entertainer whose creative efforts you block rather than receive? Or like the far section of the band—"studious, wearing glasses," not really with it? Or perhaps you are like Scoot, attentive, but asking all the wrong questions? Or could it be that you are like Valentine and Little Brother, participating in sympathy with the artist?

In short, the question that Welty asks in this last line of "Powerhouse" is whether we love her in her story. This question is unexpected because Welty herself has hindered her reader's first approach to intimacy. In a fiction that dramatizes a performer's relationship with several essentially unreceptive audiences, Welty has chosen to complicate her own author-audience relationship by adopting the technique of obstruction. Although my summary has smoothed the story over and temporarily set aside the questions that color a reader's first encounter with it, the story itself unfolds against expectations that it creates but fails to fulfill.

"Powerhouse" is likely to astonish a reader in three ways: (1) in its turn away from the question of whether Gypsy is really dead, (2) in its merging of Powerhouse's narrative invention with his musical creation, and (3) in its unannounced shifts in point of view. I have named and will discuss these narrative surprises while fully aware that the precise steps of every reader's encounter with the story will be different and reflect his or her readerly skills. I am not prescribing here readerly errors necessarily encountered by all readers of this text, but attempting to describe the process of revising expectations that Welty's text calls for, a process I will be somewhat overly deliberate about, slowing it down so that it can be discussed.

When a reader first meets Powerhouse's statement " 'I got a telegram my wife is dead,' " he may wonder why Powerhouse, who should be mourning, is on stage. If he concentrates on Powerhouse's startling announcement, he may be too preoccupied to notice that the jazzman's story is told in a musical exchange:

> "You know what happened to me?" says Powerhouse.
> Valentine hums a response, dreaming at the bass.
> "I got a telegram my wife is dead," says Powerhouse, *with wandering fingers.*
> "Uh-huh?"
> His mouth gathers and forms a barbarous O *while his fingers walk up straight, unwillingly, three octaves.*
> "Gypsy? Why how come her to die, didn't you just phone her up in the night last night long distance?"
> "Telegram say—here the words: Your wife is dead." *He puts 4/4 over the 3/4.*
> *"Not but four words?" This is the drummer,* an unpopular boy named Scoot, a disbelieving maniac. . . .
> Little Brother, *the clarinet player, who cannot now speak, glares and tilts back.* . . .
> "What the hell was she up to?" Powerhouse shudders. *"Tell me, tell me, tell me." He makes triplets, and begins a new chorus. He holds three fingers up.*

"You say you got a telegram." *This is Valentine, patient and sleepy, beginning again.*
Powerhouse is elaborate. "Yas, the time I go out, go way downstairs along a long cor-ri-dor to where they puts us: coming back along the cor-ri-dor: steps out and hands me a telegram: Your wife is dead."
"Gypsy?" *The drummer like a spider over his drums.* (pp. 133–134; italics mine)

This passage introduces both the theme of gypsy's death and the suspicion that Gypsy is not dead. A first-time reader meets it wondering how to understand Powerhouse's narrative-within-a-narrative. The temporarily obstructed reader, trying to make sense of Powerhouse's tale, may or may not notice and respond to the suggestive phrases that I have italicized. When a reader does focus on these lines, unexpected questions about the unconventionality of this passage arise. "Literary competence," the reader's conventional expectation, is leading the way here, and underlining the importance of Welty's unconventionality. When Powerhouse speaks with wandering fingers, is he literally speaking through his musical performance? His 4/4 over 3/4 and his triplets, not coincidentally, are the rhythms he develops in Gypsy's story. And when Scoot and Little Brother speak, are they speaking in turn as their performances allow and instruments direct? When Valentine begins again, is he beginning a variation on a musical theme? If a reader is attentive and recognizes the correspondence between Powerhouse's fiction and his music, what should he make of music that poses as narrative? Is Powerhouse's story perhaps the narrator's interpretation of his music as she listens intently to hear the performers' "least word, especially what they say to one another, in another language?" (p. 132). How many readers attend the text closely enough to ask these sorts of questions, and at what point in their reading process?

A reader's confusion about Powerhouse's narrative is explicitly invited to turn to skepticism when Scoot asks, "'Gypsy? Why how come her to die?'" Then a reader may be trapped for a time in Scoot's overly literal questions. Wanting to know if Gypsy is really dead, the reader asks a question that the story brushes aside. As his expectations for a literal truth are frustrated, he soon realizes that his is the wrong question, that he has been misdirected by his false expectation, and by Welty, who set up that expectation. His surprise, his obstructed expectation, may then unfold the fiction by leading him to ask why Powerhouse told the tale of Gypsy's death. Gradually, the answer to this question appears if the reader has been willing to follow Welty's text: Powerhouse's music and his story are two interactive elements in one composition on the theme of loneliness which itself is a joyful, creative means to counter it. Like Powerhouse, that person of joy who transforms the black devil stereotypes of his audience into a medium for self-expression, Welty maneuvers the expectations of her readers until they help her to create something of her own.

Welty leads her reader by indirect means to ask about the source of Powerhouse's art, about the truth of his fiction, about his need for an audience. She maneuvers the reader's own reactions—which are structured by the text, as Iser and Culler have suggested—until they create the meaning of the story, a meaning that exists in those reactions rather than in the text per se. She guides the reader with an experiment in point of view. The story's first, second, and fifth sections are told by a hypothetical someone in the audience at the dance. The third and fourth sections, however, seem to be related by a more privileged narrator who moves with Powerhouse through the rainy night. Or perhaps these sections represent the fantasy of the narrator in the audience, whose imagination responds to Powerhouse's art. Whatever the cause, the effect of the shift is clear. By shifting the point of view closer to Powerhouse, Welty moves the reader from the audience's view of him as a marvelous, but "vast and obscene" (p. 131) jazzman, to perception of the man behind that grotesque mask, the man who "seems lost—down in the song, yelling up like somebody in a whirlpool—not guiding [the band]—hailing them only" (p. 132). The shift moves the reader from the audience that views Powerhouse as alien, monstrous, "Asiatic, monkey, . . . devil," to membership in the elite who travel with Powerhouse and know his emotions and artistic strategies. In these sections of the story, the reader's privileged vision exceeds and frames that of the original narrator. The unexpected narrative shift reduces the distance between narrator and subject, and thus urges the reader into sympathy with Powerhouse and his creative need. This new relationship causes the reader to revise his first assessment and perhaps to realize that the meaning of the story was not disclosed in Powerhouse's fiction about Gypsy's death, but at the end of the first section when the narrator spoke cryptically of listening in order to learn "what it is"—that is, "what it is" (p. 132) that makes a performance great. In its way, the story has taught the reader himself to be a part of this thing, for if he has met the challenge of Welty's obstruction, he has become, like Little Brother and Valentine, part of an attentive, involved, cooperative, and loving audience.

Welty's style, then, urges a reader to attend the text, to be a reader responding to a writer. Her "obstructions," paradoxically, are a measure of her apprehension for successful interaction with her audience. Her misgivings about her readers' powers of receptivity, expressed here in fictional form, have also made themselves felt in her interviews and critical essays. I turn to these now to define more precisely Welty's attitude towards the reading encounter.

In her interviews and essays Welty has been warmly responsive to her best readers, and quick to say that—because of the help of such early supporters as Ford Madox Ford, Katherine Anne Porter, Robert Penn Warren, and her agent Diarmuid Russell—her work "has always landed safely and among friends."[21] She has appreciated critical attention, named insights it has given her, and even remained tolerant of interpretations that seemed to her "far-flung" by remembering that a writer hopes to suggest all kinds of possibilities.[22] As early as in "How I Write" (1955), she realized that a reader's commentary on a story "may go deeper than its object and more times around; it may pick up a story and waltz with it so that it's never the same," allowing that the waltz might be desirable, since the richness of fictional meaning is made over time and in more than one mind.

But Welty has also shown periodic and healthy exasperation with wrong-headed readers, an exasperation with their failure to meet her in her fictions. Then Welty seems to feel as if a portion of her audience is like Marian, the campfire girl in her story "A Visit of Charity," who set out to meet someone new but retreated when faced with the shock of encounter. In an interview with Henry Mitchell (1972), Welty joked about ordering stationery printed with a ready response for misguided correspondents: "You Just Can't Get There From Here." A reader familiar with her occasionally disturbed reactions to requests that interpretations be confirmed might guess she had a reply to some of those letters in mind. Another such correcting reply is her essay entitled "Is Phoenix Jackson's Grandson Really Dead?" (1974), in which she responded to the "unrivaled favorite" question of her public, and quietly explained that their inquiry, like those that Scoot had made, was not relevant to "the truth of the story." Earlier, in her essay "The Reading and Writing of Short Stories" (1949), she had confessed to being "baffled" by rigid analyses of her stories. "When I see them analyzed—most usually 'reduced to elements'—sometimes I think, 'This is none of me.' Not that I am too proud to like being reduced, especially; but that I could not remember starting with those elements—with anything that I could so label."[23] And in an interview with Charles Bunting (1972), she expressed surprise that some of her readers had failed to respect her as an authority on her fictions:

> I've had students write to me and say, "I'm writing a thesis to prove that *The Golden Apples* is a novel. Please send me. . . ."
> . . .So I write back and say that it isn't a novel, I'm sorry. They go right ahead, of course. It doesn't matter with a thesis, I guess.[24]

These comments all suggest Welty's mistrust of those readers who fail to meet her in her fiction. In "How I Write" she described this reader as suffering from too independent an imagination, which was also a failure of imagination. Perhaps resembling the technicians of Powerhouse's band, "studious and wearing glasses" (p. 132), he can seem "blind . . . ingrown and tedious" in his analyses because he thinks that "he is 'supposed' to see in a story . . . a sort of plant-from-seed development, rising in the end to a perfect Christmas tree of symmetry. . . ." Unlike "the reader of more willing imagination . . . [who] may find the branch-ings not what he's expecting,"[25] this reader, she went on to comment in "Words Into Fiction" (1965), errs by replacing her "mystery" with his order:

> . . . a body of criticism stands ready to provide [a] solution, which is a kind of translation of fiction into another language. It offers us close analysis, like a headphone we can clamp on at the U.N. when they are speaking the Arabian tongue. . . .
> A year or so of one writer's life has gone into the writing of a novel. . . . Does this not suggest that . . . words have been found for which there may be no other words?[26]

This sort of approach to fiction, as Welty put it in a remark about Faulkner's critics, is "to tree it."[27] She dislikes the desire to explain and restate fiction that "outside its own terms, which never were explanatory, no longer exists."[28] Convinced that meaning is not excavated from a fiction like precious metals from rubble, but is an experience one has while reading, Welty has mocked the critical impulse to explanation, saying, "I was once asked to tell one of my stories in my own words."[29] Unlike the critics who perturb her with their explications, she believes "great fiction . . . abounds in what makes for confusion. . . . It is very seldom neat, is given to sprawling and escaping from bounds, is capable of contradicting itself, and is not impervious to humor. There is absolutely everything in great fiction but a clear answer."[30] "To make a work of the imagination out to be something in another category, that can be learned in capsule terms, as an algebraic, or mathematical formula, is," she argues, "not honest."[31] Like Little Brother who feared that Powerhouse might lose his performance if he explained it, she does not trust explication. Instead, like her friend Ida M'Toy, she wants to be listened to with the whole attention, to have her "true words" remembered, and to warn us: "'Let her keep it straight, darling.'"[32]

Welty's strategy, then, for shaping and educating the reader who substitutes his own words and meaning for hers is to temporarily hinder his progress through the work. Because he looks only "for his own process in reverse," and so is in some danger of never finding Welty in her own story, she delays his appropriation of it. Her style demands that he gain perspective on his own first impressions, and coerces him to become more familiar with the limited range of possibility that is the text. Welty wants her words, the order she has created, to be held; one important effect of her style is to keep the reader close to those words while he is temporarily uncertain how to convert them into any of his own. Welty would perhaps like her stories to be too complex for analysis; and interpretations of her fictions are, in fact, rarely able to recreate the process by which a reader understands them, although that process is, after all, where the pleasure of an encounter with her fiction rests.

When Welty writes criticism herself, her key words—mystery, passion, and love—are of the affective sort that make analysts nervous. But Welty is not speaking in vague generalizations when she discusses successful fiction as "love accomplished."[33] Instead, she is outlining her expectations for her audience. What she wants from her reader is to have him find her and thereby know her. However, Welty is an author who thinks autobiographical revelations are largely irrelevant in a writer-reader exchange. Instead, the writer's project—at one level—is to transmute his or her essential, as opposed to merely real, self into fiction. When Welty praises other authors, she frequently writes of their presence in the text. For instance, Henry Green "is there at the center of what he writes, but in effect his identity has turned into the fiction. And while you the reader know nothing of Mr. Henry Green's life, as he has taken good care to see to, in the long run a life's confidence is what you feel you have been given."[34] When Welty tells us that this writer lives in his work, that his fiction "should be read instead of some account of his life," she is expressing an oblique but genuine concern that her own fiction be an encounter.

In this reading encounter, Welty expects to move her readers toward an intuition of what Wayne Booth has called "the implied author,"[35] what I have called her essential self, a construct that readers infer from the "real" author's conscious and unconscious literary choices. These choices are what Welty refers to when she writes that it is "through the shaping of the work in the hands of the artist that you most nearly come to know what can be known, on the page, of . . . [him] as apart from the others."[36] "The events of a story," she tells us, "may have much or little to do with the writer's own life: but the story *pattern* is the nearest thing to a mirror image of his mind and heart."[37] "It's our perception of this ordering"—and here I find myself thinking of Welty's own ordering for obstruction—"that gives us our nearest understanding"[38] of an author.

Welty expresses both what she hopes for and fears from interaction with her reader with a word that, in her comments and criticism, she repeatedly borrows from her photographer's vocabulary: "exposure." In her preface to *One Time, One Place* (1971), she speaks of having first recognized her narrative goal of exposure—to record the divulging gesture, to disclose the inner secret concealed in the concrete and objective by framing it—while working with a camera. She "learned quickly enough when to click the shutter, but what [she became] aware of more slowly was a story-writer's truth: the thing to wait on, to reach there in time for, is the moment in which people reveal themselves."[39] Welty seeks the perfect fictional exposure that will capture and convey her feeling and identity in words as a camera arrests a telling sign with the click of a shutter. Welty has argued that fiction, "whatever its subject, is the history itself of [the author's] life's experience in feeling"[40] and should therefore be read with love. But like the young girl in her story "A Memory" whose experience of first love contained discoveries of separateness and vulnerability, Welty understands the complexity of the reading process perfectly well enough to dread the hazards of encounter. Consequently, she is somewhat anxious as she exposes her essential, rather than merely actual, self to her audience. She writes of her need for "exposure to the world,"[41] but also of "the terrible sense of exposure" that she feels when she suddenly sees her "words with the eyes of the cold public."[42] She writes of exposure as a process that "begins in intuition and has its end in showing the heart that expected, while it dreads that exposure."[43]

The challenge of exposing an essential self in fiction rests in manipulating the external realities of words and readers to bring it into being, and certainly the project is full of risk. The most unreliable factor is the reader: the author's attempt to create and communicate herself will fail if the reader does not receive her. Like Welty's character Clytie who peers into others' faces while looking for the one that is familiar—her own—Welty sets out to meet the reader in part to find herself. It is up to the reader to reflect back to her, mirror-like, the intelligence that glances off her fiction. For this reason, the reader who first misses Welty's intention, then recomposes her text along his own lines, and finally returns to her a stranger's face, is troublesome. Still, Welty relies on this audience because she can only judge her success at constructing herself in her fiction on the basis of its reception. Her essential self is the product of her fiction's reception—the presence that her careful readers come to know as imaginative and intelligent, observant and witty, sympathetic and sharp, quite vulnerable and yet experimental and daring.

Like Powerhouse, Welty risks giving all she has to an audience that perhaps will know no better than to feel ashamed for her self-exposure. She takes this risk with feelings of vulnerability offset by the self-confidence of an artist who understands her medium and knows quite a few ways to manage the reading encounter. "Exposing yourself to risk is a truth Miss Eckhart and I had in common," Welty remarks in a self-revealing line that draws a comparison between her own passion for her life's work and Miss Eckhart's "love of her art and . . . love of giving it." The risk involved here is in the "giving it," as when Miss Eckhart gave to Virgie Rainey who, like some headstrong reader, was fortunately taking even though she appeared to reject. At the end of *One Writer's Beginnings*, the autobiographical essay in which this line appears, Welty remarks, "I am a writer who came of a sheltered life. A sheltered life can be a daring life as well. For all serious daring starts from within."[44] In these lines, I hear Welty noting the connectedness of as well as the distance between what I have called her real and essential selves. And I hear her rediscovering for herself and for us too the daring of imaginative wandering, of artistic experimentation, and of the risk she has taken when giving her fiction over to us, her readers.

Thinking about the range, publication history, and achievement of Welty's fiction, it seems possible that Welty's concern to reach her audience has affected the shape of her career. The very diversity of Welty's fiction reflects her address of different audiences and, perhaps implicitly, her exploration of the idea of audience itself. In the year when Welty discussed the potential chasm between writer and reader in "How I Write"—1955—she was already an author who had addressed a variety of audiences, a variety climaxed by the great distance between her easily accessible, democratic *The Ponder Heart* and her obscure, elitist *The Bride of the Innisfallen*, books that were published back-to-back in 1954 and 1955. And then, in 1955, there began a period which lasted for fifteen years and ended when she published *The Optimist's Daughter* and *Losing Battles* in rapid succession in 1969 and 1970. This period, sometimes inaccurately called a gap in her career, was a time when Welty wrote more than she published and experimented by reaching out to new audiences. It seems possible to me that these years reflect a productive reaction to her reader's initial failure to meet her in *The Bride of the Innisfallen*, a failure measurable through the cool response of her reviewers.[45] Did Welty reconsider her address of her audience while postponing exposure as usual?

There is some evidence to support this possibility. First, during these years, Welty's publications addressed several new audiences in new ways. She published essays that clarified her attitude toward criticism, a children's book, *The Shoe Bird*, as well as two stories responding to the Civil-Rights crisis in Mississippi which developed private themes through less private subject matter than she had taken before. What she did not publish, but instead worked on over a period of ten years, was her central fictional project, *Losing Battles*. This project was quite different from *The Bride of the Innisfallen* and problematic to Welty for the same reason that the novel is highly accessible to readers; that is, it is built almost entirely on dialogue and action. Welty commented that because she felt she had "been writing too much by way of description, of introspection on the part of [her] characters, [she] tried to see if [she] could make everything shown."[46] Then, before completing *Losing Battles* and offering it to her readers, she wrote her very personal *The Optimist's Daughter* and quickly published both books.[47] Welty herself has pointed out that during these years she was nursing her failing mother and teaching for a year at Millsaps College—two events that of course changed her usual writing habits. Constrained, she took notes and wrote scenes for *Losing Battles*, tucking "them in a box, with no opportunity to go back and revise, but writing a scene anew instead of revising it, so that the work prolonged itself." "I . . . kept thinking of more and more scenes. . . . There were extra incidents, which told the same thing in different terms, different scenes, different characters."[48] "I must have thrown away at least as much as I kept in the book. . . . I would write the scene out just to let [the characters] loose on something—my private show."[49] Of course, speculation that this change in habit and project grew up partially in response to thoughts and feelings about meeting her readers is just that, speculation. But during these years, Welty did not offer more of her very personal, or obstructed fiction to her audience through publication. Instead, she grew in new ways and produced *Losing Battles*.

At the climax of this novel Jack Renfro is able to love Julia Mortimer and so to admit her to his family circle: " 'I reckon I even love her,' said Jack, 'I heard her story.' " The familial model of author-audience interaction that this novel conveys is not at all beside the point. In her essay on Jane Austen, Welty pictures Austen "reading . . . chapters aloud to her own lively, vocative family, on whose shrewd intuition, practiced estimation of conduct, and seasoned judgment of character she relied almost as well as on her own." In that image, Welty imagines a perfect family circle as the ideal author-audience relationship. Jane Austen, Welty wrote, "must have enjoyed absolute confidence in an understanding reception of her work. [Her] novels still have a bloom of shared pleasure. And the felicity they have for us must partly lie in the confidence they take for granted between the author and her readers."[50]

If Welty has a model of her own to offer to current theorizing about the writer-reader relationship, it is this confidential family. And the function of her sometimes obstructing style is to transform the willing stranger into a member of this inner circle.[51] Welty's narrative obstacles can thus be understood as leading one to read for the sake of encounter rather than appropriation. It is the very process of unraveling difficulties that binds the successful reader to Welty with the thread of fiction; they come to share knowledge inaccessible to others who have not been so attentive, or sympathetic. As the division between reader and audience gradually diminishes, the reader is directed to complete the fiction along the lines that Welty imagined. Her obstruction of her reader's expectations more than reflects, it enacts her characteristic theme of love and separateness; it leads the reader to experience isolation and to discover communion.

In the interview I mentioned earlier, Joanna Maclay asked Eudora Welty "how [her] notion of the potential reader" affected what she did "to make [her] meaning clear." And Welty, who at first answered, "I don't know," ended by quoting Henry Green's remark: "Prose should be a long intimacy between strangers. . . ." In the context of my discussion of Welty's "Powerhouse" and her view of reading, I hope that this response has come into focus as a photograph does when rising to exposure in a developer's tray, or as Welty's fictions can in the reading process. Welty, it seems, was writing about and with knowledge of the issues of the reader-response debate two decades before it gained attention, and by adding Welty's voice to the others quoted in this article, I add the writer's point of view.

1. Here I borrow Robert Penn Warren's term from his perceptive early article, "The Love and the Separateness in Miss Welty," *Kenyon Review*, 6 (1944), 246–259.

2. Reynolds Price, "Eudora Welty in Type and Person" (1978), in *Conversations with Eudora Welty*, ed. Peggy W. Prenshaw (Jackson: University Press of Mississippi, 1984), p. 235.

3. Eudora Welty, *One Time, One Place: Mississippi in the Depression, A Snapshot Album* (New York: Random House, 1971), p. 8.

4. *Atlantic Monthly*, 183 (March 1949), 49.

5. Welty takes care to amend the impression that she values obscurity. In a 1977 interview with Jean Todd Freeman she explained that she abominates "deliberate obscurity" but that "mysterious is something else" (*Conversations*, pp. 189–190). The complex differences between being obscure—"a fault in the teller"—and being "mysterious"—a virtue in a writer—is in a sense the topic of this essay.

6. One of the earliest, best, and most relevant of these discussions is Ruth M. Vande Kieft's chapter "The Mysteries of Eudora Welty," in *Eudora Welty* (New York: Twayne, 1962). Another is Michael Kreyling's essay, "Words into Criticism: Eudora Welty's Essays and Reviews," in *Eudora Welty: Critical Essays*, ed. Peggy W. Prenshaw (Jackson: University Press of Mississippi, 1979), pp. 411–422.

7. Welty, "The House of Willa Cather" (1979), in *The Eye of the Story: Selected Essays and Reviews* (New York: Random House, 1978), p. 55.

8. Vande Kieft, p. 25.

9. Stanley Fish, *Is There A Text in This Class?* (Cambridge: Harvard University Press, 1980), pp. 25, 292.

10. Norman N. Holland, *Five Readers Reading* (New Haven: Yale University Press, 1975).

11. Wolfgang Iser, *The Implied Reader* (Baltimore: The Johns Hopkins University Press, 1974), p. 288.

12. Iser, "The Reality of Fiction," *New Literary History*, 7 (1975), 20.

13. Jonathan Culler, *Structuralist Poetics* (Ithaca: Cornell University Press, 1975), p. 116. In this passage, Culler clearly emphasizes the author's part in directing the reading process. Elsewhere, without in fact contradicting himself, he emphasizes that it is the reader's literary competence which creates the perceived structure of the text.

14. Peter Rabinowitz has also defended author-centered meaning in his article "The Turn of The Glass Key: Popular Fiction as a Reading Strategy," *Critical Inquiry*, 11 (1985), 418–431; he too is pushing against the theoretical current I have mentioned.

15. Welty modified her censure of certain kinds of readers when she prepared "How I Write" for reissue in *The Eye of the Story* and retitled the essay "Writing and Analyzing a Story." I suspect she made these adjustments in part because the readers-gone-wrong who concerned her in 1955, and earlier in "The Reading and Writing of Short Stories" (1949), concerned her less by 1978 when she had more nearly found the audience she was seeking. But the issues raised by these two early essays are very relevant to her fiction, and so I quote "How I Write" in its original form as it appeared in *Virginia Quarterly Review*, 31 (1955), 244.

16. *Conversations*, p. 282.

17. Linda Kuehl, "The Art of Fiction XLVII: Eudora Welty" (1972), in *Conversations*, p. 85.

18. Here and elsewhere in this discussion, I refer to the text of "Powerhouse" as it appears in *The Collected Stories of Eudora Welty* (New York: Harcourt Brace Jovanovich, 1980). Page references are included parenthetically in the text.

19. In *Shadow and Act* (New York: Vintage Books, 1972), Ellison explains that "the blues is an impulse to keep the painful details and episodes of a brutal experience alive in one's aching consciousness, to finger its jagged grain, and to transcend it, not by the consolation of philosophy but by squeezing from it a near-tragic, near-comic lyricism" (p. 78).

20. Welty recalls the history of this last line: "It was *The Atlantic Monthly* that published [the story] first. I remember because . . . they censored my selection of a song that ended the story. It was 'Hold Tight, I Want Some Seafood, Mama,' a wonderful record. They wrote me that

The Atlantic Monthly cannot publish those lyrics. I never knew why. I had to substitute 'Somebody Loves You. I Wonder Who' which is okay but 'Hold Tight' was marvelous. You know the lyrics with Fats Waller singing 'fooly racky sacky want some seafood, Mama!' " [Jane Reid Petty, "The Town and the Writer: An Interview with Eudora Welty" (1977), in *Conversations*, p. 209.] The original ending, then, stressed a different strand in the story's composition—Powerhouse's longing and the promise of fulfillment, in this context a metaphor for an artistic consummation. Nonetheless, Welty's choice of the new ending was deliberate, was kept in later versions of the story, and was itself fortunate.

21. Kuehl, *Conversations*, p. 86.

22. Martha van Noppen, "A Conversation with Eudora Welty" (1978), in *Conversations*, p. 247, and Jean Todd Freeman, "An Interview with Eudora Welty" (1977), in *Conversations*, p. 189.

23. *Atlantic Monthly*, 183 (February 1949), 55.

24. " 'The Interior World': An Interview with Eudora Welty," in *Conversations*, p. 43.

25. "How I Write," p. 244.

26. Welty, "Words into Fiction" (1965), in *The Eye of the Story*, p. 137.

27. Welty, review of *Intruder in the Dust* by William Faulkner, in *The Eye of the Story*, p. 210.

28. Welty, "Henry Green: Novelist of the Imagination" (1961), in *The Eye of the Story*, p. 28.

29. "Symposium: The Artist and The Critic," *Stylus*, 9 (1966), 21.

30. Welty, "Must the Novelist Crusade?" (1965), in *The Eye of the Story*, p. 149.

31. Bunting, *Conversations*, p. 62.

32. Welty, "Ida M'Toy," in *The Eye of the Story*. p. 338.

33. Michael Kreyling makes this point well in "Words into Criticism."

34. Welty, "Henry Green," p. 26.

35. Wayne Booth, *The Rhetoric of Fiction* (Chicago: University of Chicago Press, 1961), pp. 74–75.

36. Welty, "Words into Fiction," p. 144.

37. Welty, "The House of Willa Cather," p. 48.

38. Welty, "Looking at Short Stories" (1949), in *The Eye of the Story*, p. 105.

39. Welty, *One Time, One Place*, pp. 7–8.

40. Welty, "Words into Fiction," p. 142.

41. Welty, *One Time, Once Place*, p. 8.

42. Kuehl, *Conversations*, p. 76.

43. Welty, "How I Write," p. 249.

44. Welty, *One Writer's Beginnings* (Cambridge and London: Harvard University Press, 1984), pp. 101, 104.

45. See, for example, William Peden's representative review, "The

Incomparable Welty," *Saturday Review,* 9 April 1955, p. 18, a reluctant confession that he found this new work "obscure."

46. Kuehl, *Conversations,* p. 77.

47. Welty first published *The Optimist's Daughter* in *The New Yorker* (15 March 1969) and then revised the work for publication in 1972 by Random House.

48. Bunting, *Conversations,* p. 47.

49. Kuehl, *Conversations,* p. 77.

50. Welty, "The Radiance of Jane Austen" (1969), in *The Eye of the Story,* p. 6.

51. Welty has said she first sent her stories to magazines because she was too shy to show them to anybody she actually knew. "When I began to write stories, I could not have let my family or my friends see them. I thought, well, I'll send these to an abstract reader." [Scot Haller, "Creators on Creating: Eudora Welty" (1981), in *Conversations,* p. 311.] The "abstract reader," through reading, can apparently become a member of Welty's most trusted circle.

MARY HUGHES BROOKHART

AND

SUZANNE MARRS

More Notes on River Country

Getting to Rodney, Mississippi, is not easy. Established in 1828 and located forty-five miles north of Natchez, Rodney does not appear on the Official Highway Map of Mississippi. Furthermore, although the paved road to Rodney is charted, the road contains no signs to direct travelers or to confirm their arrival in the town. Once a busy cotton port on the Mississippi River, Rodney fell into decline when the river changed its course; today the Mississippi is nearly four miles away and Rodney is almost a ghost town. Nevertheless, this obscure hamlet draws a small, determined stream of visitors; some come to view the local churches, but more come to see the place Eudora Welty has recorded in many photographs, in the essay "Some Notes on River Country," and in two works of fiction. It was especially those works of fiction which prompted our trip to Rodney on a hot summer afternoon in 1983.

Rodney's Landing existed in our imaginations as an eighteenth-century port, full of the clamor, the danger, and the incipient prosperity depicted in *The Robber Bridegroom*. But it existed even more vividly for us as the twentieth-century backwater town where Jenny Lockhart lives in "At The Landing." We particularly expected to find that town, and indeed we did. Not until later did we recognize just how selectively and metaphorically Welty had portrayed Rodney in "At The landing." In her essay "Place in Fiction," Welty has stated that

. . . the writer must accurately choose, combine, superimpose upon, blot out, shake up, alter the outside world for one absolute purpose, the good of his story. To do this, he is always seeing double, two pictures at once in his frame, his and the world's, a fact that he constantly comprehends; and he works best in a state of constant and subtle and unfooled reference between the two. It is his clear intention—his passion, I should say—to make the reader see only one of the pictures—the author's—under the pleasing illusion that it is the world's; this enormity is the accomplishment of a good story.[1]

Just such a double vision, we came to realize, informed "At The Landing." Welty had not only chosen, but had also added to, altered, and omitted details from an actual place in order to create the locale of her story, a locale both credible and thematically significant. After we had visited Rodney, had reread "At The Landing" in the light of that visit, and had discovered "The Children," an early un-published sketch which prefigures the later story without having its well-developed setting, we knew that the "con-stant and subtle" reference between the outside world and the world of Jenny Lockhart was Welty's own enormous "accomplishment."

Traveling to Rodney took longer than we had planned. But after wandering the by-ways of Jefferson and Claiborne Counties for an hour or so, we finally asked directions and followed them to the bottom of a bluff, to the end of a road, and to a town which seemed to have emerged from "At The Landing." Rodney's hazy, flat, sandy, unpaved expanse seemed once to have been river bed. A smattering of wooden houses, some obviously occupied and others boarded up and abandoned, bore high water marks from recurring floods, marks like those which belted Mag Lock-hart's house; the town's most handsome structure, a two-story brick building, was crumbling away, left with only a "remnant of gallery."[2] A "rusty-red horse," like the one Billy Floyd mounted and rode so wildly, grazed freely and peacefully in front of a church (p. 243). We even saw black butterflies circle each other as they do when Jenny walks with Billy Floyd. No one came out to greet us or to disturb us, although we felt watched and intruding, just as Jenny would have felt when she came down from her grandfather's house into the town. The only sign of life we saw was a basketball game—a few men played at a single hoop in a dirt yard.

As Jenny would not have dared to do, we walked over to the men, said hello, and asked how we might get to the cemetery on the bluff. We were so convinced of the story's reality that we felt the cemetery must be there. The men were diffident but obliging. Yet when another man swaggered over carrying a pint bottle of whiskey in a paper bag, we felt the imminence of danger that Jenny's grandfather had tried to impart to her. That man's words confirmed the danger, but in more abstract terms: "You go up there and you'll see things you never seen before." His parting admonition was "Watch out for snakes."

We could not have found the path without directions, for weeds as high as our heads concealed it. But once we had walked through the weeds and climbed up a hill, we were in Jenny's world. Rodney Cemetery remains "a dark shelf above the town" with grapevines and Spanish moss hanging so densely about the graves that for us, as for Jenny, the stones seemed made of moss, the moss of stone (p. 243). Leafy vines made "pillars about the trunks of the trees and arches and buttresses all among them" (p. 257). And from the dark, secluded shelf of the cemetery, we could look down across a ravine at a sunny, grassy area—the field where Billy Floyd might have appeared on the red horse that was not his.

Rodney, of course, has changed in the years since 1943 when Welty first published her story. Not only have the path to the cemetery and the graves themselves been overgrown by weeds, but river camps like the one where Jenny hopes to find Billy Floyd have ceased even to exist. As many as 30,000 shantyboaters populated such camps in the 1940s.

The shore people feared these shantyboaters and might have expected something like Jenny's rape by the river men. Lalla Walker Lewis, in her W.P.A. report of 1940, labels many of these fishermen "retrogrades and riff-raff" and further states, "When they have no work to do their opportunities for dissipation are unlimited. There are no neighbors to object or interfere with any amount of riotous living which they choose to indulge in."[3] Welty, although much less judgmental, describes the shantyboat life as one of "timeless roaming and poverty and sameness,"[4] and her photographs of shantyboat children throwing knives at a tree suggest the sinister quality such fishing camps could have.[5] We saw no shantyboaters. Grand Gulf, where Welty saw them, is now dominated by a nuclear power plant and by a pleasant and tidy state park. A small, disorderly, and obviously poor community lies near the park, but the shantyboats are gone.

Just as the shantyboats are gone now, living on primarily in fiction, so were the Natchez Indians gone long before Welty visited Rodney—they were massacred in the 1700s. Welty, nevertheless, recalls these people in "Some Notes on River Country" and manages to create the illusion of their lingering presence in "At The Landing."

The cemetery, the river that has left Rodney but returns during floods, the vegetation, the isolated town, the threatening transient community, and the vanished Indian culture—this much of actual setting has Welty chosen to preserve in her story "At The Landing." But what aspects of setting has she blotted out or altered? In "Some Notes on River Country" (1944), Welty describes three churches in Rodney: "a little wooden Catholic church tiny as a matchbox, with twin steeples carved like icing, over a stile in a flowery pasture"; a "Negro Baptist church, weathered black with a snow-white door"; and a "rose-red" church which, Welty writes, "is the kind of little church in which you might instinctively say prayers for your friends" and in which "both danger and succor, both need and response, seem intimately near" (pp. 291–292). We saw all three of these churches: the Negro Baptist church had a fresh coat of white paint; the rose-red Presbyterian church had been gutted for restoration. And although the Catholic church was no longer in Rodney, its twin steeples decorated Grand Gulf State Park where the church had been moved. Nowhere in "At The Landing," however, do these churches bear witness to Rodney's thriving past, a past which both Welty's essay and *The Robber Bridegroom* so vividly depict. Finally, we saw no houses like Jenny's or Mag Lockhart's. Welty's many unpublished photographs of galleried houses and her single photo of a house with double chimneys and "a beautiful doorway" clearly resemble the fictional dwellings ("At The Landing," p. 246). But these pictures do not provide exact correspondences and were not taken in Rodney. The houses of "At The Landing" seem to have originated in Welty's imagination and to exist only in her story.

Welty's modifications of the Rodney locale in "At The Landing"—her decision not to describe Rodney's churches and her decision to construct fictional houses—indicate, of course, that The Landing is not ultimately Mississippi's but her own. And even those aspects of setting which Welty draws from actuality, which ground the story in a real world, are also essentially metaphoric. The river-abandoned but oft-flooded town, for instance, makes us as readers mindful of loss and danger. The setting reflects attrition through time, the continuous and irrevocable estrangement of people from a richer past; it reflects as well the power of nature to overwhelm or destroy in a moment any individual. And through Welty's imagery, her careful selection of details, and Jenny Lockhart's own perceptions, we accept the possibility of such a character as Billy Floyd, and we come to believe in the beauty, mystery, and love which do survive the ravages of time and nature.

This location speaks most loudly of what is lost through time. The town's name itself reminds the reader of a vanished past: The Landing is no longer a landing, nor has it been for decades. The galleried house of Jenny's grandfather is no more than a relic of a better day. The cemetery at the roof of the town offers further testimony to the ascendancy of loss and death in this town, and there are no churches to offer consolation or succor. The residents of The Landing nevertheless endure, as if for the sake of endurance. They come back into the town when the recurrent high waters recede, clean the slime from their places, and reduce past floods to anecdotes. The postmaster tells Jenny and Billy Floyd,

> "Some stranger lost through here says, 'Why don't you all move away?' Move away?" He laughed, and pointed a finger at Jenny. "Did you hear that, Miss Jenny—why don't we move away? Because we live here, don't we, Miss Jenny?" (pp. 248–249)

Welty associates Jenny—stranded, helpless, and already with little to hope for—with the town's actual situation. The town attempts to hold out against the forces of nature. So would the grandfather have Jenny do; specifically, it is passion that he fears might overwhelm their carefully ordered life. He deprecates "raving simply as raving, as a force of Nature and so beneath notice or mention," and keeps Jenny inside the family home or the outside pavilion which is encircled by a "thorny rose" (p. 242). Whenever she goes to the door of their house, her grandfather calls "her back, with his little murmur" (p. 242). Although shy and obedient, Jenny is not completely reconciled to life in her grandfather's and the town's constrained and repressive terms: "if in each day a moment of hope must come, in Jenny's day the moment was when the rude wild Floyd walked through The Landing . . ." (p. 243). When Jenny sees Billy Floyd, she does so from the cemetery—the one place her grandfather allows her to go because there she visits her mother's grave. By situating Jenny there and Billy Floyd on the other side of a small spring, Welty creates an image both concrete and metaphorical: "The pasture, the sun and the grazing horse were on his side, the graves on hers, and they each looked across at the other's" (p. 244). The obvious futility of anyone's holding out against the forces of nature makes this location even more appropriate for Jenny's story. The river, an overwhelming "present," can at any moment ride over and nullify this town or sweep away any of its inhabitants. Life is more dangerous, more compelling—and for Jenny, more promising—than the town or her grandfather would have it. When he dreams of high water in the story's opening scene, the grandfather associates the fisherman Billy Floyd with the danger (*and* the excitement) of the flood: " 'The river has come back. That Floyd came to tell me' " (p. 240). Jenny's danger is the town's, but unlike the townspeople, she does not try to hold out against danger. When the flood does come and high waters cover The Landing, Billy Floyd arrives in his boat to rescue Jenny: "Jenny looked in Floyd's shining eyes and saw how they held the whole flood, as the flood held its triumph . . . , and it was a vast and unsuspected thing" (p. 250). And, with the setting once again providing both the illusion of reality and a metaphor, Jenny recognizes that she and Floyd are riding right over the graves of her grandfather and her mother.

Like the triumphant but destructive river, the love which Billy Floyd brings to Jenny is both liberating and dangerous. When Floyd rescues Jenny, he also violates her. When he offers her fish to eat, she knows that "People took the fresh death and the hot fire into their mouths and got their own life" (p. 252). While Floyd's love awakens her and frees her from a repressive life, it compels her to follow him and it encroaches upon her previously "inviolate" (p. 245), although paradoxically passive, self. Following Billy Floyd means severing any ties with the town and her past, the previously established and fragilely maintained terms of her identity.

Neither the river nor the eroding but tenacious town is an element in what seems an early version of "At The Landing." "The Children" (1934?), an unpublished typescript held by the Mississippi Department of Archives and History, contains many lines which will reappear in the later story, and its protagonist, Nora, is just as trapped and susceptible to passion as Jenny is. But the credibility and rich texture that setting brings to "At The Landing" are missing from "The Children." Its setting, a rose garden, seems almost incidental because this garden in no way represents Nora's emotional life. Jenny's grandfather would "call her back" from the river, from a life of passion and risk, would "call her back" to a home which protects, confines, and represses. Nora similarly thinks "my mother . . . will call me back,"[6] but her mother would merely call Nora away from a despairing love, not away from nor toward an emblematic setting. Furthermore, Nora's passion seems foolish. Thomas, the man she loves, is unconvincing because we know nothing of the world in which he lives. In contrast, Billy Floyd emerges from his place; he is charged with the river country's vitality and mystery. Nevertheless, even if "The Children" were set in a believable and metaphoric locale, it might still be only a story of unrequited passion. In "At The Landing" Welty's use of setting provides an infinitely more complex vision.

The obvious situation of river and town are but starting points in the later story. Closer to Welty's concern in "At The Landing" are those elements of human experience which *can* survive losses through time. And, once again, this river country provides an ideal setting for such an exploration. For Welty the atmosphere of this country seems charged with a light that confirms and protects a nonmaterial world, not with one that denies or penetrates and exposes it. Indeed, she begins her essay on the river country by writing, "A place that ever was lived in is like a fire that never goes out" (p. 286), and she concludes the essay by saying, "Whatever is significant and whatever is tragic in its story live as long as the place does, though they are unseen, and the new life will be built upon these things—regardless of commerce and the way of rivers and roads, and other vagrancies" (p. 299). In "At The Landing" Welty's imagery evokes just those significant and tragic aspects of Rodney's past and allows us to share her conviction that those aspects endure. For example, she describes the town as though the departed river were still there: "Under the shaggy bluff the bottomlands lay in a river of golden haze. The road dropped like a waterfall from the ridge to the town at its foot and came to a grassy end there" (p. 241). Billy Floyd himself takes on the characteristics of a time that predates even the era when The Landing was a major river port. Just as Floyd is associated with the river, the overwhelming force of a passionate and finally indifferent present, he is also associated with the elemental vigor of the past, of the wilderness days when Natchez Indians ruled the river country. Try as the community might to define him—as gypsy, as bastard son of an old checker-player in town—he defies such ordinary definitions. The opinion of one old lady in the story, the old lady who "had books," seems closer to the truth (p. 254). Floyd's Natchez ancestors, she contends, account for his wild ways. And she looks even further back in time, tracing Floyd and the Natchez to the people of Atlantis, those men who "took their pride in the escape from that flood, when the island went under. And there was something all Indians knew, about never letting the last spark of fire go out" (p. 255).

In "Some Notes on River Country," Welty discusses the Natchez at some length, telling of their sun-worship and describing them as "proud and cruel, gentle-mannered and ironic, handsome, extremely tall, intellectual, elegant, pacific and ruthless. Fire, death, sacrifice formed the spirit of the Natchez' worship" (p. 293). The imagery Welty uses to describe Billy Floyd specifically suggests many of these traits. At one point Jenny sees Floyd in a "circle of fire" (p. 251), and later Welty tells us that the "sun had burned his skin dark and his hair light, till he was golden in the road . . ." (p. 254). Proud and perhaps cruelly indifferent to Jenny, Floyd is godlike in his primitive vitality. He is a survivor, but not in the outward, stolid sense of the towns-people. It is he who has somehow kept kindled a fire thought to have gone out, who has maintained a closeness to nature, a freedom from society's restraints, and it is he who can pass that fire on. He is a mythic figure who transcends time, an individual whom Welty has modeled in part at least upon those contemporary shantyboaters the W.P.A. report declared "riff-raff" but upon whom she has superimposed qualities of the region's distant, exotic past, a past first chronicled by French explorers.

Welty uses place in "At The Landing" in still another important way. We learn a great deal about Jenny by observing the poetic and selective quality of her vision. Passive but keenly aware of the world around her, an artist by nature, Jenny discovers what survives in spite of the devastation of time. She comes to perceive and cherish the delicacy and the mystery of the river country and of Billy Floyd himself. When she and Floyd walked on opposite sides of the spring, "two black butterflies over the flowers were whirring just alike, suspended in the air, one circling the other rhythmically, or both moving from side to side in a gentle wave-like way, one above the other." The butterflies were "always together, like each other's shadows, beautiful each one with the other. Jenny could see to start with that no kiss had ever brought love tenderly enough from mouth to mouth" (p. 244). Jenny recognizes in the actual scene a truth about love: the gentle care with which one must approach a loved one so that the "fragile mystery" (p. 245) of the other is not destroyed. Jenny will not limit Billy Floyd's identity by reducing him to the completely familiar terms the community uses. It even distresses her to find Floyd in the post office during the day; there he appears "handled and used": "For a moment Jenny thought he was going to drop his high head at being trapped in the confined place, with her between him and the door, which would be the same as telling it out . . . that he could be known in time if he were caught and cornered in a little store" (p. 248).

The strongest message in the story, above the pattern of loss, is the realization that Jenny attains midway through the story when she and Floyd meet "by the little river that came out of the spring and went to the Mississippi beyond" (p. 249); during this encounter Jenny comes to know, simply and profoundly, that love does exist in this world. She makes this discovery through a selective and sharp vision of her own setting. She knows already the impossibility of holding out against time; Floyd will go on without her; this "little staving moment" with him now by the river will end. But in watching one humble detail at the tip of Floyd's boot—a hidden mussel sending up its bubbles through the sand—Jenny finds, "It was the little pulse of bubbles and not himself or herself that was the moment for her then; and he could have already departed and she could have already wept, and it would have been the same. . . . A clear love is *in the world . . .*" (p. 250).

The story's ending is a *tour de force* in Welty's complex use of setting to tell the story of Jenny Lockhart. With the reader now fully under the illusion of the story's reality, Welty sends Jenny on a path that no one could have taken so easily in 1943 or 1983. Jenny walks to the river camp where she hopes to find Billy Floyd. Welty makes the trip physically effortless, although it could not have been. The actual camp Welty had in mind, Grand Gulf, is at least fifteen miles from Rodney. And while the description of the terrain and vegetation is exact and credible, it functions at every point symbolically. Jenny's way forward requires her to relinquish all that has shaped her life and to plunge backward towards the old simplicity, the mystery and vitality of Billy Floyd. She leaves at sunset, passing an old mimosa— "the ancient fern, as old as life, the tree that shrank from the touch, grotesque in its tenderness" (p. 256). And when she turns to look back at the town, even it is transformed. It seems a kind of seascape, a seascape which Welty clearly associates with the submerged continent of Atlantis and with Billy Floyd: "She looked behind her for the last time as she went down under the trees. As if it were made of shells and pearls and treasures from the sea, the house glinted in the sunset, tinted with the drops of light that seemed to fall slowly through the vaguely stirring leaves. Tenderly as seaweed the long moss swayed. The chimney branched like coral in the upper blue" (pp. 256–257). Through her figurative language, Welty has transformed the actual setting so thoroughly that the symbolic significance is unmistakable: Jenny can no more turn back from Floyd than she could walk out of the depths of the sea. Jenny's commitment to Floyd arises from both vision and despair; it is toward life in one sense, but it is also toward death.

Indeed, Jenny's departure from The Landing, a literal descent "down under the trees" and toward the river, recalls her earlier impulse, born of despair, to walk down into Mag Lockhart's well. Nora in "The Children" has a similar impulse, expressed in almost identical terms:

> If desperation were only a country, it would be at the bottom of a well.
>
> She wanted to arrive, from nowhere to somewhere, magically graceful and airy, in some strange blowing country wet-washed & bright, hard underfoot, greener than anywhere in the world, and walk along levelly beneath its secret sky, & have people when she passed say only "Honorable lady!" for she would be only beautiful, only a princess, she would only smile . . . She thought she could see herself rising on the breath of astonished hope and walking to the well. It was built so that it actually had steps. She saw herself walk up them, stand on top, look about in a new downward angle of [farewell (struck over)], and then go suddenly into the dark passage.[7]

Although Welty describes Nora's imagined journey into the well as she later describes Jenny's, Nora's paradoxical encounter with both "desperation" and "astonished hope" does not prefigure an actual journey through a landscape at once literal and symbolic. Jenny makes such a journey when she travels to the river camp, and setting in "At The Landing" thus intensifies a pattern of simultaneous destruction and fulfillment.

The final scene reiterates that pattern. The river camp is just as sordid and fraught with danger as the W.P.A. report said, although in Jenny's trance-like passivity, she does not appear to notice. The men take her into a grounded houseboat and one by one rape her. When the women and boys outside hear Jenny's cries and sense that "the original smile now crossed Jenny's face, and hung there no matter what was done to her, like a bit of color that kindles in the sky after the light has gone," Jenny's situation seems hopeless (p. 258); Welty's metaphoric reference to the departed sunlight, suggesting implicitly that a fire has gone out, is bleak indeed. The last paragraph moves away from Jenny and juxtaposes two additional images. The first is primarily positive; the second, corresponding directly to a Welty photograph, is not. The first suggests that something—love, passion, a life force—may endure, that the symbolic and elusive fire of the Natchez may still burn. An old woman, when she hears that Jenny is waiting for Billy Floyd, nods "out to the flowing river, with the firelight following her face and showing its dignity" (p. 258). The second and last image, however, jolts the reader into recalling violence and loss: "The younger boys separated and took their turns throwing knives with a dull *pit* at the tree" (p. 258).

Thus, despite our initial focus upon the actual town, river, and shantyboat camp depicted in "At The Landing," it is important to realize how carefully Welty selects from, adds to, and modifies details of the places we saw. In doing so, she creates the same transformation for us that the china night-light created for her as a child. "Some of us grew up with the china night-light," Welty writes,

> the little lamp whose lighting showed its secret and with that spread enchantment. The outside is painted with a scene, which is one thing; then, when the lamp is lighted, through the porcelain sides a new picture comes out through the old, and they are seen as one. . . . The lamp alight is the combination of internal and external, glowing at the imagination as one; and so is the good novel.[8]

And so is "At The Landing," we might add. We saw Jenny Lockhart's world and we see it and believe in it still. But our visit to Rodney, our examination of "The Children," and our readings of "At The Landing" have made us equally aware of the metaphoric country which lies inside that "real" world. Both glow as one for us because of the consummate skill Welty uses to make setting her own, to unite landscape and emblem in one image.

1. Eudora Welty, "Place in Fiction" (1956), in *The Eye of the Story: Selected Essays and Reviews* (New York: Random House, 1978), pp. 124–125.

2. Eudora Welty, "At The Landing," in *The Collected Stories of Eudora Welty* (New York: Harcourt Brace Jovanovich, 1980), p. 247. All future references to "At The Landing" will be made parenthetically.

3. W.P.A. State-Wide Historical Research Project, RG 60, No. 144, Mississippi River Material, Fishing and Hunting, p. 3. Mississippi Department of Archives and History, Jackson, Mississippi.

4. Eudora Welty, "Some Notes on River Country" (1944), in *The Eye of the Story*, p. 289. All future references to "Some Notes on River Country" will be made parenthetically.

5. Eudora Welty, Photographs, Z301.2, Negatives #706 and #752. Eudora Welty Collection, Mississippi Department of Archives and History, Jackson, Mississippi. The Welty Collection contains negatives of more than 1,000 photographs taken by Eudora Welty. In an exhibition catalogue entitled *Welty* (Jackson: Mississippi Department of Archives and History, 1977), Patti Carr Black illustrates significant parallels between Welty's fiction and photographs.

6. Eudora Welty, "The Children," Z301, Series 1, Box 1, Folder 3, p. 5. Eudora Welty Collection, Mississippi Department of Archives and History, Jackson, Mississippi. In the original typescript, the cited passage includes many holograph revisions and additions. Reference to "The Children" is made by permission of the Mississippi Department of Archives and History.

7. Welty, "The Children," p. 5.

8. Welty, "Place in Fiction," pp. 119–120.

DOROTHY G. GRIFFIN

The House as Container: Architecture and Myth in *Delta Wedding*

Set within the land is the dwelling—made by human hands
to hold human life. . . . the house is the physical form, the
evidence *that we have lived, are alive now. . . .*
                    Eudora Welty,
                    "The House of Willa Cather"[1]

"My imagination," observed Eudora Welty in *One Writer's Beginnings*, "takes its strength and guides its directions from what I see and hear and learn and feel and remember of my living world."[2] Most interesting in Welty's analysis of her own literary development is her close association of place—"my living world"—and the architectural constructs that contain and realize it. Welty's sense of place is generated by her family home on North Congress Street in Jackson, Mississippi, and by the Lamar Life Insurance Building that her father helped to plan and construct in the 1920's. It is "sealed" in her maternal grandparents' West Virginia mountain-top home, whose design embodied both a literal and a figurative journey: a "low, gray-weathered wooden house with a broad hall through the middle of it with the light of day at each end." Built by her grandfather "to stand on the very top of the highest mountain he could find," this house came to represent both personal and spiritual freedom in Welty's memory and imagination.[3]

Such careful crafting of an architectural, mythic, and spiritual dialectic is apparent throughout Welty's work, from the ruins of Asphodel in *The Wide Net* to the McKelva house in *The Optimist's Daughter*. Inherent in Welty's creative imagination, this dialectic is founded quite concretely in her own personal history in houses which offer sanctuary from the world while at the same time providing opportunity to venture forth from their protective retreat into that exterior world—houses whose mythic and spiritual overtones Welty constructs as deliberately as she does their edifices. Nowhere in her work is Welty more preoccupied with such construction than in *Delta Wedding* (1946). From Welty's creative imagination, rooted in her memory, come the warmth of the natural Grove, the protection of the fortress Shellmound, and the romance of the mysterious Marmion. In their mutual address, these houses not only contain the dynamic consciousness of the Delta Fairchilds, a special family of the fair and chosen, but also house in a kind of temple *mundus* their own god, the legendary George Fairchild. To follow the construction of the Grove, Shellmound, and Marmion is to part the curtain of Welty's mature vision and to see therein man's dreams and nightmares, his virtues and deficiencies. But the most compelling "*evidence* that we have lived, are alive now," resides in a fourth and culminating construct, George Fairchild, who bears the author's familiar signature of hope and praise for the human drama.

Charles Moore, in *The Place of Houses*, suggests that "the image of 'house' holds great power over the human mind," and that it "should seem the most important place in the world" to those who dwell there.[4] Houses are special places within places, separate, "the center of the world for their inhabitants, yet carefully related to the larger place in which they belong."[5] The house reflects the individual nature of its inhabitants, and the relationship of those inhabitants to each other and to the outside world. It is microcosmic.

The house is also imagistic of man's attempt to fix himself in the universe. It is imitative of nature: the floor is the earth, the ceiling is the heavens. Man sees in the universe a "larger 'tent to dwell in,' a chamber, and ultimately a most elaborate structure."[6] The house in this sense becomes mythic.

This architectural construct serves both as physical container and as the symbolic body and spirit of man. Andrea Palladio, the most imitated architect in history, compares the house to the human body: the "noble and beautiful parts" exposed, the "ignoble but essential parts" hidden. He saw the Italian villa as a compact organism, with each work designed "as if members were joined symmetrically to a central spine."[7] Architectural historian Lewis Mumford contends that the human dwelling is like the human personality: it consists of both body and spirit. Buildings have their roots in the "practical offices of life," yet they only partly fulfill their task unless they "also bear the imprint of mind and spirit."[8] Examining his own house as an individualization process, Carl Gustav Jung called his tower by the water "a confession of faith in stone."[9] Although he built "following the concrete needs of the moment," Jung also built "in a kind of a dream," thereby creating not only a physical container but a spiritual one.[10] This infusion of self into the construct not only personalizes contained interior space as called for by Palladio and Mumford but also aspires to interior "psychic wholeness": a merging of the reality and the dream, the conscious and the unconscious. It calls forth an awareness of the house as a spiritual container as well as a physical one, and thereby resonates to the man within.

Although variously defined as community and identity, atmospheric verisimilitude, retreat from civilization, estrangement, legend and real history,[11] place in the fiction of Eudora Welty also provides an actual physical construct, an artifact made by man to envelop and contain; an embracing shape, architecturally fitted to the necessity of character and theme. In *Delta Wedding*, the geographical and psychological boundary of the Fairchild world is the Mississippi Delta: flat, unvaried, shimmering in the heavy heat of September.

The town bearing the family name contains the family store, a church, a cemetery, a few houses and a cotton gin. It is the changeless world of Fairchild brightness, dimmed only slightly by a dark incident on a railroad trestle bridge.

This Fairchild world is revealed through the limited perception of a visiting cousin, the nine-year-old Laura McRaven. The novel centers on the preparations for the marriage of the second Fairchild daughter, Dabney, to the family overseer, Troy Flavin. In the midst of the bright ritual activities that focus on these preparations, there are interjected the ritualistic retelling and psychological reworkings of a "heroic" incident involving one of the Fairchild uncles, George, who saved the life of his niece Maureen when her foot became caught in the tracks on a trestle just as a train bore down on them. This incident significantly changes the perceptions of the four adult Fairchild women—Ellen, the mother; Robbie, the outsider who is wife to George; Shelley, the eldest Fairchild daughter; and the romantic Dabney, the bride. It also alters their perceptions of George. Ultimately, what each of them has confronted in her own way is mortality, and through that each, as a woman, sees the ultimate end of the family—the "house."

The central architectural construct of the novel is the principal family house, Shellmound, and it is seen, externally and internally, through the eyes of young Laura. Hers is also the consciousness which perceives the mystery and romance of Marmion, the deserted family house by the Yazoo River, deep in a forest, echoing the absence of the life with which Shellmound burgeons. The third family house is the small, past-cluttered sanctuary of the Grove, nestled in a wood.

Shellmound's exterior is Victorian, tall, white and wide-framed, with a porch completely encircling it, a bayed tower on one side and tinted windows.[12] Laura experiences the interior of Shellmound in memory before she enters it physically. As she drinks from the backyard water cooler, and later as she plays on a joggling board, there emerge from her memory parts of the body of the house. Her consciousness moves from parlor footstool (metaphoric cellarage), through the hall, into the most-remembered room, the dining room. From there her mind moves through space onto the rose-patterned carpet of the stair, through the upstairs halls, out to the sleeping porches. The house then becomes mythic as Welty grafts the image of a labyrinth onto the house of Laura's consciousness: "so many rooms" with "up and down" halls "that intersected and turned into dead-end porches and rooms" (p. 8). The labyrinth, with its connotation of an entangling and confusing representation, can also be symbolic of the unconscious; it is a man-made construct to house the unknown, to separate it from the known, and thus can be imagistic of the collective and individual Fairchild consciousness.[13]

The dining room, the room which Laura remembers most clearly, is the heart of the house; its essence is primarily social and vestigially religious in its communion function: the entire family assembles there several times a day. At Shellmound, the eating table—perhaps altar—is the central focus, but surrounding it are all the other furnishings of warmth and community: easy chairs, rockers, sewing stands, games, and a card table made from Great-grandfather Fairchild's walnut trees. There is, felicitously, at Laura's first meal with the family, a cricket on the hearth.

Young Laura's limited awareness does not allow her to see the significance of other architectural details in the house such as windows and doors, which do, however, provide for the movement outward of the reflecting consciousness of each of the four adult women. Welty, in an essay on Chekhov, observes that the window is a defining image of reality, which she sees not as a "single, pure ray," but as a "cluster of lesser lights" like "windows of a village at night, close together but not *one*."[14] In another essay, perception through a window, for Welty, becomes an "act of recognition," a seeing beyond observation.[15] The window functions as a dual conductor which provides for individual perceptions of exterior reality as well as an ultimate reality which can move inward, or, as Louis Rubin suggests, "peep in," either to promise or to threaten.[16]

Doors, simple geometric opposition like windows, open both ways; family members do come and go, but with very little actual threshold crossing. The characters are seen as being either inside or outside, with the dual nature of this spatial dialectic reinforcing the thematic dialectic of inside/outside consciousness. Gaston Bachelard, in his *Poetics of Space*, sees the phenomenon of the door as a primal image that opens to the depth of being, or closes, padlocked. Janus-like, the door opens to the world of men or to the world of solitude.[17] Shelley feels that her sister Dabney's marriage was a door shut in the family's face. And what was beyond that door: "Shelley's desire fled, or danced seriously, to an open place—not from one room to another room with its door, but to an opening wood, with weather—with change, beauty" (p. 220). Shelley desires a knowledge of the mysterious "outside" world of mutability, although almost immediately Welty brings a fragment of that world's promise into Shellmound: Shelley unlatches the door to let in her cat, just returned from hunting: "he brought in a mole and laid it at her feet" (p. 220). Death and change lie just beyond the protected world of Fairchild.

The only characters actually to be seen crossing a Fairchild threshold are the family "outsiders." The exterior, or transitional, doors are used by Robbie, George's wife, who is admitted by a servant after banging her fist on the front door, and by Troy Flavin, who enters the house—and the family—by a side door.

The absence of significant threshold movement is directly attributable to the insularity of Shellmound. It is a figurative walled fortress, whose master's name is Battle, within which the Fairchild family is contained, protected, and yet separated. "But all together we have a wall," Shelley writes in her diary, "we are self-sufficient against people that come up knocking, we are solid to the outside" (p. 84). This walled fortress is, however, continually breached by "invaders," Robbie and Troy, as well as by Welty's insistent "little messenger or reminder of death," Laura, whose mother has just died (p. 63). Not only is the exterior threat of mortality dragged across the Fairchild threshold but it is insinuated by its own members.

According to Bachelard, the house constitutes a body of images which give mankind proofs or illusions of stability. To distinguish these images, he develops a psychology of the house as a vertical and concentric being.[18] The house in other words becomes structure and soul, and this is the essence of the Fairchild family which Shellmound has so lovingly protected, shielded, encircled and encased. The soul of the house is its unchanging sameness which over the years has secreted its own protective isolation, both collective and individual. And, as will be seen, this soul is also George Fairchild, who violates that sameness and provides for the possibility of change.

In young Laura's enchanted eyes, the family sameness is apparent: a physical sameness of the Fairchilds which is reflected in their surroundings; a reckless pleasure copied by young from old. They have a fleetness, "a neatness that was actually a readiness for gaieties and departures, a distraction that was endearing as a lack of burdens." And because of this recurrent sameness, each Fairchild, even George, is "portentous" (p. 14) of future generations.

This collective sameness, this island of immunity, attempts to lock out and to ignore the intrusion of the "real" world, for the doors which the family opens reveal only another part of its interior world of self—Shellmound. But the boundaries of the Delta itself indicate that the "great confines" of Shellmound are bordered by that which the family least recognizes: mortality. The collective center of Fairchild space in the flat unchanging Delta is surrounded by the Yazoo, the river of death.

Family immortality is preserved in each of the houses, those living museums which contain relics of the past, and the incorporation of that past into the family by means of portraits, legend and memory. The library at Shellmound is a special space which serves as another dual container; it houses both the words and the people of the past, who are still present in the "living" form of books and portraits. The portraits are all of dead Fairchilds, who live again, "courteous and meditative," inside the triple safety of memory, room and house.

Unlike the library at Shellmound, the Grove, first built of the Fairchild houses, not only contains the past; it *is* the past. Fittingly, it is "a dove-gray box" with a deep porch that faces (confronts) the Yazoo (death), standing "under shade trees with its back to the Shellmound road" (p. 37). It is made of cypress wood and rests "on brick pillars now painted green and latticed over, and its double chimneys at either end were green too" (p. 37). The Grove is in and of its environment, as Shellmound can never be; and its confronting of nature, of life and death, is significant of this. Also, the house has an open deck on its roof, an access to the outside which is structurally a part of the house, which no other Fairchild house can claim.

The atmosphere of the Grove is a quiet calmness, never achieved at Shellmound; it is eternally cool "like the air of a dense little velvet-green wood [that] touched your forehead with stillness" (p. 40). This aura of serenity, natural and constructed, permeates the interior of the house, with its floor mattings, silver doorknobs, and doors which "softly" resist closing. The house was originally built with the intention of interior/exterior communication, still realized in the doors which persist in remaining open to achieve this dual access. This house, in and of the natural world, whose exterior and interior space reflects its green setting, is the Fairchild foundation, firmly holding to the soil by means of unbreakable roots from which the house, generically and structurally, draws its strength. It is the nest of the past, the family "chrysalis": a positive image of enclosure which allows for and encourages expansion and change.[19]

The Grove was used by the fledgling family until the Fairchilds outgrew it. Bachelard views the image of the nest as protected space, created by the body of the bird to house, protect and cover. Suitably, the Grove is constructed out of nature, offering the same primal image of security as the nest: "a house built by and for the body, taking form from the inside, like a shell, in an intimacy that works physically." But Bachelard also notes the instability of the nesthouse in what he calls a "paradox of sensibility"; the nest is a dream of security in a precarious reality.[20] The Grove, the primordial house, was the origin of Fairchild confidence in the world, and it gives place to Shellmound, the construct not rooted confidently in the natural, exterior world but in the family itself.

The felicity of the nest image of the Grove gives way to the image of the cage, for the family at Shellmound is seen by Laura to be like "a great bowerlike cage full of tropical birds" (p. 15), and she notes that the birds are "caged all the time and [can] not fly out" (p. 15). "Out" is where there is no security, no sameness, no protection; where a train threatens death; where the charmed life of the Fairchilds no longer extends. This image of rare birds hints, as Michael Kreyling has observed, at the captivity, the "extinction of the species," both important elements in the novel's theme.[21] The outward, confident nest of the Grove moves to the great fortress grave of Shellmound, where life is guarded from what lurks, forever threatening, outside—moves to the formalized, self-created shell of the aggregate family Fairchild.

According to Bachelard, three concepts are inherent in the shell: form, protection, and fossilization. The shell is geometric reality, a positive form protecting the softness within and thereby giving a beauty and a grace to the world with a shape formed from its own interior essence. Life becomes the building of one's house; it is process and form.[22] The shell is also a unique protection, fitted to the thing that it protects: either the soft, pliable form of a mollusk or the armored mobility of the turtle. Thus observed, the shell can be viewed in the dialectics of small and large, hidden and seen, placid and aggressive, flabby and vigorous.[23] The Fairchild house is metaphor to the family: individual and corporate, private and public, calm and passionate, old and young. Nevertheless, there is always the protective covering, the comfort and beauty of the shell.

But the shell also suggests that life begins less by reaching upward than by turning in upon itself, and thereby offers the subtle image of life as a coiling principle.[24] This is what the Fairchilds do in Shellmound; they do not grow upward and outward; they grow, if that is the appropriate word, inward, with outward observations and evaluations of life manifested through the inward processes of thought and, ironically, insight. To most family members, the past is of more immediate import than the threatening incursion of the present, and assuredly more real and prepossessing than the future. The coil allows for no achievement, material or spiritual, outside its own self. There is no reaching, no stretching, no expansion, no room for anything other than the accepted now which is generated from the past, which for the Fairchilds is also now. This coiling principle can only lead to stagnation; a living process becomes its own encasement and entombment. The house of the shell becomes a death grouping, just like the Indian mound and the Yazoo River which surround it. The house of Fairchild has become a fossil: a permanent encapsulation of the values and ideas of the past, a corporate form which cannot adapt to change or to progress.

Unlike the Grove and Shellmound, Marmion is uninhabitable. The cozy, communicative nest of the Grove could house two widows and eight Fairchild aunts and uncles as children in its natural warmth. Shellmound can protect and shield Battle, Ellen, their eight children and assorted aunts and cousins. But not so the stylized grandeur of the romantic, fantastic Marmion. Marmion is the stagnant family house, a literal lifeless shell, empty since the year it was finished, 1890. The preamble to Shellmound, "castle-like," Marmion is a Greek shell, "temple-like," archetypically Southern with white pillars, twenty-five rooms, a "wonderful free-standing stair," with a chandelier "like the stamen in the lily down-hanging." There is also a garden, a playhouse and an actual labyrinth which has become a maze (p. 122).

William M. Jones has traced the name of Marmion and of several lesser Fairchild relatives to Sir Walter Scott's *Marmion*.[25] What Welty offers with this naming is the romantic and unlivable past. It is imperative that Marmion, of all the Fairchild houses, be the expected Southern-plantation house design, columned and expansive. Marmion was built on the unreality of the Southern past, when the legend of the Old South was at its height. It is to be expected that its builder would be killed in a duel, that his wife would die of a broken heart, and that the children would be raised, pampered and spoiled by two adoring widowed aunts. The house, literally and figuratively, provides a richly spiraling staircase for the imagination, the domain of romance, which defies contained space; it soars outward through the top of the house, and from there to "the whole creation" (p. 176). Even Laura questions the reality of Marmion space by asking, " 'Is it still the Delta in here?' " (p. 175). This is not the house of predictability and sameness; it is the house of romance, of imaginative surgings upward, fostered and accentuated by a construct containing space where doors open mysteriously and where the coil principle is negated. Marmion, the heart of romance, standing structurally at the center of the novel, is the world of "Once Upon A Time," where no one lives.

In her design of the Grove, Shellmound, and Marmion, Welty reflects both the body and spirit of the Fairchild family. Through these richly detailed structures, she has provided the fair children with security and enclosure while at the same time permitting them access to the exterior world of change and mortality. This complex dialectic of enveloping and containing, restricting and protecting, made portentous by the threat of the outside world, is brilliantly summarized by the porcelain night light, the Grove aunts' wedding gift to Dabney. Pictured on this delicately painted cylinder is a "little town with trees, towers, people, windowed houses, and a bridge" (p. 46). It is the world of Shellmound, with the town of Fairchild and its houses, the towers attached to Shellmound and Marmion, and the trestle bridge. It is also Welty's familiar impress of tension and mystery. The porcelain chimney with a teapot on its top is a serenity resting on an inferno that can erupt and destroy, yet

also provide light, warmth, and security. This direct analogy to the house/world tension of *Delta Wedding* not only
summarizes the comprehensive human drama inherent in
Welty's architecture but also points unerringly to a figure of
potential release and synthesis, of achieved wholeness,
George Fairchild. His architectural construction both extends and in a sense completes Welty's remarkable building
in *Delta Wedding*.

Emerging from the dialectic of the three houses Fairchild
is a fourth construct, who houses in culminating form both
the body and spirit of the family. He alone contains their
complex dynamic of enveloping and containing, restricting
and protecting, while at the same time offering a movement
into and an acceptance of that outside world of mutability
and death. He alone offers hope for the continuance of the
Fairchild past and he alone is unthreatened by their present.
This wholeness of self, evolving from the coil of Fairchild
and augmented by a crucial awareness and perception, allows George to accept his family and their heritage without
being entrapped by them.

The container that is George is neither a coil nor a spiral;
he is represented by the geometric design of a circle, a
psychological symbol of self which expresses the totality of
the psyche in all respects. The circle also represents the
"most vital aspect of life": an "ultimate wholeness."[26] While
the inherent structure of the house of Fairchild is static and
ingrown, its ritual movements are not. Everything about the
life of the family is circular, from the heavens above Shellmound, "an unbroken circle, all around the wheel of the
level world" (p. 30), to the roundness of the earth and Ellen's
continual cycle of pregnancies, to the tangible circle which
the family makes in game and ritual. At the center, or the
heart, of this circle is George Fairchild, and it is around him
that the four perceiving female consciousnesses of *Delta
Wedding* revolve. The women have made him, just as they
have made their houses, sacred space, a magic circle of
temenos, around and through which they live—their temple
and their god. Their consciousness thus makes a profusion

of concentric circles, from the cosmos that is Shellmound, the *axis mundi*, to the cosmos that is George, who interconnects both with the cosmos that is "outside."

Through his own life-affirming sensuality George contains the life of the world, the same outside world that so frightens the other Fairchilds and sends them running "as children would do" (p. 159). Such an affirmation can and does allow for death and the confrontation with death. George, in exploring all of life, must also admit the possibility of death and, in so doing, renew the positive values of choice and experience which are at the heart of life. His confrontation with death on the trestle bridge separates him from the safety of the Fairchild world and moves him into the fearful unknown.

Just as the family asks that George become the sanctuary, the sacred container of their hopes for the house, they also ask that he be the container of the fear of its ultimate dissolution, and of their limited realization that all of life is an inward/outward, life/death dynamic. He is their past made flesh, the incarnate present, the sturdy structure of the family who houses what is best and what is worst. He is their tower of strength, raised and downfallen, who chose to marry Robbie, the unexotic, the unFairchild, and who chose to live in Memphis, the nonDelta. Yet he offers to them the hint of salvation: what is fair, bright and unafraid.

George provides a door for his family, a crossing space and a psychological threshold which allows for felicitous passage between the known and the unknown, life and death. His living admits the acceptance of the two worlds of Shellmound and "outside." He lives successfully outside and returns to Shellmound for family rituals, serving as a model for those who can see and who dare to use him as an access. It is fitting that George's ultimate confrontation with the threat of the outside world takes place on another architectural construct which provides for passage: the trestle bridge.

In his ability to "see" his family and to be "seen" by

Ellen, Shelley, Dabney and Robbie, George provides a clear window through which the four women can see beyond the tinted windows of Shellmound and which at the same time allows him to stand back from their world and to see them as they are: to love the family, "what was dark and what shone fair," and to cherish their weaknesses as "just other ways" in which experiences were going to come (pp. 193, 86). In recognizing his family's weaknesses, and his own, George is the eye, the window of the family soul, which sees them from inside, from the center, from "right in their midst." He knows what they do and do not want from life, and they are aware of that knowledge, having "long ago" made him "to be all in one their lover and protector and dreaming, forgetful conscience" (p. 212).

In his willingness to be all things to his family, George is rendered their captive as well, their sacrificial offering. The demands pull on him: to be like his dead brother, Denis, to assume Denis's mantle as the fairest, to understand them, to forgive them, to be forgiven by them. George on the trestle or George in the center of the family is caught in the ritual circle of sacrifice, offering himself as a willing victim to their needs and the expanse of his own love.

Both Robbie and Ellen see the inherent danger to George in his assumption of the roles of savior and scapegoat and formulate it in Dionysian terms. There is for George the real possibility that these roles will demand his life, a reassimilation into Shellmound, the family temple, a process in which he would be "pulled to pieces" (pp. 162, 163): a process reiterating the duality and complexity of human nature in the simultaneous pull of Shellmound and the outside world, as well as the pull of George's own individuality and the demands placed upon his life. With a willing knowledge of all life and the assumption of all responsibility, George becomes the container of the family spirit, the Fairchild god, a god of love and of light.

Finally, George is the flame of life as found in the hearth fire, again joining mythic and architectural elements. On several occasions he stands before a mantle, bringing to the dead September hearth and to the family so afraid of life the flame of loving and giving. George is the homonucleus, the eye of the house; the lamp that is the force of family light and awareness; the porcelain night light itself, warming and illuminating the interior of their world. Although various family members see him only by a "gusty lamp," exaggerated, blinded "by the lamp of their own indulgence" (p. 191), George's generosity of love allows him to see them clearly, to love them, and all men, just as they are, unconditionally. His life is a celebration of that love. So he celebrates all love, illicit or ritualized, sanctifying it by his presence and, at the same time, threatening, as the Grove aunts fear, to make the family wedding "a Saturnalian feast" (p. 47). George is the flame that gives new life and destroys old life. He can purify by ritual sacrifice in the tenderness of his burning love, the smallness and the weakness of others. George Fairchild is the flame of life, the heart of the Fairchild house, the center of its world, container and houser of its spirit. He cannot, of course, avert those changes in the Delta that will soon sweep away the old Fairchild life, a fate that Welty thought inevitable, but his firm building of the self provides irrefutable "*evidence*" of man's sustained effort to know himself and to grow through that knowledge. George Fairchild, and the houses of the Delta that he contains, is spirit.

1. Eudora Welty, "The House of Willa Cather" (1974), in *The Eye of the Story: Selected Essays and Reviews* (New York: Random House, 1978), p. 56.

2. Eudora Welty, *One Writer's Beginnings* (Cambridge and London: Harvard University Press, 1984), p. 76.

3. Welty, *One Writer's Beginnings*, p. 47.

4. Charles Moore, Gerald Allen and Donlyn Lyndon, *The Place of Houses* (New York: Holt, Rinehart and Winston, 1974), p. 51.

5. Moore, p. 50.

6. W. R. Lethaby, *Architecture, Mysticism and Myth* (1891; rpt. New York: George Braziller, 1975), p. 11.

7. James S. Ackerman, *Palladio*, The Architect and Society Series, ed. John Fleming and Hugh Honour (Baltimore: Penguin, 1966), pp. 54, 57.

8. Lewis Mumford, *The South in Architecture: The Dancy Lectures*, Alabama College, 1941 (New York: Harcourt, Brace and Company, 1941), pp. 112–113.

9. Carl Gustav Jung, *Memories, Dreams, Reflections*, ed. Aniela Jaffe, trans. Richard and Clara Winston (New York: Vintage, 1965), p. 223.

10. Jung, p. 225. Jung dreamed his childhood house, centering on cellar and subcellars, which he interpreted to be elements of his unconscious: "My dream meant *myself, my* life and *my* world, my whole reality." Carl Gustav Jung, ed., *Man and His Symbols* (New York: Dell, 1968), p. 44.

11. Lucinda H. MacKethan, "To See Things in Their Time: The Act of Focusing in Eudora Welty's Fiction," *American Literature*, 50 (1978), 258; Albert J. Devlin, *Eudora Welty's Chronicle: A Story of Mississippi Life* (Jackson: University Press of Mississippi, 1983), pp. 80–123; Louis D. Rubin, Jr., *Writers of the Modern South: The Faraway Country* (Seattle: University of Washington Press, 1963), p. 153; Michael Kreyling, *Eudora Welty's Achievement of Order* (Baton Rouge: Louisiana State University Press, 1980), p. 37; Ruth M. Vande Kieft, *Eudora Welty* (New York: Twayne, 1962), p. 92.

12. Eudora Welty, *Delta Wedding* (1946; rpt. New York and London: Harcourt Brace Jovanovich, 1979), p. 6. All citations of this work will be included parenthetically in the text.

13. M.-L. von Franz, "The Process of Individuation," in *Man and His Symbols*, pp. 175–176; Joseph L. Henderson, "Ancient Myths and Modern Man," in *Man and His Symbols*, p. 117.

14. Eudora Welty, "Reality in Chekhov's Stories" (1977), in *The Eye of the Story*, p. 63.

15. Eudora Welty, "The House of Willa Cather," p. 49.

16. Rubin, p. 131.

17. Gaston Bachelard, *The Poetics of Space*, trans. Maria Jolas (Boston: Beacon Press, 1969), pp. 211–212, 222–224.

18. Bachelard, pp. 136–139.

19. Bachelard, pp. 45, 65–66.

20. Bachelard, p. 132. von Franz sees the nest as representative of maternal warmth with associations to the female or anima figure, p. 190; Bachelard, pp. 101, 102.

21. Kreyling, p. 56.

22. Bachelard, p. 106.

23. For Bachelard's perceptive discussion of shells see pp. 107–115.

24. Bachelard, p. 106.

25. William M. Jones, "Name and Symbol in the Prose of Eudora Welty," *Southern Folklore Quarterly*, 22 (1958), 179.

26. Aniela Jaffe, "Symbolism in the Visual Arts," in *Man and His Symbols*, p. 266.

DANIÈLE PITAVY-SOUQUES

A Blazing Butterfly: The Modernity of Eudora Welty

". . . he dreams that he is a great blazing butterfly stitching
up a net; which doesn't make sense."—Eudora Welty,
"Old Mr. Marblehall"

—Vous moquez-vous de nous, Monsieur, avec une pareille
histoire?
—Est-ce qu'il n'y a pas, Madame, une espèce de tulle qu'on
appelle du tulle illusion.
—Barbey d'Aurévilly

To the late-twentieth-century reader, Eudora Welty appears
an adventurer of the mind. A spirit of challenge, of pure
exhilaration, lifts the fiction of a writer who taught her
readers how to "creep out on the shimmering bridge of the
tree," and whose figure of the artist in its protean garb is the
wanderer, defiant and heroic, brave and vain—Loch Morrison, the young rebel, hanging upside down in the hack-
berry tree to see better, thus reestablishing the truth
through his subversive vision; or Miss Eckhart, the foreign
musician, devoured by a passion for her "life work," her
"own art"; or else, Perseus the mythic hero. These examples are all taken from *The Golden Apples* (1949), that central
book in Eudora Welty's work.

A shorter version of this essay was read in Jackson, Mississippi, at the
1984 Southern Literary Festival honoring the seventy-fifth birthday of
Eudora Welty.

In "The Wanderers," Virgie Rainey meditates upon an engraving of "Perseus with the head of the Medusa" that hung above the piano in Miss Eckhart's studio: "The vaunting was what she remembered."[1] Nearly thirty years later, writing in praise of two American writers with whom she feels some spiritual kinship—Willa Cather and Mark Twain—Eudora Welty emphatically dwells on that same word "vaunt":

> Who can move best but the inspired child of his times? Whose story should better be told than that of the youth who has contrived to cut loose from ties and go flinging himself might and main, in every bit of his daring, in joy of life not to be denied, to vaunt himself in the love of vaunting, in the marvelous curiosity to find out everything, over the preposterous length and breadth of an opening new world, and in so doing to be one with it?[2]

The term is more ambiguous than it seems. Applied to Perseus, "vaunt" expresses the legitimate pride of the slayer of Medusa; to Twain and Cather, it links creative joy to ostentatious victory. And indeed there runs throughout her work evidence of Welty's secret fascination with appearances. She creates characters who delight in flaunting and shocking, from Virgie Rainey with her daredevil behavior and dress, to the "middle-aged lady" in "The Bride of the Innisfallen" who parades in a striped raincoat; or those who adore staging their response to life's drama: Fay dressed in glistening black satin, playing the part of the disconsolate widow in *The Optimist's Daughter*, or the narrator so magnificently "building up" a stage for *Losing Battles* in the first few pages. The very excess of such scenes betrays the ambiguity of Welty's feelings, the sense of ridicule that makes her laugh at the gesture while she cannot help admiring it. Etymology throws some light; the allied terms "vaunt" and "vain" are both stamped with vacuity, their common Latin origin meaning "empty" or "hollow." We come close to vainglory, at least to the idea of taking excess pride, when a more modest attitude is required.

To grasp the complex connotations of "vaunt" for Welty,

consider how she uses the word "vain" in a later work, *The Optimist's Daughter*. When Laurel McKelva comes upon a photograph of her dead mother, she remembers Becky's pride in the blouse she wears in the picture: "'The most beautiful blouse I ever owned in my life—I made it. Cloth from Mother's own spinning, and dyed a deep, rich, American Beauty color with pokeberries,' her mother had said with the gravity in which she spoke of 'up home.' 'I'll never have anything to wear that to me is as satisfactory as that blouse.' How *darling* and *vain* she was when she was *young!* Laurel thought now" (italics added).[3] The association "young-vain" is that of Perseus himself, and here "darling" softens the blame and asserts the right to glory. As for the garment itself, it is the symbol for the undaunted pioneering spirit that defied every obstacle that nature put in its way. Reflexively, Eudora Welty's praise of Twain and Cather comes to mean the celebration of two writers who wrote of America's challenge to the wilderness—not mere recorders but adventurers too in the fresh province of Western literature. But behind the very necessity and nobleness of the conquest looms its costly aftermath, as Clement Musgrove, the cotton planter in *The Robber Bridegroom*, suspects. The reverse side of the success story weighs heavily and deserves examination. Just as, figuratively speaking, on his return journey the triumphant Perseus wore the mask of the slain Medusa, which he put on the better to be seen—not the other way round—so Welty's fiction also explores the inside of the mask, examines the figure observing the other: Perseus behind the face of Medusa watching reflexively this arrogant vaunting other self that moves behind a mask. The artist is both performer and audience, watched and watching. Hence those paired characters that people her fiction, one of whom acts—often with bravado and ostentation—while the other watches. And in this onlooker's gaze (character, narrator, or the writer herself) there passes the awareness of the futility of it all, the weariness and restlessness that Eudora Welty inscribed at the very beginning of her work in a brilliant story whose trope is a key, that of the title, which functions in many ways as trope for her entire fiction. In "The Key," the stance that she gives to the red-haired man reveals a writer singularly ahead of her time:

> . . . in his eyes, all at once wild and searching, there was certainly, besides the simple compassion in his regard, a look both restless and weary, very much used to the comic. You could see that he despised and saw the uselessness of the thing he had done. (p. 37)

To complete this imaginary figure by which Welty's fiction can be represented, I should add the other two elements of the myth: the mirror-shield and the Medusa, with corresponding mirror effects in the writing, fascination and death as themes. We know how those elements, which have always been present in serious fiction, became tropes of the modernist novel, the fiction of James, Conrad, Joyce, or Virginia Woolf.

I choose to single out Perseus because he stands for "the inspired child of his times," what could be called *modernity*, and with this word we are sent traveling down the twentieth century. Eudora Welty, although influenced by and heir to the aesthetic principles of the great modernist writers—like all other writers in this century—has a much more advanced and complex position than her moment in time would lead one to expect. As early as the mid-1930s, all alone and brave, she was already displaying that new spirit and experimenting with techniques that have since become accepted as postmodernist. I will not make her a postmodernist, though, for several reasons, perhaps the chief one being that she never fails to achieve, in William Gass's phrase, "the full responsive reach of her readers."

The word *modernity* was first used by the nineteenth-century French poet Charles Baudelaire, who in many respects was one of the founding fathers of modern thinking (and a great admirer of another Southerner, Edgar Allan Poe). "Modernity," he wrote, "is what is transitory, fugitive and contingent—one half of art, whose other half is the eternal and immutable." As a corollary, he insisted on "the dual composition of the Beautiful though it is experienced as one."[4]

To Baudelaire modernity meant, even more than receptiveness to the new ideas of one's time and immersion in one's own present, a spirit of challenge, the desire to question the "given," for the truly innovative artist is he who tries to capture and represent in his work what he perceives as a new *rapport* of the human mind with the created world. This involves altering known modes of representation since any new questioning of the reality of things and the way the self perceives its position in the universe necessarily affects mimesis. For instance, Baudelaire admired Eugène Delacroix because, alone in his time, he opposed the prevalent realism of such official painters as David or Ingres, and was already trying new techniques to express the slowly emerging tendency toward abstraction. To the rendering of surface reality Delacroix preferred the suggestion of the hidden truth, to the realistic painting of a brawny sinewy arm the suggestion of *tension* produced by a new use of color and shadow. Moreover, those "brilliant modern discoveries," which somehow acknowledged the inadequacy of painting to represent, resulted in a pervasive *mood of melancholy*, that "most remarkable quality which truly signals Delacroix as *the* nineteenth-century painter." While writing this, Baudelaire was quite aware of the near impossibility of the artistic endeavor: a mood is perhaps the closest that an artist can come to modernity.

There are many moods in Eudora Welty, as Ruth Vande Kieft brilliantly stressed some twenty years ago.[5] Earlier, Robert Penn Warren had taught us how to read this "serious fiction": "the items of fiction (scene, action, character, etc.) are presented not as document but as comment, not as a report but as a thing made, not as history, but as idea." Rather than develop this symbolic aspect of Welty's writing, a "method . . . similar to the method of much modern poetry,"[6] I want to examine, first, how Welty's challenge to mimesis expresses a radical fracture of the self, then, how in the organization of experience she moves further away from modernist writers by favoring a conceptual mode of thinking that leads toward abstraction and structure rather than pattern.

The theory of representation—a word I prefer to mimesis because the Aristotelian term does not imply possible negation—rests on the human faculties of recollection and imagination. Whereas recollection dominated narrative literature in the eighteenth and nineteenth centuries, imagination rules in the present one. There has been, in Gablik's words, "a gradual shift in art from iconic modes of representation (which are essentially figurative and are linked to immediate perceptual experience, where the image closely resembles the concrete objects to which it refers) towards non-representational, non-mimetic modes which are conceptual in organization." Here she follows Piaget, who writes: "The object only exists . . . in its relations with the subject and, if the mind always advances more toward the conquest of things, this is because it organizes experience more and more actively, instead of mimicking, from without, a ready-made reality."[7] At the same time, Sartre posits irreality in his theory of the imagination. His phenomenological psychology leads him to reject the three classical theories of associationism, continuity between the different modes of knowledge (i.e., between image and idea), and strict separation of image from idea, a disjunction that takes the image for a thing and dismisses its fallacy.[8] Conversely, Sartre says, the image is "a certain type of consciousness. The image is an act, not a thing. The image is awareness of something." He thus states the dissociation between the faculty of producing images and the world of reality, then goes further when he postulates as a prerequisite for the image "the possibility to posit irreality" ("la possibilité de poser une thèse d'irréalité"). For Sartre, the negative action is constituent of the image ("l'acte négatif est constitutif de l'image").[9]

Such theories throw needed light on the more experimental side of Welty's fiction, that side which the generous, inspired tone of her criticism tends to blur. She herself, in her work, is far more daring than her literary tastes would have us believe. As early as her first collection, *A Curtain of Green* (1941), she showed her preoccupation with uncertainty. Not the modernist sense of ambiguity or the technical device of a variety of narrators each telling or recreating the truth, nor the Chekhovian juxtaposition of events or delayed exposure—rather what Ruth Vande Kieft has called "the mysteries of Eudora Welty." These mysteries lead Welty to explore the borderline situations, the reversals, shifts and crossings of borders; to attempt to submerge the frame, "to render problematical what is, as it were, inside a text and what is outside it," as Tanner says of postmodernist writers.[10] Or she twists the narrative and lets in new narrative possibilities, as in "Death of a Traveling Salesman," "Powerhouse," "A Piece of News," or "Flowers for Marjorie," one of the more accomplished stories in this respect. However, "A Memory" is most daring as an instance of Welty's exploration—it belongs to those remarkable stories in *A Curtain of Green* that are metaphors, stories whose form is the dramatization of their meaning. "A Memory" is about representation and the process of seeing and writing. Or it is a story about "the familiar and its ghostly other," as Regis Durand puts it. Durand also quotes a paper entitled "On Aspects of the Familiar World," in which Walter Abish uses the idea of the familiar and its representations to make a distinction between fictional modes:

> The need to see the world *familiarly* is a result of a preoccupation with the "self" rather than with the world. The "familiar" is to be equated with "self" preoccupation.[11]

This preoccupation with the self, supreme in a self-centered world, is what we find in the modernist novel, in James or Proust. When Proust describes the experience of the madeleine, he is dealing with an "Effet de Réel," as Barthes says; in other words, he is representing "reality," trying to see the world familiarly. The reader who has had a similar experience will identify with Marcel and be reassured in the belief they both belong to the same world, share the same reality. Proust's fiction represents the self trying to come to terms with the world.

On the other hand, a postmodernist text, according to Walter Abish, "must disavow a self-centered world in which the self continues to reign supreme," for it is essentially

> a novel of disfamiliarization, a novel that has ceased to concern itself with the mapping of the "familiar" world, for to do so would compel the characters to adopt a perception of the everyday predicated on an unquestioning affirmation of the function and role of the "self" in society, as rigidly governed by the "reality principle" and as subsumed by the logic of everyday existence as we are.[12]

Let us look closely at "A Memory." We have a first "picture" or "representation" of reality, but what do we see? Certainly not a realistic painting, not even a "virtually pastoral"[13] one:

> The water shone like *steel*, motionless except for the feathery curl behind a distant swimmer. From my position I was looking at a rectangle brightly lit, actually *glaring* at me, with sun, sand, water, a little pavilion, a few solitary people in *fixed* attitudes, and *around* it all a border of dark rounded oak trees, like the engraved thunderclouds *surrounding* illustrations in the *Bible*. Ever since I had begun taking painting lessons, I had made small frames with my fingers, to look out at everything.
> . . . . I was at an age when I formed a judgment upon every person and every event which came under my eye, although I was easily frightened. (p. 75; my italics)

What is shown here is not reality as it is experienced directly in everyday life, but a *conventional representation of a public park*, a descriptive discourse acknowledged by a group at a given time. At the same time, *this description is extremely hostile*, as the words "steel," "glaring," and "thunderclouds" imply. Third, *this picture is framed*, and framed by the Bible, so to speak.

This first picture, which the young girl sees in her innocence, will be soon shattered. In other words, Eudora Welty rejects it, and she does so for reasons that seem to me very much postmodernist. First, we are confronted with a general suspicion of the myth of reality, i.e., "the consensual discourse describing the official representation of the world in a given cultural community at a given time."[14] Then, the picture raises the problem of frames and framing. This the young girl learned when she began taking painting lessons as part of the conventional way of dealing with representation. A frame is a way of delimiting her subject, of imposing restraint and cutting out all that might crop up unexpectedly. In this context, especially with reference to the thunderclouds in the Bible, the frame represents the law, the repressive law of Jehovah. When writing about the "problematic of judicial framing and the jurisdiction of frames," Jacques Derrida refers to "all organized narration" as "a matter for the police," that is, subjected to some kind of law which, in a written work, may be simply "language," not this or that discourse, but language itself.[15] Barthes speaks too of the "fascism" of language: "fascism is not the power to prevent from saying but the power to force to say." In "A Memory" the picture is "dictated" for the child, who in placing and judging people is somehow "framed" herself, i.e., held in a false position by the oppressive prejudice of her parents that makes her feel guilty when she asserts her rights to see and know. "Breaking frames" is also what the story is about, which is as old as the novel, and it is one of the first things that Welty as a user of language learned. Heidegger envisioned the possibility of inverting this "relation of dominance":

> Man acts as though he were the shaper and master of
> language, while in fact language remains the master of man.
> When this relation of dominance gets inverted, man hits upon
> strange manoeuvers. Language becomes the means for ex-
> pression. . . .

Eudora Welty expresses much the same view in her beautiful essay "Words into Fiction": "We start from scratch, and words don't." And just as Heidegger hoped for "strange manoeuvres," Welty speaks of a "leap in the dark,"[16] or, in a superb image that reflects Heidegger's proposition, "in the boat":

> . . . it was not so much that they drifted, as that in the presence of a boat the world drifted, forgot. The dreamed-about changed places with the dreamer." ("Moon Lake," p. 360)

The third reason is linked to the deceiving quality of language—or vision. This picture is traditionally modernist, for in it "the *need* to see the world familiarly is a result of the preoccupation with the self rather than with the world." The narrator of "A Memory" says nothing else:

> To watch everything about me I regarded grimly and possessively as a *need.* All through this summer I had lain on the sand beside the small lake, with my hands squared over my eyes, finger tips touching, looking out by this device to see everything: which appeared as a kind of projection. It did not matter to me what I looked at; from any observation I would conclude that a secret of life had been nearly revealed to me— (pp. 75–76)

Framing and the need to see the world familiarly combine and represent the efforts of the self to master the world. The young girl feels such control because she can produce at will the memory of a brief encounter with a young boy, her first love:

> I still would not care to say which was more *real*—the dream I could make blossom at will, or the sight of the bathers. I am presenting them, you see, only as simultaneous. (p. 77; my italics)

At this first stage, otherness is defined as the not-self, the "world." Here the not-self is what is most familiar, the world she inhabits, the "real" society. "The paradox," Regis Durand remarks, "is that the familiar world is most familiar to us when it is least seen as it is, for what it is, but simply as the need of the self to see things familiarly: the real world treated familiarly." Modernist writers stop at this point, showing the self (as Walter Abish says) "forever striving to reach an agreement with the desirable otherness." Welty goes a step further, not only investigating the familiar, but also *looking at it for what it is*. We should perhaps bear in mind Freud's definition of the "uncanny" or *Unheimlich*: "The 'uncanny' is that class of the terrifying which leads back to something long known to us, once very familiar."[17]

The second picture presented in "A Memory" is one of violence and distortion as the child sees "a group of loud, squirming, ill-assorted people who seemed thrown together only by the most confused accident, and who seemed driven by foolish intent to insult each other, all of which they enjoyed with a hilarity which astonished my heart" (p. 77). The pleasantly controlled circle of the first picture becomes "wobbly ellipses" as the little boys chase each other. The trim white pavilion is replaced by the shapeless mound of sand built around the ugly woman. This is a painful initiation into the contingency of life as it is: in order to be true, the artist must be able to see all the violence and rage and ugliness that is part of life. But it is more than that, for in the culminating point of "A Memory," the little girl has a true vision of death. All of the images referring to the woman point to a petrified landscape. "Fat hung upon her upper arms like an arrested earthslide on a hill," her legs looked like "shadowed bulwarks" (p. 78), and when she pulled down the front of her bathing suit to empty out the "mashed and folded sand," the child "felt a peak of horror, as though her breasts themselves had turned to sand" (p. 79). This petrified landscape is the intrusion into the narrative of the face of the Medusa, the swoon into which the narrator falls, a sort of death. In "A Memory" the only escape from this "framed" condition seems to be through death; in other stories it will be through diffusion or dispersal, as in "Old Mr. Marblehall."

We see how petrifaction functions here as a strange maneuver by which Welty indicates that the girl's experience is not one of appropriation, as all her preceding ones were, but of disavowal. More important, it is one of intensification, an intensification of the radical otherness of the other, a recognition of the difference, of the unaccountable. But this disavowal, which is precisely the word used by Walter Abish, has a more complex meaning than just negation; it is, in a Freudian sense, something that involves the negation of the reality of a perception, usually a traumatic one, and it concerns itself with *the presence of an absence*. It is, as Freud has shown, the principle behind the cleavage of the self. Yet, in "A Memory" this deconstructive gesture is confronted by a very strong impulse to reestablish order, unity:

> I tried to withdraw to my most inner dream, that of touching the wrist of the boy I loved on the stair; I felt the shudder of my wish shaking the darkness like leaves where I had closed my eyes; I felt the heavy weight of sweetness which always accompanied this memory; but the memory itself did not come to me. (p. 79)

The world, the familiar world, is still present in a way, the same and not quite the same; but since the new experience is that of an *absence*, there is a fracture: "I did not know, any longer, the meaning of my happiness; it held me unexplained" (p. 79).

The third picture is that of the devastated beach. The narrator confesses: "for the object which met my eye, the small worn white pavilion, I felt pity suddenly overtake me, and I burst into tears" (p. 79). Those very tears are what Serge Leclaire, in *Rompre les charmes*, has called "the compulsion to referentiality," the illusions and displacements which the self creates to conceal the fracture, to uphold the fiction of a narcissistic whole, of an interior space. But we see how very precarious this new picture is, how pitiful our poor attempts at creating images are. It seems our lot in the end to accept the cleavage of the self, for what is the "other" but the revelation of the non-identify of self to self. This is the lesson taught in "A Still Moment."

In this story, which belongs to the second collection (*The Wide Net*, 1943), Welty pursues her reflection on representation—a reflection on the visible as it is affected by the presence of an absence. The obvious figure of the artist is Audubon, naturalist and painter. But the other two characters—Murrell, the murderer devoured by a dream of domination and the will to wrench the secret of life from his dying victims, and Lorenzo Dow, the preacher convinced in his teleological vision of the world that his fate is to save all souls—stand for the artist's darker selves or tempters. Their passion is the artist's and so is their awareness of "the object," the white heron, perceived by Murrell as a projection of himself, by Lorenzo as a part of God's creation, and by Audubon as a thing of beauty to be painted.

Just as the artist is seen in three, so is the creative process. In the first stage there must be a deep immersion in the sensible world, which prevails over the world of ideas, and an intimate knowlege of its workings. We note Welty's (or Perseus's) joy in the created world because it holds wonder, but this does not mean, however, that evil of all manner is not forever present, as "A Still Moment" reveals. The mirror surface of the story functions very much like one of those mirrors used by painters after the fashion of Claude Lorrain, framing and reflecting what is not seen directly—control and indirection in technique. In the second stage the artist must accomplish some form of severance; he must acknowledge the inevitable fracture, which is symbolized in "A Still Moment" by the killing of the heron. The third stage is that of representation. It states the impossibility of drawing from memory and restoring to wholeness an instant's vision of absolute beauty. Instead, the artist will reconstruct that vision through fragments, which is a deconstructive gesture:

> [Audubon] knew that the best he could make would be, after it was apart from his hand, a dead thing and not a live thing, never the essence, only a sum of parts; and that it would always meet with a stranger's sight, and never be one with the beauty in any other man's head in the world. (p. 198)

The artist faced with the impossibility of representing pure essence has become a cliché, as Welty, the avid reader of Virginia Woolf's fiction and diaries, knows all too well. But

I think Welty departs from her modernist predecessors when she shows how representation involves a fracture, a construction which amounts to deconstruction ("never the essence, only a sum of parts"), and, still more pointedly, when she acknowledges the presence of an absence through the symbolism of the dead bird used to represent a live one. I would even suggest that "separateness" in this context— that of Lorenzo's dismay—means "an endeavour to dispose of causality," in Claude Richard's phrase. Let me quote again that well-known passage in "A Still Moment":

> He could understand God's giving Separateness first and then giving Love to follow and heal in its wonder; but God had reversed this, and given Love first and then Separateness, as though it did not matter to Him which came first. Perhaps it was that God never counted the moments of Time; Lorenzo did that, among his tasks of love. Time did not occur to God. Therefore—did He even know of it? How to explain Time and Separateness back to God, Who had never thought of them, Who could let the whole world come to grief in a scattering moment? (p. 198)

If time no longer ordains, the whole logically organized sequence of a narrative no longer matters. And indeed, the text is about a "still moment." Moreover, as the necessities of likeness or unlikeness disappear, representation may move further away from the original object. It becomes, in effect, a reflection on the distorting power of absence over presence, an absence which is a sort of echo but not the thing itself. This is the crux of Audubon's method: to represent a bird alive, the painter must kill it.

This experience of "otherness" in the familiar occurs again in *The Golden Apples*. "Moon Lake" is a story about the other (whether he be a boy for the girls, a grownup or an orphan for Nina and Jinny Love), a story about disavowing a self-centered world, with a lesson similar to that of "A Memory." To discover the other is to acknowledge one's own mortality, to become aware of the other side of the mirror, of the self.

The story begins with an exploration of differences, which, in our need to see the world familiarly, we tend to categorize. This is deeply ironic since the camp at Moon Lake was intended to abolish all differences, especially between the orphans and the respectable little girls of Morgana, but it has only succeeded in making them more bitterly felt. Nina's initiation consists in renouncing her own system of differentiation to acknowledge true "separateness." Her first intimation of the presence of the other *as presence* comes of a denial, when she realizes that Easter will not return or acknowledge her gaze—that is to say, when Easter refuses to be *seen*, possessed by Nina; in other words, when Nina's need to see the world familiarly fails. For although Nina has already "placed" the orphans, it is not without ambiguity—as the "not answerable" already hints with disquieting otherness:

> The reason orphans were the way they were lay first in
> nobody's watching them, Nina thought. . . . They, they were
> not answerable. Even on being watched, Easter remained not
> answerable to a soul on earth. Nobody cared! And so, in this
> beatific state, something came out of *her*. (p. 352)

Then, for the first time, Nina is able to enter Easter's mind and know what she thinks after they have played together in the boat. To signify this development in the narration (told from Nina's point of view), all "as if" and "it seemed" constructions are dropped; we have pure affirmative sentences, as the following modulation suggests:

> A dragonfly flew about their heads. Easter only waited in her
> end of the boat, not *seeming* to care about the disappointment
> either. If this was their ship, she was their figurehead, turned
> on its back, sky-facing. She wouldn't be their passenger.
> (p. 356; my italics)

For the first time, the voice we hear is no longer Nina's but Easter's.

The next step occurs through writing when Nina becomes capable of seeing herself as an object, just as she has seen Easter as the other. She writes side by side "Nina," then "Easter." The fine point made later about the spelling of Easter's name is that this *other* is totally unaccountable, not "wholly calculable," as Henry James said. It lives its own life and escapes our power of naming it; this is why *Easter* can spell her name *Esther*, which is at least a real name, not a nickname, and can proudly say in a world defying all laws of causation—that new world which Welty's fiction ceaselessly explores—"I let myself name myself" (p. 357).

I will not insist on Nina's education as a writer, which implies the experience of death and, ultimately, becoming the other. Yet, I wish to make one more point in this exploration of the unfamiliar: somehow, Easter's proud declaration brings us close to "A Still Moment." The reflexive pronoun becomes warped on the way back. "I let myself name myself" does not describe the same/identical, i.e., what Nina expected—Easter. Instead, there rises from the depth of time the Other—Esther. Duration and time are challenged as Nina is brought face to face with the mirror of writing: it reflects the person whom we call but his true character is never spelled correctly. Instead of the foundling, the Biblical heroine faces Nina. The silvering is now *before* the mirror, not behind, thus turning it into a medal (a coin). What is sent back to Nina is no longer her own image but that of other women unknown to her:

> Easter's eyes . . . were neither brown nor green nor cat; they had something of metal, flat ancient metal, so that you could not see into them. Nina's grandfather had possessed a box of coins from Greece and Rome. Easter's eyes could have come from Greece or Rome that day. (pp. 347–348)

The fine quality of Welty's writing comes from this dual texture. Beneath the apparently familiar world—shall we say realistic?—spreads the huge territory of the never quite known or mapped, the wholly elusive. Here I mean more than the unconscious, which has always been explored by writers; I mean the very questioning of the possibilities of the human mind to conceive and represent the world. In work after work, Welty tries to represent the functioning of the human mind, to evoke the duality between an extreme susceptibility to the sensuousness of the created world and the desire to grasp it and show it through figures. This abstracting tendency in her fiction I would now like to examine in relation to the way she constructs her stories. This will be a discussion of structure as opposed to pattern.

In the modernist aesthetics of the earlier part of this century, the formal and symbolic resources of the novel were emphasized; "form," "pattern," and "myth" were of paramount importance. Traces of this can be seen in *The Wide Net*, but we see in a later story such as "Circe" (1955) how Welty has decisively broken new paths. Let me quote from both a postmodern writer and a postmodern critic to make my point. John Hawkes writes in 1965:

> I began to write fiction on the assumption that the true enemies of the novel were plot, character, setting and theme, and having once abandoned these familiar ways of thinking about fiction, totality of vision or structure was really all that remained. And structure—verbal and psychological co-herence—is still my largest concern as a writer.[18]

And Robert Scholes in 1967:

> Fabulation, then, means a return to a more verbal kind of fiction. It also means a return to a more fictional kind. By this I mean a less realistic and more artistic kind of narrative: more shapely, more evocative; more concerned with ideas and ideals, less concerned with things.[19]

This could be compared with what Welty writes in "Words into Fiction," where we note her essential preoccupation with form, the "totality of vision and structure":

> The novel or story ended, shape must have made its own impression on the reader, so that he feels that some *design* in life (by which I mean esthetic pattern, not purpose) has just been discovered there. And this pattern, shape, form that emerges for you then, a reader at the end of the book, may do the greatest thing that fiction does: it may move you. And

however you have been moved by the parts, this still has to happen from *the whole* before you know what indeed you have met with in that book.[20] (my italics)

The important words, of course, are *design* and *whole*. In this deep awareness of form, what matters is the ultimate shape of the finished work, the concern for the *figures* that graphically represent the written work, just as a building is represented by the blueprint of an architect. In this can be traced Welty's surest right to innovation. Claude Simon in *Les Georgiques*, his latest novel, points out this fictional mode and insists on the fact that to read the blueprint correctly one must be aware of the code; otherwise the design is indecipherable. This is somewhat akin to Welty's story of the caves in "Words into Fiction." We need an interpretation.

The difficulty of her work comes from the fact that Eudora Welty used those codes at a time when few could decipher them. The reading of more avant-garde fiction has since taught the public how to look for another representation beneath or behind the story, how to seize, hidden in the visible broken pattern, a more secret pattern. Out of the wide range of figures by which this fiction reveals itself, I will select two, equally beautiful, although the more daring and brilliant may well be the earlier one. Both show, however, the extremely lucid and original way in which Eudora Welty deals with the South—I mean "Old Mr. Marblehall" and "Kin."

"Old Mr. Marblehall" is a story about the imposture of writing; it shows the creation, the "fabrication," of a character, and its limitations. Once again, the surface is deceptive; the apparent subject of the narration is a picture of the decadent society of the Old South, the South seen as myth, if you prefer, and consequently reduced to staging with sets and costumes. In reality, the story shows what Genette argues in *Figures III* about the *recit*, the narrative, which is related both to the story as story and to the act of telling a story. In other words, "Old Mr. Marblehall" stages the specificity of the literary act, the questioning of the very nature of poetical invention and what happens at the moment invention becomes a narrative. In large measure, Eudora Welty's innovative art rests upon this constant shifting towards narration: the *telling* of the story as opposed to the story proper. In "Old Mr. Marblehall," the story is always shown as something elusive, uncertain, in great danger of complete dissolution. Along with this postmodernist tendency to destroy all certainties and reduce the story to its mere constituent parts, we have another well-known trope, constant in Welty's fiction, which I shall call "narrative reversal." Apparently, we shift from what is seen to what is written, but this is pure illusion for it is just the reverse.

To create her character, Eudora Welty raises the two basic questions at the same time: How do we define a character? How do we give him a fictional existence? For this, she relies entirely on a stylistic device often adopted by later writers (William Gass, for instance), that of stylization or the use of stereotypes. It enables her to satirize a number of clichés about the South, to expose hypocritical attitudes, and to insure the active critical participation of her reader. This discourse, founded on a number of infallible and reiterated signs, aims at producing all the marks of what is conventionally known as the Old South, *including its reverse*. The two possible dangers of stylization, imitation and parody (i.e., excessive admiration for one's model or harsh criticism), are brilliantly avoided. This results in Eudora Welty's inimitable tone—her unique voice—which transmutes into poetry the displacement inherent in parody. No labored effects, rather arabesques and flights of the imagination. Writing becomes "a great blazing butterfly" (p. 97).

Character as it appears in the nineteenth-century novel and still quite often in the twentieth-century English novel is defined by family, house, and social life. In "Old Mr. Marblehall," Welty plays on doubles that are not quite identical in order to deconstruct such traditional conception of character. Thus, instead of drawing a portrait of Mr. Marblehall as a Southern gentleman, she paints a full-scale

portrait of Mrs. Marblehall as a Southern gentlewoman—
hyperbolic if not hysterical. The reality of the couple is
denied by the deliberately Balzacian effect of the portrait,
doubled by the poor histrionic origins of the husband on
another level, and also by the fabricated existence of their
child, whose portrait is a series of collages from nineteenth-
and twentieth-century writers. For Mr. Marblehall's other
more common family Welty follows the same process in the
reverse. The whole story, then, is based on the deconstruction of the characters; by stressing their unimportance and
artificiality, Welty presents them as *literary constructions*.
The signifier becomes the signified, form becomes matter.
Poor insignificant Mr. Marblehall, unnoticed by his fellow
citizens, comes to nothing, or rather to that illusion which
the story represents. That Welty changed old Mr. Grenada
into old Mr. Marblehall and the town of Brewster into
Natchez corroborates her wish to satirize at the same time
the artificiality and anachronism of any literature about the
Old South and its myth *and* the traditional way of creating
character. She inaugurates here a new kind of character
without past existence, which heralds the heroes of the
nouveau roman.

Duly provided with a stylized mansion, ancestors, and a
wife, Mr. Marblehall still lacks what would make him exist:
a life. This is the narrative problem which is presented
when we read that Mr. Marblehall, in his desire to catch up
with time, or the others, is a bigamist. To insert oneself into
the flow of time by claiming a past, a present, and a future,
and to force the town's attention, is to accede to existence.
But this existence is kept doubtful throughout the story:

> Nobody cares. Not an inhabitant of Natchez, Mississippi,
> cares if he is deceived by old Mr. Marblehall. Neither does
> anyone care that Mr. Marblehall has finally caught on, he
> thinks, to what people are supposed to do. This is it: they
> endure something inwardly—for a time secretly; they estab-
> lish a past, a memory; thus they store up life. He has done
> this; most remarkably, he has even multiplied his life by
> deception; and plunging deeper and deeper he speculates

upon some glorious finish, a great explosion of revelations . . . the future. (pp. 96–97)

It all amounts to a matter of vision, and vision is what founds the dialectics used in "Old Mr. Marblehall": *to see and to show on the narrative level, to show oneself and [not] be seen on the narrated level.* The injunction to "watch" is the key word of the text; added in the revised version, it centers the whole story on the creative act which takes place between the puppeteer and his audience. This injunction is obviously addressed by the narrator to the reader, but it is also addressed by Mr. Marblehall to the other characters in the narrative. The positive exchange in the first case becomes negative or null in the second. If we look at the last scene, when old Mr. Marblehall imagines he is discovered by his second son, we are warned that it *cannot happen*, for the *whole* passage is based on the sum of all the different signs attached to his different lives. This scene is purely fictitious in the narrative with no other reality than the writing to give it existence. The text, then, can be read as a kind of staging of Welty's *ars poetica:* writing is a matter for illusion; it begets it while it feeds on it. "Old Mr. Marblehall" fictionalizes the process of writing; it is the imposture of narration.

"Kin" also deals with imposture: what a fraud a family portrait is. Here the structure is based upon the principle of the play within a play. André Gide noted this device in his *Journal*, in reference to the famous Van Eyck painting "The Wedding of the Arnolfi." In it, the guests, that is to say, the witnesses, those who testify to the truth of the event, are not shown directly but as reflections in a mirror. In "Kin," Welty also uses the device of a mirror to represent opposition, but the shift is no longer in space as with the Arnolfi (the witnesses standing where we stand, so to speak) but in time. The mirror does not reflect directly a part of the scene which is presented to the spectator or reader, but the fragment of another scene, of which it constitutes the only material proof, thus putting the first picture into perspective. The beauty of the story comes from the perfect adequacy of the medium for the subject: one must look at the portrait of the great-grandmother in order to understand the meaning of a story about people coming to have their picture taken. "Kin" treats the myth of the Old South after the manner of Monet or Vuillard: only fragments on the shimmering surface. Certainly, Eudora Welty satirizes the nostalgia, but at the same time she celebrates the South, whose essence remains immortal because it is steeped in vivid sensations.

"Kin" is a comedy whose obvious target is Sister Anne, vulgar, money-grabbing, without scruples or delicacy, who relinquishes her duties to the dying Uncle Felix and desecrates the house by letting an itinerant photographer use it. Her gain will be her own picture taken for free.

Two objects form the critical distance, the portrait of Great-grandmother Jerrold and the stereoscope. By a narrative perversity the point of view is Dicey's, who, like Laurel McKelva, is the Southerner gone North who comes back home to visit. The aptness of her remarks is such that we believe her—we are, in fact, in great danger of being taken in by Dicey's lively, charming speech. The extreme impressionistic—and postmodern—fragmentation of the narration, the intermingling of the present and the past, hides the counterpoint, which we see only at the end of the story. In "Old Mr. Marblehall," the Southern way of life was doubled; here it is tripled as it would be in a series of mirrors endlessly reflecting the same picture, producing an effect of closure. Thus three versions of Southern life are presented almost identically (Welty uses the same words). They consist of a present positive image (Dicey revisiting the South), a negative one (Sister Anne), and a much earlier one (the heroic past of the family). The function of the first scene is to establish, *en transparence*, that conventional code by which we can appreciate the structure. For all its beauty and polished appearance this society is essentially racist, materialistic, frivolous and irresponsible. But these flaws, so deeply engrained in the Southern way of life, appear unpleasant only after they are *repeated* in the text:

It was two-thirty in the afternoon, after an enormous dinner at which we had had company—six girls, chattering almost like ready-made bridesmaids—ending with wonderful black, bitter, moist chocolate pie under mountains of meringue, and black, bitter coffee. (p. 539)

"What do I see? Cake!" (*CS*, p. 548) (Sister Anne's first words of greeting.)

. . . Uncle Harlan, who could be persuaded, if he did not eat too much, to take down the banjo later. (p. 557)

Welty deepens this critique of the family by holding the portrait of Great-grandmother Jerrold in tense relation with the photograph of Sister Anne. Their differences are only superficial, for Anne's photograph is the comical version of the portrait of the great-grandmother—the same vanity, the same desire to appear to advantage in both instances, above all, the same artificiality in the setting. The photographer uses a backdrop—a "blur of . . . yanked-down moon-light"—just as the itinerant painter did, to produce "the same old thing, a scene that never was" (p. 560).

The evocation of the heroic life of the great-grandmother, the founder of the family, is tinted with the same nostalgia and exotic overtones as the views shown in the stereoscope by Uncle Felix: wonderful cities to which the optical machine added the fascination of haziness. In effect, the heroic has become a postcard, rather, a yellowed photograph, something that can be discarded like the old Confederate musket which is kept behind the door like a broom. What the short story "Kin" presents is a series of old-fashioned portraits on the art of living in the South, but it also shows how they were *made up*. Did this legend ever exist? Or was it born out of a series of conventional embellishments? Welty requires that we remove all that is artificial, all that depersonalizes, just as we know that the veil behind the photograph or the canvas is not true. Dicey realizes this when she looks at her great-grandmother's eyes, which are her own, strangely authentic in this artificial portrait. As she leaves Mingo, she takes away with her one last "photograph," another faded and yellowed one too, the blurred, indistinct vision of the country neighbors waiting under the porch. Their faces are identical, yet each carries its impenetrable secret, its identity.

The counterpoint upon which the story is built functions like a stereopticon or a stereoscope, both of which juxtapose images that are seen in relief. Whatever the specific mechanism, the principle is one of duality with the result either of increased distinctness or blurring. This provides the key to "Kin." The superimposition of diverse attitudes, nearly identical throughout the ages, gives a unique picture which both permits one to see what is called "the Old South," and at the same time suggests something evanescent. On this apparent contradiction rest the dialectics of "Kin": to seize the myth one must start from the present, not the other way around. "Kin" is a fraud. The fraud of a family picture, the fraud of a loving family. By choosing appearances, artificiality, and the absurdly false, the living perpetuate an *illusion*. Yet, true values are seen, true courage exists. By rejecting false romanticism, Welty says, people can live authentically: the beauty and idealism of the South are all there. In this respect, "Kin" is a plea for the South, this South, which in a purely postmodern reading may amount to *traces* only. Memories are, paradoxically, as evanescent and immortal as smells, the exquisite smells of the pinks and four-o'clocks that Aunt Beck would give to her visitors as she walked them to the gate—as if, what is left of people, and life, amounted to no more than mere traces.

In an essay entitled "Literary History and Literary Modernity," Paul de Man arrives at the insight that "one is soon forced to resort to paradoxical formulations such as defining the modernity of a literary period as the manner in which it discovers the impossibility of being modern."[21] Paradoxical formulations are what would best define Euroda Welty's fiction. The first, as suggested by Paul de Man, is the urge repeatedly to try new techniques to express deeper truths about man, and at the same time, the awareness that this is illusory. There is also the effort to imprison the spirit of the moment and to know that it is past already—which is but one aspect of man's old quarrel with time since he is bound to meet defeat in his very accomplishment. The second paradox is to be very much a Southerner and at the same time to transcend, even disavow, the South, to stand outside in order to see better inside and to know the very desperation and impossibility of the enterprise. And, more important perhaps, it is to be alert and critical and distant and yet to use that very distance to encompass with greater love, with more comprehending love, all that is human. At the heart of Welty's modernity there is a lucidity that is never cold or ruthless even when scalding, a despair that can still love, and is above all a saving comic spirit.

1. Eudora Welty, *The Golden Apples*, in *The Collected Stories of Eudora Welty* (New York: Harcourt Brace Jovanovich, 1980), pp. 459–460. Subsequent references to the stories of *A Curtain of Green*, *The Wide Net*, *The Golden Applies*, and *The Bride of the Innisfallen* follow the text of *The Collected Stories*. Pagination is noted parenthetically.

2. Eudora Welty, "The House of Willa Cather" (1974), in *The Eye of the Story: Selected Essays and Reviews* (New York: Random House, 1978), pp. 51–52.

3. Eudora Welty, *The Optimist's Daughter* (New York: Random House, 1972), p. 136.

4. The word *modernité* was coined in 1849 by Chateaubriand and used, disparagingly, to oppose a romantic landscape with storm and gothic architecture to modern bureaucracy. A few years later Baudelaire took up the word to praise Constantin Guys, "the painter of modern life," for his desire to record moments and scenes from contemporary life. He valued this painter's efforts to extract poetry from fashion, eternal beauty from transience. *Curiosités Esthétiques*, "Le peintre de la vie moderne" (1863).

5. See Ruth M. Vande Kieft, *Eudora Welty* (New York: Twayne, 1962).

6. See "The Love and the Separateness in Miss Welty," *Kenyon Review*, 6 (1944), 257.

7. Quoted by Ihab Hassan in "Wars of Desire, Politics of the Word," *Salmagundi* (1982); rpt. in *Representation and Performance in Postmodern Fiction*, ed. Maurice Couturier (Delta 1983), pp. 47–55, 50.

8. For detailed discussion of postmodernist fiction, see *Representation and Performance*, especially the first part entitled "Theory," and Regis

Durand's brilliant essay, "The Disposition of the Familiar." This essay is centered on James and Walter Abish, and started my own reflections on the unfamiliar in Welty.

9. See Sartre, *L'Imaginaire; Psychologie phénoménologique de l'imagination* (Paris: Gallimard, 1940), p. 232, and *L'Imagination* (Paris: PUF, 1981), p. 162.

10. See Tony Tanner, "Frames and Sentences," in *Representation and Performance*, pp. 21–32, 25.

11. See Regis Durand, "The Disposition of the Familiar," pp. 73–84, in *Representation and Performance*. Durand quotes from a typed version of Walter Abish's paper that was circulated at the Nice conference on Postmodern fiction, April 1982.

12. *Ibid.*

13. This is Chester Eisinger's perceptive reading of the scene, although I think the scene too "framed" in the threatening sense of the word to be truly pastoral. See "Traditionalism and Modernism in Eudora Welty," in *Eudora Welty: Critical Essays*, ed. Peggy W. Prenshaw (Jackson: University Press of Mississippi, 1979), p. 10.

14. I am quoting here from Couturier's "Presentation of the Topic," pp. 3–8, in *Representation and Performance*.

15. Derrida, "Living ON: Border Lines," quoted by Tanner in *Representation and Performance*, p. 22.

16. Eudora Welty, "Words into Fiction" (1965), in *The Eye of the Story*, p. 144.

17. Freud, "The Uncanny" (1919), in *On Creativity and the Unconscious* (New York: Harper, 1958), pp. 122–161.

18. Quoted by Robert Scholes in *The Fabulators* (New York: Oxford University Press, 1967), pp. 68–69.

19. Scholes, *The Fabulators*, p. 12.

20. Welty, "Words into Fiction," p. 144.

21. Paul de Man, *Blindness and Insight: Essays in the Rhetoric of Contemporary Criticism* (New York: Oxford University Press, 1971), p. 144.

PATRICIA S. YAEGER

"Because a Fire Was in My Head": Eudora Welty and the Dialogic Imagination

Woman's language has recently become the subject of a set of elaborate and contradictory mystifications. While a number of American feminist critics have begun to join French theorists in asserting that language is a patriarchal institution, French feminists like Hélène Cixous, Marguerite Duras, and Luce Irigaray additionally insist that this institution can be transcended, that woman's writing is an ecstatic possibility, a labor of mystery that can take place in some fruitful void beyond man's experience. "We the precocious, we the repressed of culture," says Cixous in "The Laugh of the Medusa." "Our lovely mouths gagged with pollen, our wind knocked out of us, we the labyrinths, the ladders, the trampled spaces, the bevies—."[1] If past repressions have become the source of woman's strength, the discovery of her secret and self-perpetuating language will give woman "access to her native strength; it will give her back her goods, her pleasures, her organs, her immense bodily territories," delivering paradise and more (p. 250). In a 1975 interview in *Signs* Marguerite Duras echoes and extends parts of Cixous' theory, arguing not only that

This is a revised version of an essay which first appeared in *PMLA*, 99 (October 1984), 955–973, and is reprinted by permission of the Modern Language Association of America.

woman can discover her own private and libidinal realm of connotation through writing but that men and women live in different linguistic cultures; they write from radically different perspectives. "Men . . . begin from a theoretical platform that is already in place, already elaborated," she says. "The writing of women is really tanslated from the unknown, like a new way of communicating rather than an already formed language. But to achieve that, we have to turn away from plagiarism."[2] Plagiarism, as Duras defines it, is any complicity with masculine ideology, theatricality, or rhetorical style. "Feminine literature is a violent, direct literature," she insists. "To judge it, we must not—and this is the main point I want to make—start all over again, take off from a theoretical platform" (p. 425). "Translated" from subterranean depths, women's writing must resist cooperation with the tradition, must avoid the temptation to be patrilineal. In this essay I wish to argue, however, that women's writing employs a *useful* form of "plagiarism." Women who write are not only capable of appropriating myths, genres, ideas, and images that are "populated" with patriarchal meaning; they are continually endowing a male mythos with their own intentions and meanings. According to this argument women write about their own lives by appropriating masculine traditions and transforming them, adapting what has been called "phallocentric" diction to fit the needs of "feminocentric" expression. While this view is necessarily controversial it will lead, I hope, to an interesting thesis: although the plots that women construct for their heroines continue to focus on, and therefore in a sense to privilege, the dominant sex/gender system, the language that women writers have begun to develop to subvert or deconstruct this system is at once traditional and feminocentric. Language is not a reductively patriarchal system but a somewhat flexible institution that not only reflects but may also address existing power structures, including those conditioned by gender.

"Language," as Mikhail Bakhtin argues in his essay "Discourse in the Novel," "is never unitary. It is unitary only as an abstract grammatical system of normative forms, taken in isolation from . . . the uninterrupted process of historical becoming that is characteristic of all living language."[3] Disruptive, emotional, nonhegemonic, language, according to Bakhtin, is open to intention and change. Moreover, both spoken and written language are dynamic and plural, and, as such, language resists all attempts to foster a unitary or absolute system of expression within its boundaries. This does not mean, however, that language itself is either nonpossessive or free from obsession. As Bakhtin explains, "language is not a neutral medium that passes freely and easily into the private property of the speaker's intentions; it is populated—overpopulated—with the intentions of others" (p. 294). The process of its transformation is dialogic; that is, this process involves a dialectical interaction between words, between styles, between points of view. According to Bakhtin, this interaction is highly visible in the novel:

> The prose art presumes a deliberate feeling for the historical and social concreteness of living discourse, as well as its relativity, a feeling for its participation in historical becoming and in social struggle; it deals with discourse that is still warm from that struggle and hostility, as yet unresolved and still fraught with hostile intentions and accents; prose art finds discourse in this state and subjects it to the dynamic-unity of its own style. (p. 331)

Bakhtin argues that we are accustomed to think of the novel in terms of thematic unities or structural polarities but that the novel is neither univocal nor dialectical in structure. "The style of a novel is to be found in the combination of its styles; the language of a novel is the system of its 'languages'" (p. 262). The novel, then, is polyphonic; it is composed of various styles, speech patterns, and ideologies that interact dynamically as a "heteroglossia," or many-languaged discourse. In the novel various stratifying forces come together and diverge, styles speak or argue with one another, barely constrained by the shifting framework of the author's intentionality. The novel, Bakhtin explains, is not a closed system in which style is controlled by authorial monologue. Instead, it represents, or results from, a dynamic conversation, a dialogue between those heterogeneous styles that, even as they are woven into a new plot and reinterpreted by an author, still speak with the intentions of their previous contexts.

Bakhtin's theories of linguistic evolution, of dialogism, and of heteroglossia will give us a useful vocabulary and a new perspective from which to examine the central tensions between men's and women's writing. Using his framework of ideas I will discuss Eudora Welty's *The Golden Apples*, a beautifully crafted and gender-preoccupied novel whose emphasis on sexuality and intertextuality has not been fully comprehended.[4] By focusing on Welty's dialogue with the "already formed" language of the masculine canon, specifically on her appropriation of themes and images from the poetry of William Butler Yeats, we will see that Welty's appropriation of Yeats's poetic imagery is neither a destructive form of "plagiarism" nor a source of disempowerment but a potent rhetorical and ideological strategy.

In the final moments of "June Recital," the second story in *The Golden Apples*, Cassie Morrison is possessed—erotically—by a poem:

> Into her head flowed the whole of the poem she had found in that book. It ran perfectly through her head, vanishing as it went, one line yielding to the next, like a torch race. All of it passed through her head, through her body. (p. 330)[5]

The poem is William Butler Yeats's "Song of the Wandering Aengus," which tells the story of a man driven by the "fire" in his mind to seek an object equal to his desire. He finds this object in "a glimmering girl / With apple blossom in her hair / Who called me by my name and ran / And faded through the brightening air." After calling his name she disappears, but in her echoing image the wanderer discovers his vocation:

Though I am old with wandering
Through hollow lands and hilly lands,
I will find out where she has gone,
And kiss her lips and take her hands;

And walk among long dappled grass,
And pluck till time and times are done
The silver apples of the moon
The golden apples of the sun.[6]

Yeats's poem focuses on the simultaneous impotence and persistence of the male poet's will to define himself through a feminine muse. And yet the final tone of the poem is one of self-assurance: "I will find out where she has gone," the speaker says, equating his discovery of the "glimmering girl" with a capacity to conjure presence out of absence, closure out of uncertainty, eroticism out of ennui. The feminine persona who enables the poet to create this sense of presence has the quality of a projection: she is the shadow or penumbra of the speaker's mind, the figment of *his* imagination. Although she enters the poem as an Ovidian enigma, returning briefly to human form after an immersion in nature, by the end of Yeats's poem she has been reabsorbed not only by nature but by the poem itself, her body becoming metaphor for the sexual plenitude of the landscape where the poet gathers his images. In Yeats's poem, in other words, the "glimmering girl" is assimilated into a masculine story. Even though she has been the first to call him by his name, she is also echoing the sound he wants to hear—"the name of the father"—enabling him to speak as she gives birth to his poem.

Although it has become a commonplace of feminist analysis to argue that patriarchal culture and writing undermine women's creativity, throughout *The Golden Apples* Eudora Welty makes extensive use of the "Song of the Wandering Aengus" as well as of "Leda and the Swan." Paradoxically, she finds these texts useful because of their masculine bias; they provide tropes of the imagination that must be redefined to include women as well as men. On the most primary level Welty borrows images from the "Song of the Wandering Aengus" to describe those women characters who find themselves in a situation like that of the glimmering girl. At the end of "June Recital" Cassie Morrison is dispossessed by Yeats's poem; she utters only a few words from the Aengus' song before falling back "unresisting" into her dreams. Maideen Sumrall, whose very name, with its sense of warmth and seasonality, its alliterative syllables, resembles that of Yeats's muse, is another avatar of the glimmering girl and commits suicide soon after sleeping with Ran MacLain and preventing his suicide. Maideen's lover and the narrator of her story, Ran is the son of Miss Snowdie and King MacLain, a couple who are avatars not only of the glimmering girl and the Wandering Aengus but of the folk heroine Snow White and her wandering prince. As true to her name as Maideen is to hers, Snowdie is an albino who must stay out of the light; her house becomes both coffin and palace where she is always at home, always on view for her prince's pleasure. Snowdie is not simply kept out of the light; she is deprived of the vision and will to wander. "We shut the West out of Snowdie's eyes of course," her neighbor and friend Katie Rainey explains, referring to more than Snowdie's feeble vision (p. 270). Snowdie's husband, King, by contrast, is a roustabout who wanders through the forest, wild-eyed and white-suited, in search of maidens to distress. King is not only the legendary maker of community babies but the designated wanderer, the procreator of the more erotic and exuberant aspects of the communal plot.

Strangely, it is this most stereotypical of male roles that Welty reverses first in *The Golden Apples*. King becomes both "muse" and narrative subject in the fables that the women of Morgana tell themselves as they go about their work. "With men like King, your thoughts are bottomless" (p. 274), says Katie Rainey at the end of "Shower of Gold." King, like the glimmering girl, has the capacity to disappear and reappear, not just in fact, but in women's fancies.

Why is this role reversal important in our estimation of

Welty's stories? In order to understand Welty's expropriation of Yeats's poetry, we need to examine Bakhtin's theory of the novel at closer range. For Bakhtin, novels are "multiform in style and variform in speech and voice" (p. 261); they are created by mingling many styles and genres. This "mingling" is progressive and dialectical. The novel, Bakhtin argues, both enacts and represents "a radical revolution in the destinies of human discourse" (p. 367). The novelist joins disparate languages and inserts disruptive points of view into dominant discourses and ideologies. As a result, the novel records a situation and becomes the site of struggle. At the same time, although the novel's openness to historical change can provide an increasingly flexible medium for deconstructing dominant mythologies, in numerous situations counter-mythologies remain difficult to voice. Since language is "overpopulated with the intentions of others," the novelist has at his or her disposal only those words that are already qualified or inscribed by others; writing occurs within a hostile linguistic environment. "Not all words for just anyone submit equally easily to this . . . seizure and transformation into private property: many words stubbornly resist, others remain alien, sound foreign in the mouth of the one who appropriated them and who now speaks them" (p. 294). This struggle against constraining ideologies is complicated by the fact that words may not submit easily to the writer's will. The limiting "intentions and accents" of a language system can be inscribed to such a depth that words become difficult to reappropriate even in new dialogic contexts. As linguistic and social patterns reinforce one another over time, language may change only to remain the same.

What feminist critics have come to call "patriarchal" discourse is clearly a variant of this general linguistic tendency. But women writers have begun to find voices: they continue to free language from the constraints of a mother or "father" tongue; and they have discovered within the multi-vocal structure of the novel fertile ground for their own reappraisals of history. Welty, for example, incorporates Yeats's poetry into *The Golden Apples* in order to reveal the limitations of his mythology of gender while extending the imaginative power that this mythology brings to male speakers to women as well. Welty uses the energy generated by Yeats's traditional images to question the source of these images and to challenge the masculine nature of his themes.

In order to reveal the hidden zone of women's desires, Welty employs several rhetorical strategies. First, to describe those women characters who wish to become wanderers or storytellers and to protest their positions in a hierarchical and gynophobic society, Welty needs a discourse that is adequate to her characters' complexities—a discourse that is articulate, resonant, and capable of expressing women's aspirations. Instead of abandoning the tradition and creating the new dispensary of images that feminists like Duras have envisioned, Welty expropriates and redefines images from the masculine tradition; she places her own prose or prose intentions in dialogue with what has already been said. "The prose writer," Bakhtin explains, "makes use of words that are already populated with the social intentions of others and compels them to serve . . . new intentions, to serve a second master" (pp. 299–300). But in order to create this dialogic tension Welty must simultaneously call on and interrupt the singularity of Yeats's fictions; she must rupture his language with an intensity of her own. Welty's strategy, then, is to preserve, to intensify, and yet to anatomize Yeats's poems. She inserts fragments from Yeats's "Song of the Wandering Aengus" and "Leda and the Swan" into her own prose contexts, simultaneously challenging and calling upon a well-known male plot.

For example, in "Sir Rabbit," the third story in *The Golden Apples*, Mattie Will, a young woman bored with her sedentary marriage, imagines making love to King in the forest. As she sits on her front porch, churning and dreaming, she stages his gargantuan approach: "When she laid eyes on Mr. MacLain close, she staggered, he had such grandeur, and then she was caught by the hair and brought down as suddenly to earth as if whacked by an unseen shillelagh." While Mattie Will's fantasy begins as a clever parody of "Leda and the Swan," it develops into a serious commentary on the poem itself: "But he put on her, with the affront of his body, the affront of his sense too. No pleasure in that!" Quarreling with Yeats's mythology of gender, Welty recontextualizes his diction; she bestows several of his most memorable phrases on her own female speaker.

> She had to put on what he knew with what he did—maybe because he was so grand it was a thorn to him. Like submitting to another way to talk, she could answer to his burden now, his whole blithe, smiling, superior, frantic existence. (p. 338)

While Mattie Will's precursor Leda had no power to control her own fate, Mattie Will has a measure of control over her own story. Welty's references to "Leda" enable us to measure the relative autonomy of Mattie Will's fantasy even as they remind us that women's desire for pleasure is still inscribed by a male economy: "And no matter what happened to her, she had to remember, disappointments are not to be borne by Mr. MacLain, or he'll go away again" (p. 338). King's "burden," or song, replicates the masculine impositions of the Wandering Aengus, and yet Welty herself could be said to answer to Yeats's "burden" in this story; she submits his language to her own system of accents, her own "way to talk."

Some readers have taken Mattie's fantasy of lovemaking for a real encounter with King in the forest.[7] Why does "Sir Rabbit" have this effect on its readers? Certainly, there is no first-person narrator, as in "A Shower of Gold," to cast doubt upon the narrator's reliability. In addition, Welty invites us to identify—here, and in other stories—with the structures of idealization and fable that add a patina of glamor to the everyday tedium of women's lives. But Mattie Will is day-dreaming; her dreams are inspired by the very taboos that deny them: "Junior Holifield would have given

her a licking . . . just for making such a story up, supposing, after she married Junior, she had put anything in
words. . . . Poor Junior!" (p. 333).

Readers may mistake Mattie Will's imaginary adventure
for reality because they confuse the shared ideology of
Welty's Morgana with the painful and contradictory reality
this ideology works to hide. An ideology is a set of beliefs
that allows individuals to experience themselves as unified
or coherent in a society that is neither. In "A Shower of
Gold," King MacLain and Snowdie are asked, within the
communal mythos, to represent the ideological extremes of
male and female identity. By representing these extremes,
they play delicious roles in the fantasy lives of Morgana
women, but insofar as these women talk about the extremes
of King's and Snowdie's identities as if they were inevitable,
the "naturalness" of these extremes is bolstered or rein-
forced. If it is natural for men to be boisterous, libidinal,
and free-spirited like King, and for women to be pale,
patient homebodies like Snowdie; if it follows that men are
afraid of home and family since children are both silly and
burdensome, then the women of Morgana must be content
with yarning and churning; they must put up with their lot.
What Welty emphasizes, however, as she moves from "A
Shower of Gold" to "Sir Rabbit" is something far more
liberating: the restrictive myths that the neighborhood
women need to fantasize about King lead them paradoxically to identify with his power. "He was going like the
wind, Plez swore to Miss Lizzie Stark. . . . But I bet my
little Jersey calf King tarried long enough to get him a child
somewhere. What makes me say a thing like that? I
wouldn't say it to my husband, you mind you forget it"
(p. 274).

In "Sir Rabbit" Mattie Will also imagines that her husband is conveniently missing from the story. Junior Holifield has been knocked cold, made oblivious not just to
King's desire but to Mattie's as well. The dialectical structure of *The Golden Apples* prepares us for this subterfuge.
After discovering the controlling gender myths of the Mor-

gana community in the first story, we learn their results in "June Recital." Since the community only idealizes wandering men and sedentary women, there is no space in Morgana for women wanderers. Women who want to be visionaries like the Wandering Aengus, or roustabouts like King MacLain, must either become self-destructive or deviant (that is, commit suicide like Mrs. Morrison, go crazy like Miss Eckhart, or become unhappily promiscuous like Virgie Rainey), or—they may let this impulse go underground by imagining wild, compensatory stories about themselves and King, the designated wanderer.[8]

Thus mythos and ethos work together. But while this imaginative wandering is limited in scope, it also provides a motive for liberation. Throughout the novel, Welty uses Yeats's poems "to write what cannot be written," to extend the scope of Mattie Will's story. Though Mattie Will can only draw on the limited myths of her community, she tries, in a rush of sexual energy conveyed through the images Welty has borrowed from "Leda and the Swan," to reinscribe these limits, to become the author of her own sexuality. And while the images that Welty selects to describe Mattie Will's revisionary reading of her world are comic, they hint at something beyond community:

> Then when he let her fall and walked off, when he was out of hearing in the woods, and the birds and woods-sounds and the wood-chopping throbbed clearly, she lay there on one elbow, wide awake. A dove feather came turning down through the light that was like golden smoke. She caught it with a dart of the hand, and brushed her chin; she was never displeased to catch anything. Nothing more fell. (pp. 338–339)

In imagining what happens to Mattie Will after the rape, Welty revises both of Yeats's poems; she is in dialogue not only with his sense of an ending but with his reading of women's creativity as well. In "Sir Rabbit" it is not King but Mattie Will who ventures imaginatively through the forest, alone with whatever her imagination can conjure. "In the woods she heard sounds, the dry creek beginning to run or a strange man calling, one or the other, she thought, but she walked right up on Mr. MacLain again, asleep—snoring" (p. 339). Like the Wandering Aengus, Mattie Will hears the call of a stranger whom Welty has deliberately associated with the glimmering girl. " 'You boys been sighting any birds this way?' the white glimmer asked courteously, and then it passed behind another tree. 'Seen my dog, then?' " (p. 334).

> His coat hung loosely out from him, and a letter suddenly dropped a little way out from a pocket—whiter than white.
> Mattie Will subsided forward onto her arms. Her rear stayed up in the sky, which seemed to brush it with little feathers. She lay there and listened to the world go round. (p. 340)

Like a cherubic version of Zeus, Mattie Will could almost be said to resemble a baby swan as King's letters (his quills, his white and authorial feathers) fall from him and begin to describe Mattie Will's fledgling, if less than philosophic imagination. But these feathers are also signs of Zeus/King's sexual triumph, and Mattie Will's sense of vocation is short-lived:

> . . . presently Mr. MacLain leaped to his feet, bolt awake, with a flourish of legs. He looked horrified. . . .
> "What you doing here, girl?" Mr. MacLain beat his snowy arms up and down. "Go on! Go on off! Go to Guinea!"
> She got up and skedaddled. (p. 340)

Yeats's mythology is both temporalized and satirized in Welty's prose, and a modicum of creative power is translated to woman from man. But while King becomes the "other" that Mattie Will's fantasy transforms, he also blocks her deeper hearing; she misses the "dry creek beginning to run or a strange man calling" and stumbles instead upon an old man who is swearing and snoring. Seeking a romance within herself, Mattie Will rediscovers the limits of domesticity: "Junior Holifield would have given her a licking . . . just for making such a story up, supposing, after she married Junior, she had put anything in words" (p. 333). Although Mattie Will's fantasy becomes a lyric of sexual subordination in which only King's sons can inherit his freedom and power, her exuberant metaphors in this fantasy within a fantasy give evidence of a playful—if not yet powerful—imagination, unfairly constrained.

> But as she ran down through the woods and vines, this side and that, on the way to get Junior home, it stole back into her mind about those two gawky boys, the MacLain twins. They were soft and jumpy! That day, with their brown, bright eyes popping and blinking, and their little aching Adam's apples—they were like young deer, or even remoter creatures . . . kangaroos. . . . For the first time Mattie Will thought they were mysterious and sweet—gamboling now she knew not where. (pp. 340–341)

The bitter memory of Mattie Will's earliest sexual experience has been transformed by this forbidden seizure of linguistic and imaginative power, and it is in this capacity of imagination that Mattie Will Holifield née Sojourner most resembles Eudora Welty herself. We must distinguish, however, between Mattie Will's persona and Welty's own authorial voice. "The activity of a character in a novel is always ideologically demarcated," Bakhtin suggests. "He lives and acts in an ideological world of his own[;] . . . he has his own perception of the world that is incarnated in his action and in his discourse" (p. 335). Mattie Will makes her own mistakes, and yet her "ideological world" is useful to Welty as an arena in which Yeats's authoritative language and Welty's own intended themes begin to clash. If Mattie Will is a figure of the artist as a young woman, she is also a symbolic site where the dialogic interactions of text and intertext become visible. Since she is unable to imagine terms for herself beyond those provided by the erotic plot, Mattie Will's fantasy represents the limited scope of creativity that Morgana society confers—even on women of strong imagination.

In *The Golden Apples* Welty has invented a complement of

characters who replicate even as they relativize the patterns of Yeats's poetry. She achieves this primarily by giving the figure of Yeats's glimmering girl a literary if not a social status equal to that of Yeats's wanderer. Women like Mattie Will, Snowdie MacLain, Maideen Sumrall, and Cassie Morrison do not remain peripheral to Welty's plot; they become instead the central "actors" on the stage of her story. Welty not only redefines female desire in her revisions of "Leda"; she also breaks the "Song of the Wandering Aengus" into a series of quotations spoken by Cassie and a set of fragmentary images defining both male and female characters. She alters the poem's context and its meaning by insisting that Yeats's poem has two protagonists and that each protagonist incarnates a different aspect of woman's story. If at times Welty's female characters resemble the passive, mysterious figure of the glimmering girl whom Yeats portrays as the object of man's desire, in other moments they resemble the ostensible subject of Yeats's poem, the Aengus, in their imagination and their desires.

In "The Wanderers," for example, the last story of Welty's novel, King MacLain reminisces that he once nicknamed Katie Rainey "Katie Blazes" because of her tendency as a child to set her cotton stockings on fire at a dare. " 'Whsst! Up went the blazes, up to her knee! Sometimes both legs. Cotton stockings the girls used to wear—fuzzy, God knows they were. Nobody else among the girls would set fire to their legs. She had the neighborhood scared she'd go up in flames at an early age' " (p. 438). Throughout *The Golden Apples* this imaginative fire is associated with woman rather than with man. And yet, in describing Katie's charred stockings Welty has overliteralized the opening images of Yeats's poem to emphasize that Katie's desires and the social limits of those desires are in conflict. The stockings become an image of impotence, of Katie's inability to go "out to the hazel wood" because a fire was in her legs. But it is in the character of Miss Eckhart, one of Snowdie MacLain's boarders, that Welty has invented the most direct and disturbing counterpart to Yeats's male wanderer. Miss

Eckhart, a piano teacher fiercely devoted to her pupils and her art, sets a literal "fire in her head" the day she escapes from the county asylum and returns to Morgana. Having given the daughters of Morgana's community a forbidden vision of the passion, the genderless ecstasy available to the woman artist, Miss Eckhart is ostracized and incarcerated—punished more severely for her iconoclasm than are the men of Morgana. But Miss Eckhart tries, in her own peculiar way, to remain close to both the male economy of power and the female economy of nurturance. She passes the gift of her insight and her disobedience to Virgie Rainey, her protégée and Katie Rainey's daughter: "Miss Eckhart had had among the pictures from Europe on her walls a certain threatening one. It hung over the dictionary, dark as that book. It showed Perseus with the head of the Medusa" (p. 459). The threat of the picture comes from its frightening invitation to female passion and creativity:

> Miss Eckhart, whom Virgie had not, after all, hated . . .
> had hung the picture on the wall for herself. She had
> absorbed the hero and the victim and then, stoutly, could sit
> down to the piano with all Beethoven ahead of her. With her
> hate, with her love, and with the small gnawing feelings that
> ate them, she offered Virgie her Beethoven. She offered,
> offered, offered—and when Virgie was young, in the strange
> wisdom of youth that is accepting of more than is given, she
> had accepted *the* Beethoven, as with the dragon's blood. That
> was the gift she had touched with her fingers that had drifted
> and left her. (p. 460)

After Katie Rainey's funeral Virgie Rainey not only contemplates the community that has constrained both her and her mother; she also accepts Miss Eckhart's "gift," her absorption of "the hero and the victim" embodied in the frightening picture of the Medusa and Perseus. In "Women's Time" Julia Kristeva outlines a similar pattern of feminist inquiry: "the habitual and increasingly explicit attempt to fabricate a scapegoat victim as foundress of a society or a countersociety may be replaced by the analysis of the potentialities of *victim/executioner* which characterize each identity, each subject, each sex."⁹ Virgie begins to propound for herself a pattern of meditation and self-engagement in which she achieves a freedom she has always sought—not by enacting the violent stories that have been thrust on heroic men like Perseus but by achieving a dialectical vision of the rhythms of victim and victimizer that are the pulse of every heroic and gender-specific plot. "In Virgie's reach of memory a melody softly lifted, lifted of itself. Every time Perseus struck off the Medusa's head, there was the beat of time, and the melody. Endless the Medusa, and Perseus endless" (p. 460).

This dissociation of the story of Perseus from its mythic origins is characteristic of Welty's writing. Her prose is an absorbing exercise in freeing language from previous meanings. As Bakhtin explains in "Discourse in the Novel," the seizure and redefinition of any story whose traditional meaning has seemed synonymous with "truth" has far-reaching consequences:

> By "dissociation" we have in mind here a destruction of any absolute bonding of ideological meaning to language, which is *the* defining factor of mythological and magical thought. An absolute fusion of word with concrete ideological meaning is, without a doubt, one of the most fundamental constitutive features of myth, on the one hand determining the development of mythological images, and on the other determining a special feeling for the forms, meanings and stylistic combinations of language. (p. 369)

If it is mythological thinking that makes language seem absolute in its affirmation and expression of a "patriarchal" authority, then by subverting the seemingly inviolable fusion of word and ideology, by converting "authoritative discourse" into a new form of metaphor, Welty also challenges the view of reality this language represents. Perseus, as Virgie understands, is finally as culpable and as benign as the Medusa herself. Their terrible and seemingly archetypal hatred and love are only elements in an endlessly painful linguistic melody through which our gender differences are maintained. But finally it is more than the gender-specific structures of Yeats's poems or the gynophobic nature of Greek myth that Welty protests in *The Golden Apples*. She protests, as well, that "dark" dictionary which sits beneath Miss Eckhart's picture, a dictionary as blinding as the picture's frame. "Around the picture—which sometimes blindly reflected the window by its darkness— was a frame enameled with flowers, which was always self- evident—Miss Eckhart's pride. In that moment Virgie had shorn it of its frame" (pp. 459–460). Welty begins to "free" language systems that have encouraged us to associate gynophobia and heroism. Like Virgie she has altered their reflections, released them from their frames, allowing lan- guage to express something more powerful: the "fire" in women's minds that it has sought to contain.

While it could be argued that Welty's transformations of the canon's "alien" mythologies should come under the auspices of Harold Bloom's theory of "the anxiety of influ- ence" or Gilbert and Gubar's theory of "the anxiety of authorship," clearly Welty's intertextual dynamics are of a different order. Welty, for example, does not deny, repress, or disguise her obligation to Yeats; she emphasizes her own comic resourcefulness by expropriating Yeats's poems in unexpected ways. Welty has, moreover, taken the title of *The Golden Apples* from the "Song of the Wandering Aengus," as if to signal Yeats's complicity in her story. But her title is also ambiguous; it evokes Atalanta's golden apples and the fruit of the Hesperides. Yeats's poem resonates from the beginning, then, in a number of different contexts. Neither a strong misreading nor a simple repetition, Welty's use of the "Song of the Wandering Aengus" is dialogic.

We can define dialogic discourse, or what Bakhtin calls "dialogic heteroglossia," as the reciprocal action or play that occurs among a novel's collective and heterogeneous systems of language. "In it the investigator is confronted with several heterogeneous stylistic unities, often located on different linguistic levels and subject to different stylistic controls" (p. 261). The novel's incorporation of poetry, however, presents a different set of opportunities and problems. Unlike the novel, the poem tries, Bakhtin argues, to be monovocal:

> Poetry also comes upon language as stratified, language in the process of uninterrupted ideological evolution, already fragmented into "languages." . . . But poetry, striving for maximal purity, works in its own language *as if* that language were unitary, the only language, as if there were no heteroglossia outside it. Poetry behaves as if it lived in the heartland of its own language territory. . . . (p. 399)

When the poem is incorporated into a prose text, however, the poetic voice ceases to possess the illusion that it is "alone with its own discourse": it can be altered—even violated— by a new prose context.

> As soon as another's voice, another's accent, the possibility of another's point of view breaks through the play of the [poetic] symbol, the poetic plane is destroyed and the symbol is translated onto the plane of prose. . . . In this process the poetic symbol—while remaining, of course, a symbol—is at one and the same time translated onto the plane of prose and becomes a double-voiced word: in the space between the word and its object another's word, another's accent intrudes, a mantle of materiality is cast over the symbol. (pp. 328–329)

The prose writer who quotes another's poem in her or his text changes that poem's meaning and orientation by representing the poem's symbols in a different light. This operation occurs in Welty's prose when Yeats's figural fire becomes the fire literally blazing up Katie Rainey's legs or the "fire in the head" of Miss Eckhart. And yet, even within these simple examples, Welty's transformation of Yeats's images acquires new complexity. Welty may impose a new accent or point of view onto Yeats's poem (women, like men, have imaginations or fires in their minds), but she also allows Yeats's poem to work on her own images and characters (women who have "fires" in their minds are still unable to escape the role of victim, of literally "glimmering girl"). Although Welty reaccents Yeats's poem with her own powerful intentions, at the same time this process is limited by the recalcitrance of Yeats's language and plot.

The woman in *The Golden Apples* who is compared most frequently to Yeats's glimmering girl is Cassie's mother, Catherine Morrison. Like many of the women Welty portrays in *The Golden Apples*, Mrs. Morrison sees herself as a failed artist: "'Could you have played the piano, Mama?' 'Child, I could have *sung*,'" she tells her daughter with bitter pride (p. 293). To inscribe Mrs. Morrison's now-frivolous life, Welty transposes the imagery associated with Yeats's muse into a modern key. While the wanderer sees "a glimmering girl, with apple-blossom in her hair," who fades into "the brightening air," Cassie Morrison experiences her mother as a vanishing or evanescent fragrance. "Her bedroom door had been closed all afternoon. But first her mother had opened it and come in, only to exclaim and not let herself be touched, and to go out leaving the smell of rose geranium behind for the fan to keep bringing at her" (p. 287). Cassie's younger brother, Loch, Mrs. Morrison's favorite child, is also disturbed by his mother's disappearances.

> By leaning far out he could see a lackadaisical, fluttery kind of parade, the ladies of Morgana under their parasols, all trying to keep cool while they walked down to Miss Nell's. His mother was absorbed into their floating, transparent colors. Miss Perdita Mayo was talking, and they were clicking their summery heels and drowning out—drowning out something. . . . (p. 280)

If Welty's prose suggests a transposition of the call the Wandering Aengus hears as he begins his quest, these women hear nothing as they chatter mindlessly on the way to a summer party, "drowning out—downing out something. . . ." At this moment Mrs. Morrison, like the glimmering girl, disappears from view, "absorbed" by the other women's transparency. Later in the novel she fades altogether, for we learn in "The Wanderers" that she, like Maideen Sumrall, has committed suicide. Just as Yeats's glimmering girl becomes an object, a mirror for the Aengus' desires, so Mrs. Morrison has become an "object" to herself, a mirror to the desires of her community, and only through suicide can she speak her despair. Ironically, it is not until after her death that someone calls Mrs. Morrison by her name. To commemorate her mother's death, Cassie first marks the grave with a stone angel and then plants her own front yard with a bed of narcissi that spell out "Catherine." By writing her mother's name in floral letters, Cassie is attempting to bring her mother back into the communal garden: she does not allow Catherine Morrison to have a plot of her own even in death. Moreover, Catherine Morrison's death is reincorporated into the myth of Narcissus, making her once again the "echo" of a masculine story.

But beneath the lackadaisical surface of Mrs. Morrison's life as it is described in "June Recital," Welty invites us to see something unvoiced and ominous—the glimmer of an untold story. From the beginning of "June Recital" Cassie's mother is more absent than present, reluctant to fulfill the chores of mothering, guilty about the fates of other women. Even Loch notices her vacant presence. "It was not really to him that his mother would be talking," Loch observes, "but it was he who tenderly let her, as they watched and listened to the swallows just at dark. It was always at this hour that she spoke in this voice—not to him or to Cassie or Louella or to his father, or to the evening, but to the wall, more nearly" (p. 328). In this moment we are allowed to see beyond the plot that has been scripted for her by her community and to look into the margins of Catherine Morrison's own story. As her voice moves back and forth in the fading light, she tells Loch her story about the garden party. Heard in this darkening context the garden "plot" becomes liminal, and we begin to read between the lines, to realize that Mrs. Morrison's speech is more nearly a parable about the permissible range of feminine creativity in this small Southern town than it is an anecdote about a ladies' social:

> "Listen and I'll tell you what Miss Nell served at the party," Loch's mother said softly, with little waits in her voice. She was just a glimmer at the foot of his bed.
> "Ma'am."

"An orange scooped out and filled with orange juice, with
the top put back on and decorated with icing leaves, a straw
stuck in. A slice of pineapple with a heap of candied sweet
potatoes on it, and a little handle of pastry. A cup made out of
toast, filled with creamed chicken, fairly warm. A sweet
peach pickle with flower petals around it of different-colored
cream cheese. A swan made of a cream puff. He had whipped
cream feathers, a pastry neck, green icing eyes. A pastry
biscuit the size of a marble with a little date filling." She
sighed abruptly.
"Were you hungry, Mama?" he said. (p. 328)

If a number of characters in *The Golden Apples* are "just a
glimmer at the foot" of someone's bed, if they replicate,
even as they comment on, the limited powers of Yeats's
muse, others, like Cassie's piano teacher, Miss Eckhart,
initially appear as figures of capable imagination. Although
by the end of "June Recital" Miss Eckhart has been ostracized and packed off to the County Farm, she maintains
throughout the story a strange nobility and a will to
wander. Even after she has taken leave of her senses, she is
still able to resurrect a private teleology; she returns to the
house where she taught piano lessons, as determined as the
Aengus to finish her story.

Miss Eckhart's attempted recreation and destruction of
past events become the central dramatic action in "June
Recital." As Cassie Morrison looks forward to an evening's
hayride and creates a "tie-dye scarf" according to communal
formula, her brother, Loch, watches the world outside his
window and composes stories about the vacant house next
door. Already the separation between genders has begun.
Cassie's attention is focused on an object of feminine adorn-
ment that is safely unpredictable. Loch allows his mind to
wander freely; his stories are fantastic, his metaphors inventive. As he watches Virgie Rainey and a "friendly" sailor
making love on the second floor of the vacant house, Loch is
established as a naive and unbiased observer who is already
attempting to construct a metaphoric language to account
for a world he does not understand. At first he is the only

one to see an old woman enter the house and begin to putter about downstairs. Her behavior is strangely festive:

> The old woman was decorating the piano until it rayed out like a Christmas tree or a Maypole. Maypole ribbons of newspaper and tissue paper streamed and crossed each other from the piano to the chandelier and festooned again to the four corners of the room, looped to the backs of chairs here and there. When would things begin? (p. 283)

This is the room where Miss Eckhart used to give her June recitals, the room where every year she would come to life for one handsome, perfectible evening:

> Then she would look down ceremoniously at the sleepiest and smallest child, who had only played "Playful Kittens" that night. All her pupils on that evening partook of the grace of Virgie Rainey. Miss Eckhart would catch them running out the door, speaking German to them and holding them to her. In the still night air her dress felt damp and spotted, as though she had run a long way. (p. 315)

In her sweaty garment she resembles a benign goddess, in love with the world she has made, for like Yeats's wanderer she is a creator who has struggled, who seems to have "run a long way." Thwarted in love and in art she sustains herself by giving June recitals and imagining an artistic life for Virgie Rainey, who, at thirteen, is still passionately absorbed in her music:

> She played the *Fantasia on Beethoven's Ruins of Athens*, and when she finished and got up and made her bow, the red of the sash was all over the front of her waist, she was wet and stained as if she had been stabbed in the heart, and a delirious and enviable sweat ran down from her forehead and cheeks and she licked it in with her tongue. (p. 313)

Images of sweating, of licking, of violence, of delirium bind child and woman together and reveal the price both must pay for their art. Too eccentric, too foreign and impassioned for Morgana, Miss Eckhart loses her pupils and Virgie her inspiration. "Perhaps nobody wanted Virgie Rainey to be anything in Morgana any more than they had wanted Miss Eckhart to be," Cassie reminisces, "and they were the two of them still linked together by people's saying that" (p. 306). Miss Eckhart's return from her banishment to the County Farm is poignantly ceremonial: she comes back to the place where she organized recitals and cultivated a talent in Virgie Rainey as beautiful and as violent as her own.

In decorating the room for the final recital Miss Eckhart refurbishes it with numerous mementos. The piano is crowned with magnolia blossom—Virgie's perpetual and too fragrant gift to her teacher. Earlier in the story the magnolia has been an emblem of exuberant and rebellious female energy, but at this final recital it becomes—like the nest Miss Eckhart weaves in the piano—a symbol of woman's defeat. Miss Eckhart is preparing her beloved objects—piano, magnolia, metronome, empty house—for a small and funereal conflagration:

> She wanted things to suit herself, nobody else would have been able to please her; and she was taking her own sweet time. She was building a bonfire of her own in the piano and would set off the dynamite when she was ready and not before.
>
> Loch knew from her actions that the contrivance down in the wires—the piano front had been taken away—was a kind of nest. She was building it like a thieving bird, weaving in every little scrap that she could find around her. He saw in two places the mustached face of Mr. Drewsie Carmichael, his father's candidate for mayor—she found the circulars in the door. (p. 316)

Just as this collage contains patriarchs who will be burned in effigy, so the house contains Virgie Rainey, whose participation in the erotic play overhead (an eroticism that, we are led to believe, has helped disconnect Virgie from her art) may be permanently ended. But in spite of the fire Miss Eckhart envisions in her head, her plot is poorly conceived from the start. As Loch explains to himself, watching her clumsy activities through his bedroom window, "only a woman" would try to start a conflagration in a breezeless room where the windows are down, their cracks stuffed with paper. Unlike Yeats's wanderer Miss Eckhart lacks the freedom or knowledge to take her fire to that traditional source of inspiration—the hazel wood with its attendant rhetoricity.

> She bent over, painfully, he felt, and laid the candle in the paper nest she had built in the piano. He too drew his breath in, protecting the flame, and as she pulled her aching hand back he pulled his. The newspaper caught, it was ablaze, and the old woman threw in the candle. Hands to thighs, she raised up, her work done. (p. 317)

This Promethean and painful act is thwarted at once. Two husky wanderers who have spent the day fishing have been watching Miss Eckhart through the window as she painstakingly decorates her recital hall and builds her empty nest. As she holds her candle to the paper they jump into the house with a yell.

> Old Man Moody and Mr. Bowles together beat out the fire in the piano, fighting over it hard, banging and twanging the strings. Old Man Moody, no matter how his fun had been spoiled, enjoyed jumping up and down on the fierce-burning magnolia leaves. So they put the fire out. . . . When a little tongue of flame started up for the last time, they quenched it together. . . . (p. 320)

Woman's "fierce-burning magnolia leaves," her "little tongue of flame," and her fiery piano are amusing objects to these men. But even in the moment when they play, child-like, with woman's fire, their pleasure edges toward sadism.

> She rose up, agitated now, and went running about the room, holding the candle above her, evading the men each time they tried to head her off.
> This time, the fire caught her own hair. The little short white frill turned to flame.
> Old Man Moody was so quick that he caught her. He came up with a big old rag. . . . He brought the cloth down over her head from behind, grimacing, as if all people on earth had

to do acts of shame, some time. He hit her covered-up head
about with the flat of his hand. (p. 322)

Her hair aflame, Miss Eckhart becomes an archetype of
woman's fury and desire. Like Yeats's wanderer she has a
"fire in her head," and yet the image turns in on itself and
becomes parodic as she strikes back, not at society, but at
herself. Her fire becomes a masochistic flame: it scorches
before it illuminates. Miss Eckhart's resemblance to Yeats's
wanderer, then, at once expands and collapses. Her aspirations are mediated by her culturally inscribed role as victim,
as literally "glimmering girl."

"Old Man Moody was so quick that he caught her. . . ."
Her hair in flames, her victimizer still in pursuit, woman is
caught in a periphrasis, but her desire to change roles is not
so much thwarted by Yeats's poem as it is expressed *through*
the poem:

> When heteroglossia enters the novel it becomes subject to an
> artistic reworking. The social and historical voices populating
> language, all its words and all its forms, which provide
> language with its particular concrete conceptualizations, are
> organized in the novel into a structured stylistic system that
> expresses the differentiated socio-ideological position of the
> author amid the heteroglossia of his epoch. . . . in the novel
> heteroglossia is by and large always personified, incarnated in
> individual human figures, with disagreements and oppositions
> individualized. But such oppositions of individual wills and
> mind are submerged in *social* heteroglossia[,] . . . surface
> manifestations of those elements that play *on* such individual
> oppositions, make them contradictory, saturate their con-
> sciousness and discourses with a more fundamental speech
> diversity. (Bakhtin, pp. 300, 326)

Within the context of Welty's novel Yeats's poem becomes
one of the voices that both describe and explain women's
predicament within a society that represses their desires.
His poem provides a set of differential images describing
gender roles that Welty refracts with an even more frightening "speech diversity." Old Man Moody prevents Miss

Eckhart from acting out her chosen role, and although he saves her life, his act is mediated by violent images of suffocation ("he brought the cloth down over her head from behind") and of sadism ("he hit her covered-up head about with the flat of his hand").

Shadows of an older mythology, the men portrayed in "June Recital" have been demystified in Welty's prose, brought down to earth. But if they move through Welty's world clumsily, ineptly, their cruelty is not abated; Welty asks them to enact, as if by rote, their older roles of victor and victimizer. Miss Eckhart and her pupils are harassed, for example, by the second roomer at Miss Snowdie's boarding house, the encyclopedia saleman Mr. Voight, who "would walk over their heads and come down to the turn of the stairs, open his bathrobe, and flap the skirts like an old turkey gobbler. . . . he wore no clothes at all underneath" (p. 294). Welty's humor is a mediating device to keep these stories about human derangement dialogic. But neither the humor nor the dialogism obscures the fact that sexual, economic, and linguistic restraints are imposed on women at an early age. Cassie "herself had told all about Mr. Voight at breakfast, stood up at the table and waved her arms, only to have her father say he didn't believe it; that Mr. Voight represented a large concern and covered seven states. He added his own threat to Miss Eckhart's: no picture show money" (p. 295). Those women in Morgana who step outside traditional roles, who attempt to speak in the culture's excluded heteroglossia, either are denied scripts altogether or have scripts foisted on them. " 'Listen. You should marry now, Virgie,' " Jinny Love Stark shrieks at Katie Rainey's funeral. " 'Don't put it off any longer.' . . . She was grimacing out of the iron mask of the married lady. It appeared urgent with her to drive everybody, even Virgie for whom she cared nothing, into the state of marriage along with her" (pp. 444–445). But while the community tries to prevent another outbreak of pyromania, the reader who is attuned to Welty's revision of Yeats's poem sees another story altogether. The Morgana community acts together, man and woman alike, to prevent *feminine* acts of Prometheanism: woman is not allowed to steal man's holy fire.

In her essay "The Difference of View" Mary Jacobus asks for a feminist criticism that does more than reaffirm the concept of gender difference as opposition. Instead, Jacobus envisions an alliance of feminism and the avant-garde in which the traditional terms of linguistics, of psycho-analysis, and of literary criticism "are called in question—subverted from within." "Such a move has the advantage of freeing off the 'feminine' from the religion-bound, ul-timately conservative and doom-ridden concept of dif-ference-as-opposition which underlies Virginia Woolf's reading of the 'case' of George Eliot," Jacobus argues. "*Dif-ference* is redefined, not as male *versus* female—not as biolog-ically constituted—but as a multiplicity, joyousness and heterogeneity which is that of textuality itself."[10] In forging an alliance between avant-garde literary practice and femi-nist criticism, textuality "becomes the site both of challenge and Otherness; rather than (as in more traditional ap-proaches) simply yielding the themes and representation of female oppression" (p. 12). This redefinition of difference should, according to Jacobus, encourage the transgression or "transversal" of gender boundaries and expose these boundaries "for what they are—the product of phallocentric discourse and of women's relation to patriarchal culture" (p. 12). A new feminist poetics should begin, then, to ad-dress the heterogeneous languages, the dialogism, the "plea-sure edge" in women's writing, since this writing will be in conflict, in conversation, and, to some degree, in correspon-dence with the ideologies it is trying to dislodge.

In this essay I have begun to show how such an alliance of feminist criticism and "those pleasurable and rupturing as-pects of language" that Jacobus identifies with the avant-garde may work together in the analysis of a literary text. One of Welty's strengths as a writer is her recognition that she need not be coerced by those stories that coerce her female characters; she feels small compunction at her own Promethean acts.

In the last sentence of *The Golden Apples* words and images that have been appropriated from the poetic contexts of the "Song of the Wandering Aengus" and "Leda and the Swan" begin to reappear as part of the irresolution and diversity of Virgie's final vision:

> She smiled once, seeing before her, screenlike, the hideous and delectable face Mr. King MacLain had made at the funeral, and when they all knew he was next—even he. Then she and the old beggar woman, the old black thief, were there alone and together in the shelter of the big public tree, listening to the magical percussion, the world beating in their ears. They heard through falling rain the running of the horse and bear, the stroke of the leopard, the dragon's crusty slither, and the glimmer and the trumpet of the swan. (p. 461)

Is Welty hinting at her text's demythologization not only of Yeats's poetry but of that "sixty-year-old smiling public man" who dreams so poignantly "of a Ledaean body" in "Among School Children" and celebrates organic beauty in the "chestnut-tree, great-rooted blossomer"? Welty has transformed Yeats's wished-for organicism into a series of dissolving images; she links the death of the mythological "King" with Virgie's own multiple vision. And finally, in subjecting Yeats's poetic discourse to the heteroglossia of her own story, Welty has displaced the ending of his story with a beginning of her own: the unresolved yet resolute image of "the big public tree" sheltering two marginal and intemperate women who are, nonetheless, afoot with their visions.

1. Hélène Cixous, "The Laugh of the Medusa," in *New French Feminisms*, ed. Elaine Marks and Isabelle de Courtivron (Amherst: University of Massachusetts Press, 1980), p. 248. Further references to this work will be cited in the text.

2. Marguerite Duras, "An Interview with Marguerite Duras," by Susan Husserl-Kapit, *SIGNS*, 1 (1975), 425. Further references to this work will be cited in the text.

3. Mikhail Bakhtin, "Discourse in the Novel," in *The Dialogic Imagination*, trans. Caryl Emerson and Michael Holquist, ed. Michael Holquist (Austin: University of Texas Press, 1981), p. 288. Further references to this work will be cited in the text.

4. Only a few of Welty's critics have begun to discuss her prose in terms of feminist analysis or theory. For fine examples of such analysis see Mary Anne Ferguson's "*Losing Battles* as a Comic Epic in Prose," in *Eudora Welty: Critical Essays*, ed. Peggy Whitman Prenshaw (Jackson: University Press of Mississippi, 1979), Carol Manning's *With Ears Opening Like Morning Glories: Eudora Welty and the Love of Storytelling* (Westport, CT: Greenwood Press, 1985), and Louise Westling's *Sacred Groves and Ravaged Gardens: The Fiction of Eudora Welty, Carson McCullers, and Flannery O'Connor* (Athens: University of Georgia Press, 1985).

5. References to *The Golden Apples* (1949) follow the text of *The Collected Stories of Eudora Welty* (New York: Harcourt Brace Jovanovich, 1980). Page numbers are cited parenthetically in the text.

6. William Butler Yeats, *The Collected Poems of William Butler Yeats* (New York: Macmillan, 1968), p. 57.

7. See, for example, Carol Manning's reading of "Sir Rabbit" in *With Ears Opening Like Morning Glories: Eudora Welty and the Love of Storytelling*, pp. 100–103. Manning's analysis is representative of recent readings of "Sir Rabbit" in which the critic assumes the actuality of the episode; otherwise her analysis is very perceptive, especially her descriptions of King's mock heroism and Welty's comic flair.

8. Although a complete analysis of Welty's reading of gender in *The Golden Apples* is beyond the scope of this essay, the rest of the novel focuses on gender issues with a thorough dialectical force. After exploring the constrictions that an asymmetrical sex/gender system imposes on women, Welty begins in "Moon Lake," and then in "The Whole World Knows" and "Music from Spain," to address the pain this asymmetry creates for men as well. For a reading of this dialectic in "Moon Lake," see my "The Case of the Dangling Signifier: Phallic Imagery in Welty's 'Moon Lake,'" in *Twentieth Century Literature*, 28 (Winter 1982).

9. Julia Kristeva, "Women's Time," trans. Alice Jardine and Harry Blake, *SIGNS*, 7 (1981), 34.

10. Mary Jacobus, "The Difference of View," in *Women Writing and Writing about Women*, ed. Jacobus (New York: Barnes and Noble, 1979), p. 12. Further references to this work will be cited in the text.

The Loving Observer
of *One Time, One Place*

Eudora Welty has often said that her work for the WPA in the mid-1930's opened her eyes as a writer, showing her the real Mississippi that her sheltered life in Jackson had kept her from seeing.

> It took me all over Mississippi, which is the most important thing to me, because I'd never seen it—except Jackson and Columbus—never. . . . that experience, I think, was the real germ of my wanting to become a real writer, a true writer. It caused me to seriously attempt it. It made me see, for the first time, what life was really like in this state. It was a revelation.[1]

Something similar was happening all over the country in the 1930's, as WPA writers and photographers fanned out along the nation's roads, surveyed its farmlands, analyzed its towns and cities. The photographs that record Welty's observations, from which she selected the group published in 1971 as *One Time, One Place*, are part of a nationwide documentary phenomenon, also represented by Dorothea Lange and Paul Taylor's *An American Exodus*, Erskine Caldwell and Margaret Bourke-White's *You Have Seen Their Faces*, Richard Wright and Edwin Rosskam's *12 Million Black Voices*, and the classic of them all, James Agee and Walker Evans's *Let Us Now Praise Famous Men*.[2] The general aim of these publications was to shock the nation into awareness of poverty and the need for reform; thus both photographs and accompanying texts emphasize political injustice and the physical facts of hunger, dirt, and domestic squalor in general.

Eudora Welty's particular sympathies set her work apart from the general run of documentary writing of the thirties and made her contribution unique. She chose to concentrate on black Mississippians, but instead of seeing her subjects as sociological data or political victims, she approached them with a sense of kinship and celebration. Because she was a woman and self-effacing in temperament, she was allowed glimpses into the lives of her black neighbors that no white man could have had. In *One Time, One Place* she has given us photographs that celebrate the dignity and grace of black Southerners in spite of the poverty and the humiliation that often surrounded them.

As we consider Welty's place among documentary photographers and writers, we should compare her to two exact contemporaries who were also writers from the South involved in the documentary effort: Richard Wright and James Agee. Born within a year of one another (Wright in 1908, Agee and Welty in 1909), all three left the South for education and crucial development, and all three used their pens to complement the photographs that tell their people's story. Welty differed in taking her own photographs and in using her camera instead of her pen to provide her record of the Depression. Later she subtly transmuted the raw material of her WPA travels into her first collection of short stories, *A Curtain of Green* (1941). Welty's sensitivity to the lives of the people whom she photographed is closely related to Wright's desire "to seize . . . upon that which is qualitative and abiding in Negro experience, to place within full and constant view the collective humanity whose triumphs and defeats are shared by the majority" (p. 5–6).

Agee, too, shared this awareness of universal experience in the midst of poverty, even though his work focused primarily on poor whites. The two months of late summer, 1936, when he and Walker Evans lived with tenant farmers in Alabama and documented their lives, were as profound a revelation for him as Welty's WPA experiences were for her. Agee's friend, the poet Robert Fitzgerald, recalled that it was "a shaking kind of experience for him," and Agee himself wrote Father Flye at the time that it was "certainly one of the best things that ever happened to me."[3]

Alfred Kazin analyzed the documentary photography and writing of the Depression very soon after the fullest outpouring of that remarkable process of national self-discovery. In "America! America!" the final chapter of *On Native Grounds* (1942), Kazin sees the work of WPA agents as "a repository as well as a symbol of the reawakened American sense of its own history." Just as Welty discovered the richness and variety of her native state for the first time and Agee discovered a part of the South which brought forth his deepest literary powers, so the writers of the WPA guides "uncovered an America that nothing in the academic histories had ever prepared one for, and very little in imaginative writing."[4] The spectacle of American life revealed by the WPA and similar documentary projects awakened a new sense of democratic community in the nation and stimulated new kinds of fiction in the hands of such writers as John Steinbeck and Erskine Caldwell.

Valuable as the documentary effort may have been in promoting national self-awareness, it embodied techniques which Kazin saw as morally troubling. The camera was at the center of this enterprise, symbolizing a kind of passive objectivity.

> Indeed, the technical and psychological fascination of the camera may be considered even to have given a new character to contemporary prose, a transformation which can be appreciated only in terms of its moral example, since it was the camera's essential passiveness that made for its technical influence over so many writers.[5]

In Kazin's view, a *posture* of objectivity came to be assumed by the photographer and was accompanied by a prose style that sought pure denotation. The camera was nevertheless controlled by a person who chose what to photograph and when to click the shutter. Photographers have long been aware of the predatory and potentially disruptive nature of their work. Henri Cartier-Bresson has said that he prowled the streets of Marseilles, "feeling very strung-up and ready to pounce, determined to 'trap' life," while Dorothea Lange has likened the photographer to a lion tamer.[6] Walker Evans states that he and Agee "bought" the sharecroppers who were the subjects of *Let Us Now Praise Famous Men*. "We went into their houses as paying guests, and we told them what we were doing, and we sort of paid them for that." When asked by students how to treat subjects anxious about facing a camera, Evans replied that "any sensitive man is bothered by a thing like that unless the motive is so strong and the belief in what he's doing is so strong it doesn't matter. The important thing is to do the picture."[7]

Agee was more troubled by this problem. Richard King has perceptively analyzed Agee's revulsion against the pretense of objectivity and his rejection of documentary prose style, as well as his realization of the impurity of his own motives and the violation of the dignity of the three families that he and Evans studied so closely.[8] James Agee's admission of these problems gives a painfully honest, if ironic, fullness to *Let Us Now Praise Famous Men* as a complex embodiment of the whole documentary effort. At the beginning of the book, he describes the greatest danger of this kind of voyeurism.

> It seems to me curious, not to say obscene and thoroughly terrifying, that it could occur to an association of human beings drawn together through need and chance and for profit into a company, an organ of journalism, to pry intimately into the lives of an undefended and appallingly damaged group of human beings, an ignorant and helpless rural family, for the purpose of parading the nakedness, disadvantage and humiliation of these lives before another group of human beings, in the name of science, of "honest journalism" . . . , of humanity. . . . (p. 7)

"Obscene" and "thoroughly terrifying" are appropriate terms for the extremes of cruelty that photographers can achieve. Susan Sontag's major example in *On Photography* is the work of Diane Arbus that created such a sensation in the early 1970's. Sontag sees such work as predatory and sensational tourism performed by members of a privileged class. "Who could have better appreciated the truth of freaks than someone like Arbus, who was by profession a fashion photographer—a fabricator of the cosmetic lie that masks the intractable inequalities of birth and class and physical appearance."[9] In recent years Arbus has been succeeded and perhaps surpassed by another fashion photographer from New York, Richard Avedon, whose *In the American West* reveals not the wide open spaces but the horrors of grotesquerie among ordinary people. He claims that his subjects are beautiful and that he has merely allowed them to reveal their poignant selves, yet the frontal poses and harsh lighting of his portraits strip these people to a nakedness that reveals every pimple, wart, and sag of skin. Avedon seems to admit this selectivity when he says, "I don't think the West of these portraits is any more conclusive than the West of John Wayne."[10]

Eudora Welty also felt that her photographic subjects were beautiful and that she was allowing them to reveal themselves. Yet in her technique and selection she is as far removed from Arbus and Avedon as it seems possible to be. She is also very far removed from Walker Evans, whose photographs in *Let Us Now Praise Famous Men* emphasize the bareness and stark poverty of his Alabama sharecroppers' lives. Evans's frontal poses and direct lighting sharply etch the stubble of beard on the men's thin faces, the safety pins holding together the deeply soiled and sacklike dresses of women and girls, and the blank or tired or wary expressions in the eyes of all his people. Many of his photographs also emphasize the sparse furnishings and dilapidation of the unpainted buildings in which they lived. He later said that he loved this bare quality and the grain of the wood and regretted seeing such structures painted.[11] Welty's subjects in *One Time, One Place* are usually very poor and often ragged, living in the same kind of wooden shacks that Evans photographed, but she captures the basic human courage and grace beneath the superficial badges of class and race. "Boy with his Kite" is almost a frontal pose, similar to those characteristic of Evans's work, but Welty caught the moment at which the boy held up his homemade toy, looking at it with a determined pride, rather than at the camera. The smudges and holes in his sweater or the uneven length and dusty look of his knickers are unimportant in comparison to his achievement. In other pictures, many of mothers and children, smiles and animated gestures similarly overshadow signs of poverty such as ill-fitting clothes or holes in the fabric. In one, entitled, simply, "Coke," a big sister or young mother balances a baby on her knee as she balances herself on her other foot and stands leaning against the porch wall with her free hand resting, Coke in hand, on a windowsill. Her sacklike dress has slipped from one shoulder, and a ragged edge is noticeable on one side of her hem, but the major impression of the image is a jaunty relaxation expressed by the graceful alignment of the girl's limbs with the baby's. In the picture of mother and child entitled "To Find Plums," there is harmony in the pose of the smiling mother holding her daughter in her arms, both in dresses and bright hats, facing the same way in anticipation perhaps of the fruit they will find, mother with a large bucket and daughter with her own miniature made from a coffee tin.[12] Welty explains that she and her subjects shared a kindred spirit.

> Whatever you might think of those lives as symbols of a bad time, the human beings who were living them thought a good deal more of them than that. If I took picture after picture out of simple high spirits and the joy of being alive, the way I began, I can add that in my subjects I met often with the same high spirits, the same joy. Trouble, even to the point of disaster, has its pale, and these defiant things of the spirit repeatedly go beyond it, joy the same as courage. (p. 6)

Something more than personal attitude and selection was at work in her relationship to those whom she photographed. Most of the people in her pictures are blacks, and Welty sees these pictures as testimony to a kind of trust between white people and black which she believes "dates the pictures now, more than the vanished years" (p. 6). The relaxed poses, gestures, and facial expressions of her portraits testify indeed to a remarkable trust, more marked in her photographs of blacks than of whites. Such trust was not, however, a deep and natural part of relations between blacks and whites in Mississippi, or the rest of the South, any more then than it is now. Individuals might achieve it, but the appearance of easy relations between the races in the 1930's was only an external accommodation to a troubled caste system whose tensions were always in danger of exploding. Richard Wright described the underlying reality of life for black people in the South during the 1930's in *12 Million Black Voices*.

> Fear is with us always, and in those areas where we black men equal or outnumber the whites fear is at its highest. Two streams of life flow through the South, a black stream and a white stream, and from day to day we live in the atmosphere of a war that never ends. (p. 46)

In order to protect themselves in this atmosphere, blacks "strove each day to maintain that kind of external behavior that would best allay the fear and hate of the Lords of the Land" (p. 41). The result was a dual reality of which most whites knew only one part. "They have painted one picture: charming, idyllic, romantic; but we live another: full of the fear of the Lords of the Land, bowing and grinning when we meet white faces . . ." (p. 35).

James Agee was painfully aware of this gulf between the races. He and Walker Evans avoided serious confrontation with racial tensions by concentrating almost exclusively on white subjects, but occasionally Agee records an incident which reminds us of the barriers that probably would have excluded them from any effective documentation of black tenant farmers' lives. One such incident occurred on a Sunday morning when he and Evans accompanied a white landowner on a visit to his Negro tenants' farms. As the white men arrived in their cars, the peaceful family gather-

ing broke up, and most of the blacks moved uneasily out of
sight after first respectfully nodding, smiling, and touching
their foreheads. Several older men and boys remained behind to speak with their employer, staying at a careful
distance "as if floated, their eyes shifting upon us sidelong
and to the ground and to the distance. . . ." The landlord
asked questions about crops and chores, and then shifted
the subject. "And you, you ben doin much coltn lately, you
horny old bastard?" he asked the oldest man. Shy giggling
and whining denials followed, and then the white man
increased the humiliation of the blacks by insinuating that
the old man's sons—"colts"—were too strong and handsome
to be legitimate. Once again the old man deferentially ob-
jected, while the others laughed and "the two boys twisted
their beautiful bald gourd-like skulls in a unison of
shyness . . . ; meanwhile the landowner had loosened the
top two buttons of his trousers, and he now reached his
hand in to the middle of the forearm, and, squatting with
bent knees apart, clawed, scratched and rearranged his
genitals" (pp. 28, 29).

No Southern lady would have been allowed to see such a
thing, and yet it was a display of exactly the kind of power
exercised by the white men of the South to maintain their
domination of social and political and economic life. The
Negro men and boys were playing their subservient part in
this grotesque scene, adapting their behavior to the demands of their white overlord in order to protect themselves.

The fear that Wright describes as motivating this pretense
was unexpectedly revealed to Agee on another occasion
outside a little country church which Evans wanted to
photograph. A young black couple walked by, glanced grav-
ely at the two white men, and continued down the road.
Agee wanted to ask permission to photograph their church
and so began following them in an effort to catch up. As he
walked, he admired their beauty and grace.

They were young, soberly buoyant of body, and strong,
. . . and I remembered their mild and sober faces . . . and
their extreme dignity, which was as effortless, unvalued, and

undefended in them as the assumption of superiority which
suffuses a rich and social adolescent boy. . . .

Unable to catch up quickly by walking, Agee increased his
pace to a trot and was horrified to see the transformation
which the sound of his footsteps wrought in the young man
and woman. Both twisted around, the woman almost falling
and then preparing to run like "a suddenly terrified wild
animal," and the man freezing in an instinctive gesture of
protection toward her. Agee reports his excruciating sense
"of the shattering of their grace and dignity, and of the
nakedness and depth and meaning of their fear, and of my
horror and pity and self-hatred. . . ." When he reached
them, and they had all regained some composure, he recalls
that "their faces were secret, soft, utterly without trust of
me, and utterly without understanding; and they had to
stand here now and hear what I was saying, because in that
country no negro safely walks away from a white man . . ."
(pp. 40–42).

White men enforced a racial and sexual hierarchy whose
levels they could move up and down at will. Historically,
the exercise of their power included sexual humiliation of
black men, sexual exploitation of black women, violent
punishment of insubordination, and careful segregation of
white women from knowledge of these arrangements. Eudora Welty grew up in a family world of peace, courtesy,
books, music, and morally decisive women, a world which,
as she describes it in *One Writer's Beginnings*, seems largely
sheltered from poverty and violence. Her fiction only rarely
betrays any knowledge of the violent enforcement of white
male authority that Richard Wright and James Agee see at
the base of Southern life. We do catch a glimpse of this
undercurrent in *Delta Wedding*, when Shelley Fairchild
stumbles upon a confrontation between the overseer of her
father's plantation and several black field hands. Shelley has
unwittingly broken a taboo by witnessing the shooting
which ensues, and although she returns safely to the big
house, her sense of security in her protected world will

never be quite the same.[13] She is much like Eudora Welty in her contemplative nature, her love of books, her habit of holding herself somewhat aloof, observing the behavior of those around her, and then writing about it. It is tempting to imagine the young Eudora Welty as having had similar experiences in Jackson, glimpsing the hidden violence beneath the gracious surface of Mississippi life but never really having the opportunity or perhaps desire to see it closely.

Eudora Welty's experiences in traveling through Mississippi for the WPA taught her how protected her life had been, but she nevertheless remained a Southern lady who would always be outside the lives of the people whom she met and photographed. Her sex, her class, and her manner worked to her advantage as a photographer, however. As a woman, she was clearly removed from the sphere of white male authority, and she represented no sexual threat. As a young, gentle, and shy person, she seems as well to have been able to put her black subjects at their ease. Because she was white, they were perhaps required by the racial code to cooperate with her, but because she was female and shy, they had nothing to fear. Alice Walker describes the impression Miss Welty made upon her when as a young black woman involved in Civil Rights work in Jackson, she came to interview the older writer on a hot summer day.

> When we face each other, talking at first in starts, I think how odd it is that I feel entirely relaxed, entirely comfortable. Considering how different we are—in age, color, in the directions we have had to take in this life, I wonder if my relaxation means something terrible. For this *is* Mississippi, U.S.A., and black, white, old, young, Southern black and Southern white—all these labels have meaning for a very good reason: they have effectively kept us apart, sometimes brutally.
>
> She is modest, shy, quiet, and strong as the oak tree out in the yard. Life has made a face for her that concentrates a beauty in her eyes.[14]

Pictures of Welty from the 1930's show that she appeared equally modest and shy and quiet in her youth, and the combination of this gentle manner with her way of taking photographs may well have allowed the rare trust which is reflected in her results. Barbara McKenzie has pointed out that Welty probably used a camera that was held at the waist for focusing and thus required the photographer to look down rather than straight at the subject as we would do with most cameras today and as Walker Evans did with the Leica he used for the majority of the pictures in *Let Us Now Praise Famous Men*.[15] The indirect scrutiny of a waist-held camera would help subjects to relax into natural poses, instead of freezing with the embarrassment of gazing into a naked mechanical eye held up like a weapon before a stranger's face.

James Agee's experience with the young black couple by the country church illustrates why he and Walker Evans would never have seen a young black woman lounging gracefully on the brick wall of her front porch and smiling easily as Welty did when she photographed her in "Saturday Off." It is hard to imagine a black mother grinning at white men with the same openness that we find in Welty's photo of the "Hairdressing queue," or a mother and daughter holding up a baby and smiling intimately the way they do in Welty's "With the baby," or the two girls in "With a chum" (pp. 27, 31, 34–35). These pictures clearly support her claim that "I was in the position of being perfectly accepted wherever I went, and everything was unselfconscious on the part of both the people and myself. There was no posing, and neither was there any pulling back or anything like that. Our relationship was perfectly free and open, so that I was able to get photographs of things really as they were."[16]

Of the more than 1,200 negatives and prints in the Welty Collection of the Department of Archives and History in Jackson, most of those concerned with people are photographs of blacks.[17] When she made a careful selection of these images more than thirty years after taking them, Welty chose only one hundred for *One Time, One Place*. This "snapshot album" contains three times as many photos of blacks as of whites, some sixty-one as opposed to twenty-one. The proportion is the same in the special section of portraits at the end of the volume. Welty used her privileged position as an unobtrusive female observer to explore many of the same themes in the lives of blacks which she would later dramatize in her fiction: domestic life, women with children, courtship, children's games, feminine rituals of work and recreation, strong independent women in the community, and the overall comedy of manners which makes her fiction sometimes reminiscent of her favorite Jane Austen's.

Beginning with the noble frontispiece image of an old woman standing in her buttoned sweater and hat and looking straight into the camera, Welty includes thirteen pictures of lone female figures. Silhouetted against the sky, one young woman stands arrested with her hoe in the air "Chopping in the field" as a graceful symbol of the intense labor exacted by cotton. Three other pictures of women working alone include one of a woman tending a boiling pot, one of a woman supervising the work of a cane press, and another of a washerwoman sitting in determined rest on her front steps as the wash dries on a line in the background. Independent professional women include "Nurse at home" in her uniform, ready to leave for the day's work, a formidable "Schoolteacher on Friday afternoon" standing with hand on hip in immaculately starched and stylish clothes beside her suitcase while waiting for her ride or bus, a solemn fortuneteller with cards outspread, and a playful lady bootlegger with ice-pick raised in mock attack. The leader of the Pageant of Birds sits in formal and quiet dignity in another picture, book in hand, in the Baptist church sanctuary (pp. 11, 14, 16, 19, 22, 23, 64–65, 91). All the other pictures of lone women are of figures intent, sure of themselves.

Many photographs capture the domestic world of women and children, while others are images of women together in town, shopping or standing with arms affectionately intertwined as they gaze up at the lighted signs and rides of the fair they are about to enter. Five pictures celebrate the bond of mother and child, some as solemn portraits, some as laughing moments of affection, and a number of pictures show children at play in gaily circling groups or in pairs or occasionally alone.

Welty's emphasis on black women's lives seems to be her tribute to their special strength and community. The photographs of solitary female figures establish an overall image of competent, determined independence. Welty explains that the heroic face of the woman in the buttoned sweater had to come first in her book because of the story of her life written there. "Her face to me is full of meaning more truthful and more terrible and, I think, more noble than any generalization about people could have prepared me for . . ." (p. 7).

Another series of pictures in the collection makes a profound commentary on women's spiritual strength in the black community. Three of the five pictures of Sunday activities in the Holiness church feature white-robed women in tableaux-like poses with backlight flooding into the time exposure in a halo effect (pp. 82–83, 86). One remarkable image presents a woman in white like a sibyl or priestess surrounded by little girls with rapt expressions. On the facing page we see an ascending file of three large women in white with veils flowing down over their shoulders. The closest woman to the camera almost fills the lower half of the picture, while above her on her right another woman similarly robed gazes into the camera, and just above her a third holds large cymbals poised on either side of her head. Behind the two large figures that dominate the foreground, the preacher stands with his Bible in hand, his face almost obliterated in shadow. The women are enor-

mous, dazzling presences who dwarf the faint image of the preacher.

Welty described her visit to this church at some length in a 1945 *Vogue* article, emphasizing the remarkable dominance of this shriveled little preacher in his congregation. Apparently all money collected during the services was given to him, and he was the center of absolute devotion for his largely female flock.[18] Yet the photograph in which he appears removes him from the center of attention and concentrates power in the hieratic white-robed figures of his deaconesses. One thinks of how beloved males are also the objects of adoration in Welty's novels but in a world seen from a woman's point of view. George Fairchild serves such a function in *Delta Wedding*, Uncle Daniel Ponder does in *The Ponder Heart*, Judge McKelva is the center of attention in *The Optimist's Daughter*, and Jack Renfro is doted upon by all the women in *Losing Battles*. In each of these fictions, men

are seen through the eyes of women, and stability and authority are fixed in women's relationships and rituals.

The effects of lyricism, mysticism, intimacy, and celebration which Welty achieved in her amateur way with her simple camera would never have been sought by a professional photographer engaged in documentary work. Walker Evans said near the end of his life that he had admired the "old America" he found in the sharecroppers' world of rural Alabama, for to him these people represented classic American pioneering stock.[19] He was able to convey a static quality of timelessness about them in his photographs, but he sometimes did so by artificially flattening their images with a long lens.[20] At other times, with closeups, he sought the direct, frontal image of faces in clear light with clearly etched lines and sharp detail. His relationship with his subjects was that of a strongly marked outsider from the North and from a privileged class, who moved into their homes to study them and who changed the circumstances of their lives in the process. He ate their food, followed them through their ordinary routines, posed them for photographs, and paid money for these intrusions.

Welty, by contrast, used unobtrusive equipment and generally seemed a natural part of her subjects' world; she did not seek to pose them or otherwise interfere with their ordinary activities. "It will be evident," she says of her photographs, "that the majority of them were snapped without the awareness of the subjects or with only their peripheral awareness. . . . The snapshots made with people's awareness are, for the most part, just as unposed: I simply asked people if they would mind going on with what they were doing and letting me take a picture" (pp. 4–5).

One result is that many pictures are taken from the side or from the back, capturing gestures of the body arrested in expressive motion. Pictures of men lounging on the wooden porch of a store or gossiping beside the town square, two ancient Confederate veterans in silhouette on a park bench, three young black women walking down the sidewalk in long dresses whose lines flow with the movement of their stride, an older black woman seen from the side as she stands on a street corner in a paper-bag hat, and two couples in easy stances of conversation and courtship (pp. 53, 51, 61, 56, 60, 62–63)—all of these capture the postures and movements of daily life in both city and town. Welty describes the effectiveness of oblique approaches in fiction which she may well have learned from taking these pictures. "Anything lighted up from the side, you know, shows things in a relief that you can't get with a direct beam of the sun."[21]

These indirect perspectives are also better suited to the self-revelations Welty sought in her subjects. "The human face and the human body are eloquent in themselves, and stubborn and wayward, and a snapshot is a moment's glimpse (as a story may be a long look, a growing contemplation) into what never stops moving, never ceases to express for itself something of our common feeling" (p. 8). She learned through photography how to wait for the moment of revelation and to recognize the telling gesture when it came. In the process, she was learning also that she would need to go beyond the photographic glimpse, "to hold transient life in *words*—there's so much more of life that only words can convey. . . . The direction my mind took was a writer's direction from the start, not a photographer's, or a recorder's."[22]

As Elizabeth Meese remarks, the year 1936 was a critical point in Eudora Welty's life.[23] Her WPA job ended, she had a one-woman show of photographs at Lugene's Gallery on Madison Avenue in New York, and she published her first two short stories, "Death of a Traveling Salesman" and "Magic."[24] She had been writing as well as taking photographs on her own from the early 1930's, but after the WPA work was over and she began publishing fiction, she put her camera away. For the rest of her life, she would explore the human comedy with the more discursive and narrative medium of language. All her fiction, however, would be affected by the visual lessons she had learned from photography and would manifest the same sympathy for its subjects that characterizes the photographs.

In spite of the fact that she moved away from photography after 1936, she had used her status as a privileged observer to gather a unique documentation of life in Mississippi during the Depression, particularly among the black population, which documentary collections of the thirties and forties had generally slighted. In *One Writer's Beginnings* she describes an early experience which helped to define her character as an observer and make her photographs possible. Bedridden for some weeks at the age of six or seven, she was allowed to stay in her parents' bed until they were ready to sleep. There she would lie, feigning sleep and listening to the murmur of her mother's and father's voices as they talked in another part of the room.

> What I felt was not that I was excluded from them but that I was included, in—and because of—what I could hear of their voices and what I could see of their faces. . . .
> I suppose I was exercising as early as then the turn of mind, the nature of temperament, of a privileged observer; and owing to the way I became so, it turned out that I became the loving kind.[25]

When she returned to her photographic experiment in 1971 to publish the carefully selected pictures of *One Time, One Place*, Eudora Welty shaped her contribution to the national self-discovery of the thirties—a tribute to her black contemporaries made by a loving observer.

1. Jean Todd Freeman, "An Interview with Eudora Welty," in *Conversations with Eudora Welty*, ed. Peggy Whitman Prenshaw (Jackson: University Press of Mississippi, 1984), p. 178. For two important earlier discussions of Welty's photographs, see Barbara McKenzie, "The Eye of Time: The Photographs of Eudora Welty," and Elizabeth Meese, "Constructing Time and Place: Eudora Welty in the Thirties," in *Eudora Welty: Critical Essays*, ed. Peggy Whitman Prenshaw (Jackson: University Press of Mississippi, 1979), pp. 386–400, 401–410. McKenzie's essay emphasizes photographic craft and links between the photographs and Welty's fiction. Meese differentiates Welty from the better-known WPA photographers in her concentration on subject matter rather than on dis-

tinctive photographic style, and provides a description of the 1,200 photos and negatives Welty made in the 1930's, which are now collected in the Mississippi Department of Archives and History in Jackson.

2. Lange and Taylor (New York: Reynal and Hitchcock, 1939); Caldwell and Bourke-White (New York: Viking Press, 1937); Wright and Rosskam (New York: Viking Press, 1941), and Agee and Evans (1941; rpt. Boston: Houghton, Mifflin, 1960). Subsequent references to Wright-Rosskam and to Agee-Evans will be included in the text. Julia Peterkin and Doris Ulmann's *Roll, Jordan, Roll* (New York: R. O. Ballou, 1933) has not been included in my list of documentary works of the 1930's because it is a blatant apology for the Old South; its text romanticizes the lives of blacks under the system of segregation and Jim Crow, and its photographs are posed and "picturesque" images of "happy darkies."

3. Ross Spears, Jude Cassidy, and Robert Coles, eds., *Agee: His Life Remembered* (New York: Holt, Rinehart, and Winston, 1985), p. 75.

4. Alfred Kazin, *On Native Grounds* (New York: Reynal and Hitchcock, 1942), pp. 501, 502.

5. Kazin, p. 494.

6. Quoted by Susan Sontag, *On Photography* (New York: Farrar, Straus and Giroux, 1977), p. 185.

7. *Walker Evans at Work*, with an essay by Jerry L. Thompson (New York: Harper and Row, 1982), p. 125.

8. Richard King, *A Southern Renaissance: The Cultural Awakening of the American South 1930–1955* (New York: Oxford University Press, 1980), pp. 213–226.

9. Sontag, p. 44.

10. "Background," *In the American West* (New York: Abrams, 1985), unpaginated.

11. Quoted in Bill Ferris, *Images of the South: Visits with Eudora Welty and Walker Evans* (Memphis: Center for Southern Folklore, 1977), p. 34.

12. Eudora Welty, *One Time, One Place: Mississippi in the Depression, A Snapshot Album* (New York: Random House, 1971), pp. 29, 30, 47. Subsequent references will be included in the text.

13. Eudora Welty, *Delta Wedding* (New York: Harcourt Brace, 1946), pp. 195–197.

14. Alice Walker, "Eudora Welty: An Interview" (1973), in *Conversations*, pp. 131–132.

15. McKenzie, p. 387, and Evans in *Walker Evans at Work*, p. 13.

16. Jo Brans, "Struggling against the Plaid: An Interview with Eudora Welty" (1980), in *Conversations*, pp. 296–297.

17. Meese, pp. 403–405.

18. "Literature and the Lens," *Vouge*, 104 (1 August 1944), 102–103.

19. Ferris, p. 34.

20. Thompson, *Walker Evans at Work*, p. 12.

21. Charles T. Bunting, "'The Interior World': An Interview with Eudora Welty" (1972), in *Conversations*, p. 53.

22. Eudora Welty, *One Writer's Beginnings* (Cambridge and London: Harvard University Press, 1984), pp. 84–85.

23. Meese, p. 409.

24. Elizabeth Evans, *Eudora Welty* (New York: Ungar, 1981), p. xi; Don Lee Keith, "'I Worry Over My Stories'" (1973), in *Conversations*, pp. 146–147.

25. *One Writer's Beginnings*, p. 21.

Mothers, Daughters, and One Writer's Revisions

It is widely known that the book version of *The Optimist's Daughter*, published in 1972 by Random House, is a revision of the story by the same name which appeared in the *New Yorker* in 1969, but the nature of those revisions has not yet received much attention.[1] Eudora Welty, indirectly, has invited us to note the significance of those revisions through her memoir, *One Writer's Beginnings* (1984), and in her introduction to the Franklin Mint edition of the novel. In that 1980 introduction, she attributes the three years between the *New Yorker* story and book publication to "its nearness to me. . . . The passage of time had perhaps this result," she reflects, "that the degree of intensity shows more openly."[2] That degree of intensity bears examination. Welty does not deny her emotional involvement with the story, but her authorial observations on the revised novel suggest that a more than customary degree of self-knowledge evolved through its rewriting. The process of revision itself, in fact, becomes a remarkable drama of self-revelation, and the differences between the *New Yorker* version and the revised novel may well provide a rare glimpse of Welty herself as what Reynolds Price has called woman at the "center."[3]

In 1969 Price offered an early reading of the story which anticipates the later revisions. Welty "has found the point, the place to stand to see this story—and we discover at the end that she's seen far more than that."[4] In many of Welty's earlier works, Price notes, "the final look in the onlooker's eye is of puzzlement"; in "The Optimist's Daughter," however, "the end clarifies. Mystery dissolves before patient watching," before "the unbroken stare of Laurel McKelva Hand," who is "finally merciless—to her dead parents, friends, enemies, herself; worst, to us."[5]

After publication of the book, Ruth Vande Kieft related Price's discussion of woman at the "center" to the novel and reaffirmed that "through the character of Laurel McKelva [Welty] is standing squarely inside, looking out from involvement in the most intimate of human love relationships."[6] Perhaps the "mystery" has dissolved before Welty's "patient waiting," before her "unbroken stare," and she, like Laurel, moves forward. The two versions have markedly different intentions, and the differences may very well suggest that a personal growth has transpired through the rewriting. The original is a story of memories painfully touched upon; the revision is a story of resolution, wherein Laurel's final comprehension of the "continuity of life"[7] may be attributed in part to the author's discovery of and emphasis upon wholeness.

In both versions of *The Optimist's Daughter*, Welty portrays people whose lives are suspended in a particular moment in time. We all know the plot. Judge McKelva, his only child, Laurel Hand, and his young second wife, Fay, meet in New Orleans for the Judge's eye surgery; while there they confront the realities of that particular time, including the stark reality of how they relate to each other. They bring with them their own special needs and visions, and the experience takes them in radically different directions. Judge McKelva moves away from life itself and never recovers from the surgery; Fay, by contrast, is impatient to get on with the trivialities which have already made her life so fruitless; Laurel probes for answers with keen perception, then shields herself by retreating into the past as she remembers it.

After Judge McKelva's death, the setting changes to Mount Salus, Mississippi, and both versions move into a pattern of shifting memories and present realities that brings the character of Becky, Laurel's mother, into greater prominence. These memories, which dominate the two middle sections of the novel as well as the story, force Laurel to examine life closely. Finally, with major additions to the last portion of the story, the novel becomes more intimately involved with Laurel's memory of Phil, her long-deceased husband. Here Laurel comes to terms with her past, present, and future, and finds freedom from the constricting memories that have contributed to her tendency to withdraw from life. She leaves Mount Salus with a mature confidence, sensitive to the pain of those memories, but free to examine and control them rather than to be intimidated by them.

Michael Kreyling has noted several changes in the revised novel which focus on the "vital area of Laurel's condition as a family member who is not yet fully aware of what that family embraces." He observes that these changes deepen Laurel's experience in the novel and he argues that love is "the emotion the new Laurel discovers."[8] I would suggest, however, that in the revision Laurel first learns how to feel anger: "For there is hate as well as love . . . in the coming together and continuing of our lives" (RH, p. 177), Laurel thinks, in one of the culminating epiphanies that Welty adds toward the end of the novel. The original Laurel clearly comes to feel and recognize love, just as the new Laurel does; but it is her inability to accept hate, too, as a natural part of her emotional range that troubles her. The significance of this new sentence may be suggested by a brief comparison of the two versions of the climactic confrontation between Laurel and Fay.

In the conclusion of the *New Yorker* story, Laurel's discovery of her mother's breadboard in its scarred, grimy condition brings the word "abuse" to her mind, the same word that Mrs. Martello, the bold hospital nurse, had shouted down the corridor (in both versions) on the night that Judge McKelva died. In the original story Laurel feels shame when she finds the breadboard, shame that "she had conspired with silence, when she ought to have shouted

'Abuse!' And perhaps shouted also 'Love!' " She senses that while she *should* have expressed her feelings, she has instead only made the house into a "shining surface" with her cleaning and sorting, and that as a result it seems "to have died" (NY, p. 127). She confronts Fay with the breadboard, but when Fay responds with accusations of her own, Laurel cowers and uses the board as a defense. In contrast, the new Laurel realizes that "she had been ready to hurt Fay. She had *wanted* to hurt her, and had known herself capable of doing it" (RH, p. 178, emphasis mine). This recognition of her own strength supports her, and the recognition comes just as she raises her mother's breadboard, "a raft in the waters, to keep her from slipping down deep, *where the others had gone before her*" (RH, p. 177, emphasis mine). Becky, having a clear view of her own courage and capabilities, was moved to action at times of crisis; Laurel's father was one of *"the others,"* and that, perhaps, explains why he slipped away. But because in the novel Laurel can acknowledge her anger and feelings of passion, she can pardon and free herself too, and then see that Fay, pitifully, "could no more fight a feeling person than she could love him." Fay is "without any powers of passion or imagination," and has "no way to see it or reach it in the other person" (RH, p. 178).

An important difference between the old and the new Laurel is that the new Laurel now understands that side of herself—of anyone—which feels anger, and learns that in her new-found maturity she can acknowledge her anger and hatred *without guilt*. She has loosed the restraint of help-lessness that caused her dying mother to cry out, "I despair for you" (RH, p. 151); and this may well be the leap she has made to become her mother's daughter, shedding the primary trait she acquired from her "optimist" father—the inability to recognize and accept anger.

Just as Laurel traveled backward in order to go forward again, Eudora Welty seems to be taking a journey backward too. In her introduction to the Franklin Mint edition, she explains that she first wrote the story while coming to terms with the deaths of her mother and brother, both of whom had died in the same week following lengthy illnesses, and that the writing of the story helped her to know her own emotions. "But it was important to me to get another chance to shape it and sharpen it. In fact, I think I deepened it in some ways. I tried to because things happened to my thinking in the meanwhile and I could see it more clearly."[9] The sincerity of the author's tone is evident in both versions, but in the original her emotions are guarded, although their urgency of expression surely forms the impetus of the work. With the perspective of a few years, however, Welty has deepened and clarified her thinking and endowed Laurel with new vision. The Laurel of the original story confronts her crisis and works through it, but she does not reach a point of comprehension; one imagines her returning to Chicago to nearly the same life she had before. In the revision, however, she reaches a new level of understanding through the resolution of the crisis and emerges at the close of the book with a wholeness that is not evident in the first version.

The original four chapters of the story are expanded from approximately 28,000 to 40,000 words and supply the framework of the novel, which is similarly divided into four sections. The nature of Welty's revisions varies from one section to the next. For example, revisions of Part One consist of many small changes—words and phrases that were added or deleted and are significant to the general direction and intensity of Welty's rewriting. Changes in Parts Two and Three are primarily of character, or are structural and aesthetic revisions that seem pertinent to her intention in rewriting the story. The culmination of these revisions occurs in Part Four, where Welty makes major and significant additions.

Welty defines principal characters in *The Optimist's Daughter* by their differences not only in background, personality, and interest, but more particularly in their depth of vision and their relation to time. Part One of the novel closely parallels the first chapter of the original story in chronology, description, and dialogue. But visual images and references to time attain greater importance in the novel, sometimes through expansion and emphasis, sometimes through a refinement of detail. Words such as "saw," "look," "eyes," and "reflections," among other additions to and rewordings of the revised version, form a pattern that points to what each character sees or wants to see. Clocks and watches are more noticeable, and the direction that time takes for each character is made more explicit. Welty has re-scored the novel to show precisely what Laurel, Fay, and Judge McKelva see and how they measure time.

Judge McKelva begins to see behind him—an uncommon view for this community leader—at the onset of his "disturbance." While pruning Becky's Climber, described elsewhere in the book as a rose from an old root that refused to die, he sways in a saraband-like dance step, as though "bowing to his partner" (RH, p. 6). Suddenly he sees flashes of light which he thinks are Becky's reflectors in the fig tree, but the fig tree is behind him. That the first symptoms of failing vision occur in relation to Becky and during Fay's absence is more than coincidence, and the word "slipped," used three times in reference to the incident, works to confirm this suspicion. Fay had "slipped out somewhere" (RH, p. 4) when his retina slipped; he says of the incident, "Of course, my *memory* had slipped" (RH, p. 5).

Judge McKelva's vision, it appears, takes him away from the present, and from Fay and Laurel. Numerous small changes emphasize how his vision becomes further removed from the present and the optimism he professes. After surgery, even his good eye closes: "Perhaps, *open*, it could see the *other eye's* bandage" (RH, p. 18, italicized words are new). As if to confirm the vision turned backward and his loss of optimism—if, indeed, Judge McKelva ever was an optimist—Welty adds two new passages: "He never asked about his eye. He never mentioned his eye" (p. 18), and "He didn't try any more to hold [Laurel] in his good eye. He lay more and more with *both* eyes closed" (RH, p. 24, emphasis mine).

It may well be that Judge McKelva *chooses* to remain in the dark. In the revision, his expression at the moment of death gives him "the smile of a child who is hiding in the dark while the others hunt him, waiting to be found" (RH, p. 34). The original version is more precise concerning his retreat into darkness: he has "the smile of a child who is *deliberately* waiting in the dark to be found, not knowing yet that the rest of the players have slipped over to the other side" (NY, p. 44B–C, emphasis mine). In the revision Welty deletes the latter portion of that sentence as well as another reference to "taking sides": in the hospital room when her father is dying Laurel hesitates to leave "because she thought that Dr. Courtland, for all his born kindness, was now in great haste and might not have time to remember whose side she was on" (NY, p. 44C).

The past controls Laurel too, but not in the same sense as it does her father. She does not pretend to be an optimist and seems, on the surface, at least, to live realistically in the present. Her present, however, persistently yields to her memories and she often defines herself through the past. As a result, Laurel's vision in the novel is partially concealed; although she is always looking, she sees in patches, through mirrors, and with blinds lowered. A significant addition to the novel reveals that her present job in Chicago is to design a theater curtain. When she rushes into the hospital shortly before her father's death, she notices, for the first time, the design of the floor tiles in the corridor. In the *New Yorker* version, she thinks that "to go and inquire after her father was like walking into a diagram of perspectives, or taking a test in optical illusions" (RH, p. 43C). In the revision, she finds in the tiles "some clue she would need to follow to get to the right place" (RH, p. 31). Her delay in noticing the "clue" is typical of her limited vision, but it does suggest that she eventually looks for answers in the design of experience.

One of the most revealing passages about Laurel's vision

is the description of her view from the hospital window. In the original story, Laurel thinks that

> . . . the rooftops below the high window might have been the rooftops of anywhere, colorless and tar-patched, with here and there a pool of rainwater. The bridge lay out there dull in the distance, as tall in the sky as if it were only another building, with windows opposite to this one. She looked at her watch. (NY, p. 39B)

In the novel, Welty expands the passage in order to modify Laurel's vision:

> This was like a nowhere. Even what could be seen from the high window might have been the rooftops of any city, colorless and tarpatched, with here and there small mirrors of rainwater. At first, she did not realize she could see the bridge—it stood out there dull in the distance, its function hardly evident, as if it were only another building. The river was not visible. (RH, p. 14)

In the revision, the river, the vigorous, life-giving Mississippi which elsewhere in the book suggests her father's life as well as her own, is entirely hidden from Laurel's sight; and the bridge, whereby that river is crossed, is barely visible. Welty's addition of the words "patched" and "mirrors," of the phrases "at first she did not realize" and "its function hardly evident," suggests Laurel's refracted vision, a suggestion that is not in the original text at this point. Moreover, the revision adds that she lowers the blind against the white light of the sky that reflects the river (RH, p. 14). This is one of the first indications of Laurel's tendency to stop time by shutting out life. Welty deletes the reference here to Laurel's glance at her watch and adds that it seemed to Laurel "that the grayed-down, anonymous room might be some reflection itself of Judge McKelva's 'disturbance,' his dislocated vision that had brought him here" (RH, pp. 14–15).

Laurel is capable of much greater perception than she allows herself. Her tendency to limit her vision, perhaps because its depth would open her to great pain, is further noted by her careful arrangement of the blind, which, Welty adds, allows only a *two-inch* strip of light to come through (RH, p. 20)—just enough to fall on her book so that she can read to her father as her mother had read with him, just enough light to preserve a ritual of the past. Still, Laurel sees more than the others in the hospital room. Her final view of that room and its occupants as she leaves for the last time before her father's death is poignant: "Judge McKelva, like Mr. Dalzell, lay in the dark, and Fay *crouched* in the rocker, one cheek on the window-sill, with a *peep* on the crack" (RH, pp. 29-30; new words italicized). Laurel "reluctantly" left them this way.

Finally, Laurel sees symbolism in the journey that carries her father's body back home to Mississippi. As the train leaves New Orleans, passing through a "black swamp," images of time, flight, and journey are subtly focused by a white seagull that appears in the broad expanse of sky and water. Watching the gull, Laurel dozes until the bird's wings, "fixed, like a stopped clock on a wall" (RH, p. 45), become the hands of a clock in the lighted courthouse dome, symbol of her father's life in Mount Salus. This passage is a personal one for Welty: in designing the Lamar Life Building in the mid 1920s, her father (an officer of the company) had a lighted clock placed atop this distinctive structure in downtown Jackson.[10]

In contrast to Laurel, Fay throws blinds open wide (p. 33). In her pitiful hunger for life, she tries to reach out and grasp it, but she lacks the depth of vision to be successful. She and Mr. Dalzell would tear down the blinds (RH, p. 20), frightened as they are of the dark, because they want to see more than their perceptions allow. Even when Fay must abide the closed blind, she peeks through the crack, but with her narrow vision, she sees only the earthy, the superficial, and such fantasies as make her feel loved. Fay also sees herself as having been shortchanged by life. She hungers—Laurel thinks she might have gone undernourished as a child—and she stares; by telling us what Fay looks at, Welty tells us about Fay.

In a new passage Laurel attempts to become better acquainted with Fay at the hotel. Fay gives a fictitious version of her family, which has them now all dead (RH, p. 27). In her fantasized vision she recalls a warm, self-sacrificing family and projects herself as a dutiful, adored daughter. Laurel, by contrast, is indicted for having "run off and left" her family (RH, p. 28). In the earlier story, Fay's regret about her separation from her family is that *they* don't get to see *her*: " 'And my poor family's gone for two years *without laying eyes on me* '" (NY, p. 46B, emphasis mine). Of her grandfather too, it is not that she hasn't seen him, but that " '*He* hasn't seen *me* for nine whole years' " (NY, p. 46B, emphasis mine). Everything in her vision, it is clear, leads back to Fay.

Fay's repeated requests to leave the eye condition "to Nature" (RH, p. 6) are additions that contrast her platitudinal view of nature with Becky's reverence for it, and suggest the Judge's need to concern himself about his physical condition, something he never had to do for himself before. In a family where mutual concern for health and well-being prevailed once, Fay "keeps on telling him" now of his ailment's insignificance. Her own importance in the matter, however, does concern her. Dr. Courtland, Judge McKelva, and Laurel did not defer to Fay in making plans, and an addition to the novel, spoken as she follows them out of the examining room, clearly explains why: " 'Isn't my vote going to get counted at all? . . . I vote we just forget about the whole business. Nature's the great healer' " (RH, p. 10).

Several minor characters are more sharply defined in Part Two of the novel. It is Miss Adele Courtland, for example, who metaphorically restores order on the day that Judge McKelva is buried, righting his overturned smoking chair during Fay's melodramatic exhibition. Welty develops this scene from the original, in which Laurel sees Adele "drop" into the smoking chair that Mrs. Chisom has vacated and "sit waiting" with her forehead "drawn" against its wing (NY, p. 76). In the novel Adele doesn't merely *reclaim* the chair from the Chisoms; through the implication that she rights it, she restores in effect a semblance of dignity and order to Judge McKelva's memory. Welty's original hint of Adele's personal affection for the Judge and of her forbearance as she "sit[s] waiting" gains greater importance in the revision through Laurel's realization that Adele must have been there all the time.

In the Franklin Mint introduction, Welty speaks of the social forces that meet in the town. Adele is as much a part of the traditional society as Judge McKelva was, and much more than Becky; but in the novel, through her calm endurance, she seems to serve a unifying purpose between the young and the old, the new and the established. More importantly, Adele helps Laurel to face the reality of her life and to seek the continuity of its love. Welty observes that "neither blood-kinship nor the relationship of marriage proves, in the course of the novel, to be tie enough to ensure loving-kindness. An affinity that is neither is sometimes more merciful" (FM). Passages added to the novel show that Adele perceives the rivalry at work in the McKelva home in the hours preceding the funeral, and that she too cringes at the vulgarity of the Chisoms and the pain they bring to Laurel; but for herself she accepts their human weakness with tolerance and some humor too. She also indulges the imperfection of her fellow townsmen and tries to communicate to Laurel an understanding of their needs, "people being what they are," as she says in the novel (RH, p. 83). At times like this, she seems to be almost the voice of Welty arguing with herself. Adele, for example, realizes how hard the townspeople are trying, for Laurel's sake, to avoid saying anything untactful about her father's marriage to Fay. Welty adds these significant lines:

> "What's happening isn't real," Laurel said, low.
> "The ending of a man's life on earth is very real indeed," Miss Adele said.
> "But what people are saying."
> "They're trying to say for a man that his life is over. Do you

know a good way? . . . They're being clumsy. Often because they were thinking of you." (RH, p. 82)

Laurel resents clumsy people and refuses to comprehend. She presses:

"He never would have stood for lies being told about him. Not at any time. Not ever."

"Yes he would," said Miss Adele. "If the truth might hurt the wrong person." (RH, p. 83)

Here, for the only time in the novel, Laurel pulls a little apart from Adele. But Adele has led her to the point of realizing that her own memory may be fallible. Standing apart, she gazes at the bookcase in her father's library. A revealing sentence added to this paragraph marks the beginning of Laurel's self-discovery, and perhaps of Welty's as well:

The shelf-load of Gibbon stretched like a sagging sash across one of them. She had not read her father the book he'd wanted after all. The wrong book! The wrong book! *She was looking at her own mistake, and its long shadow reaching back to join the others.* (RH, p. 83, new words italicized)

In *One Writer's Beginnings* Welty notes her dark sense of helplessness, even as a child, when faced with the deficiencies of the human memory, with the dehumanizing effects of man's clumsiness. She comments on the *long shadow* of her father's mistake in giving her the wrong name: "But when I was named Eudora for my Andrews grandmother, I had been named for [my Welty] grandmother too. Alice was my middle name. Her name had been Allie. Too late, after I was already christened, it came out that Allie stood for not Alice but Almira. Her name had been remembered wrong. I imagined what that would have done to her. It seemed to me to have made her an orphan. That was worse to me than if I had been able to imagine dying" (*OWB*, p. 65).

Perhaps Welty, writing of Laurel's first, tentative admission of error, gains an understanding of her own parents' inadequacies and capacity for error. The novel, Welty says, taught her, "all the way," and may be teaching her still. "Though the story was not 'like' my own, it was *intimate* with my own—a closer affinity. Writing it involved my deepest feelings, their translation into the events of the story was demanding of my ability as no other novel, so far, has been" (FM).

The four chapters in Part Three alternate in mood and style and closely follow the original story. The first and third chapters place Laurel in social settings, the first in the backyard with ladies of her mother's generation and the third on a friend's patio with ladies of her own generation. In revising, Welty adds a wry musical counterpoint to the gossip in each setting, a counterpoint of raucous birdsong in the one case and of blaring popular music in the other. Both sets of friends have shed the formalities of the funeral day and are, no doubt, trying to console Laurel; but their conversations revolve around Fay, and the music mocks them. Perhaps more than any other, chapter three focuses on change. The contrast between generations is evident and Welty sharpens that contrast in revising; the new generation—Laurel's generation—and the social change they bring are juxtaposed with the older generation, which does not quite understand it all, which is dying out. It is a quiet comment on the eternal separation enforced by time. That it follows the retrospection of chapter two and precipitates Laurel's awakening in chapter four is appropriate.

Laurel, alone in her father's library in chapter two, faces all of the silent reminders of his life and work; but in both versions she discovers that there is nothing of her mother in the room "for Fay to find, or for herself to retrieve" (NY, p. 95; RH, p. 123). She realizes that Fay has been in the library ahead of her, but, more importantly, she realizes that her father has not kept his personal letters—he attended to them immediately and discarded them. Welty adds in revising that "The only traces there were of anybody were the drops of nail varnish" (RH, p. 123).

Laurel finds a file of papers on the '27 Flood, renamed the

"Big Flood" in the novel, and becomes annoyed that everyone has forgotten about this part of her father's life—"his *drudgery*," Welty adds (RH, p. 120). In the *New Yorker*, Laurel, too, had forgotten about this part of his life, but there is one significant passage deleted here in revision that gives a different slant to Laurel's emotional response. In the *New Yorker*, she becomes angry, feeling that the town and Fay are not worthy of her father: "Anger was always the first emotion to penetrate her numbness after something had happened, as her mother had pointed out to her, warned her about, when she was a child: 'Laurel, why is it that when one of us is the least bit threatened with something out of the ordinary you always get mad about it?'" (NY, p. 95). This passage suggests the original Laurel's guilt at feeling anger and recalls both Welty's own struggle with anger and her mother's attitude toward her children's tempers.[11] Perhaps the passage also explains the shame Laurel experiences later when the word "Abuse" comes to mind. Welty, however, does not want Laurel to perceive her anger yet and deletes the passage in revising. In the novel Laurel simply moves to the window and looks out, suppressing her annoyance. Miss Adele, at the clothesline, sees Laurel and waves, "a beckoning sort of wave" (RH, p. 120); and Laurel realizes that the old lady must have been there many times while her father stood at that same window, but he never saw her. He was, it seems, as shortsighted as the townspeople in recognizing a neighbor's constancy—her *"drudgery."*

The last chapter of Part Three is very close to the original story until the closing paragraphs when Laurel confronts her memory of Phil. This revision leads into the most significant rewriting of the book. Laurel enters her parents' bedroom—now Fay's—in fear of a bird that she finds trapped in the house, wondering why she is afraid, what she "is in danger of here" (RH, p. 130). In revising Welty adds *"here"* and deletes the revealing phrase "Am I not safe from *myself*?" (NY, p. 100). In both versions Laurel reflects upon Fay's abuse of her father in the hospital, and she takes an important step toward unburdening herself by admitting that she wants retribution for Fay's actions, that she cannot feel pity for her until Fay has been exposed. Welty adds Laurel's admission that "I can't pretend [to feel pity], like Mount Salus that has to live with her. I *have* to hold it back" (RH, p. 131; emphasis mine). In both versions Laurel wants her mother to know what has happened, and in wanting that she feels she is reduced to Fay's level.

With the bird's insistent beating against the door, Laurel retreats further into the interior of the home, into the womb-like sewing room where she slept as an infant. Now Welty gives free rein to her own memory. The few changes in the text in this central section of the novel may be attributed to Welty's certainty of her own direction here as she wrote the *New Yorker* story. The reader who compares reminiscences from *One Writer's Beginnings* will see why: Welty is not just casually using her parents as models; she is reliving anecdotes that are a part of her life. The childhood incident of pigeons feeding, sticking their beaks into each other's throats, could be Welty's memory as well as Laurel's; in *One Writer's Beginnings*, the author speaks of her "agitation and apprehension" of her West Virginia grandmother's "over-familiar pigeons" (*OWB*, pp. 56–57). The germ of the idea that people feed off each other in their hunger and need—an act which with all its repulsiveness is as natural as life itself—was surely carried by Welty as long as by Laurel before becoming a part of *The Optimist's Daughter.*

While sorting through her mother's personal effects, Laurel relives experiences that are a part of Welty's own past. Laurel's revulsion at the feeding habits of the pigeons, at the way they waddle on worm-like feet, alike, yet each with slightly different markings, at the sound of their voices—these recall her revulsion from the Dalzells, from the Chisoms, and to some extent from the more refined towns-people of Mount Salus. Had Welty's sensitive nature also felt the effrontery of human clumsiness in times of her own deep personal need? Had she too heard the "unmistakable sound . . . of people *blundering*" and retreated into a self-protective shell? The child Eudora was told by her grandmother that the pigeons would "eat out of her hand if she would let them" (*OWB*, p. 55). In both versions Laurel's grandmother extends this counsel: "They're just hungry, like we are" (NY, p. 111; RH, p. 141). In *One Writer's Beginnings* Welty acknowledges her mixture of fear, revulsion, and her desire to understand, to *tolerate*, even as a child, and her own childhood becomes a part of her story.

Birds are described throughout the novel as well as the story. Starlings that had "wrinkled away" in the sky as the funeral party approached return, in the revision, as the mourners leave the cemetery. "Down on the ground, they were . . . all on the waddle, pushing with the yellow bills of spring" (RH, p. 93), oblivious in their feeding to human crisis or grief. The image of feeding is carried a step further by Welty; the Dalzells feed, figuratively and literally, in the hospital waiting room. The Chisoms are no better. In the revision, Bubba, Fay's brother, hands back an empty plate that he had filled immediately after the funeral; now that it is empty he has no time "to spare," no time to "fool around here" any longer (RH, p. 95).

The distinction that Laurel discovers is that she is confronted by people who, like the birds, do not feel; they meet basic needs but have not found another dimension to their lives. The birds are engrossed in gratifying themselves; they do nothing else. Laurel, in her revulsion from their "naturalness," has retreated from human relationships and denied a necessary part of her life. Now, with the unexpected memory of the pigeons, Laurel moves a step closer to truth. Albert J. Devlin has observed that "it is the immemorial hunger of all humans, whether expressed in joy or humiliation, belonging or exile, that Laurel now shares on an intimate, dramatic level."[12]

It is here that Welty does not probe more deeply in the original version; with the distance of a few years, however, she provides a last paragraph to Part Three. Laurel recalls Phil, and for the first time faces her brief marriage in its reality and the reality of her life without him. The original story does not tell us about Phil, but Welty revises the story to include Laurel's memories of him. Laurel remembers that Phil had taught her to use her artistic talent "to work toward and into her pattern, not to sketch peripheries" (RH, p. 161), and now she applies that skill to her search. She recognizes within herself that tendency which conceals, which refuses to *see* reality fully, which holds on to a child-like desire to preserve memories intact; and finally she courageously delves into the past. She realizes that she has been "living with the old perfection undisturbed and un-disturbing"; it was "sealed away" and "nothing . . . re-mained except in her own memory." This self-revelation comes *"by her own hands"* (RH, p. 154, emphasis mine).

The image of hands, sometimes ugly, often beautiful, and occasionally comical, here signals the most portentous self-revelation of the work: at some point in each of our lives, we see our parents not as our parents, but as the frail, vulnera-ble human beings they are. Welty, in *One Writer's Beginnings*, has made this discovery. "Through learning at my later date things I hadn't known, or had escaped or possibly feared realizing, about my parents—and myself—I glimpse our whole family life as if it were freed of that clock time which spaces us apart so inhibitingly, divides young and old, keeps our living through the same experiences at separate dis-tances" (OWB, p. 102).

At a similar point in Laurel's drama she too glimpses the unity of all human experience. She has reached the nadir in her search for answers and for the solace she hopes they will bring; now with an insight that has heretofore evaded her, she discovers that answers are to be found within, *"By her own hands."* As Laurel raises her own past, she sees Phil looking at her—"here waiting, all the time, Lazarus" (RH, p. 154). The answers are all there but it is Laurel who has to find and make personal meaning of them. In the last lines of *One Writer's Beginnings* Welty, speaking of her own life, con-firms in effect Laurel's insight and courage: "A sheltered life can be a daring life as well. For all serious daring starts from within" (OWB, p. 104). Laurel accepts the challenge and resurrects Phil's memory.

What Laurel sees when she raises the memory of Phil is a man "wild with the craving for his unlived life" (RH, p. 154). Phil, who was not an optimist, wanted life in spite of its reality. She thinks of his rejecting that division of the armed forces which employed the use of camouflage, and later, of his getting close enough to "shake hands" with the *kamikaze*. Now his mouth—like the pigeons', "open like a funnel's"—cries out to her for the life they did not have: not for the perfect, idyllic days of early marriage that are preserved in her memory, but fearlessly for a marriage that might have been pulled and torn by change and, perhaps, different visions, and for the fulfillment that comes to those who can accept and love through those changes. Phil, who knew that the best one could do still might not be enough, courageously wanted it. In the storming of Laurel's emotions, his voice melds with the wind of the storm outside. It roars around the house, " 'I wanted it!' " (RH, pp. 154–155). The truth of these powerful additions made between 1969 and 1972 speaks for Welty, for the reader, and for Laurel: "She wept for what happened to life" (RH, p. 155).

In revising *The Optimist's Daughter*, Welty organized each part of the book except Part Four into four chapters. She rewrote the powerful conclusion of the novel in one long, flowing chapter. Noting this structure, Peggy Prenshaw relates it to Jungian symbolism in which "the number four has been regarded from time immemorial as an expression of wholeness, completeness, totality."[13] Perhaps knowing this, or perhaps simply by instinct, Welty's expression of wholeness—Laurel's sense of completeness—is final here.

The chapter opens with a suggestion of memory as journey, and it closes as Laurel leaves for her home and work in Chicago, one journey completed and a new one about to begin. In the revision, however, a sense of urgency, importance, and hints of resolution accompany the opening lines. The *New Yorker* version implies that Laurel's journey is over: "Bright day woke her. Laurel stood up stiffly, like a traveller who has ridden all night" (NY, p. 119). Revised, it reads:

"She had slept in the chair, like a passenger who had come on an emergency journey in a train. But she had rested deeply" (RH, p. 159). The slight change involves the most basic difference in the themes of the two versions: Laurel of the original story concludes her evening of soul-searching when she weeps in "grief for love and for the dead" (NY, p. 119). She wakes, still fatigued, but no doubt renewed by the emotional catharsis, and picks up at the same point where she entered her reminiscing. As she goes through the quiet house, she is aware of its being "more still than she could remember its being even when she woke as a child and her parents were *not yet ready to open their eyes* in the next room" (NY, p. 119, emphasis mine). She goes through the house, and *puts on her glasses* in order to see the bird. Here, Laurel has not changed a great deal. Suggestions of visual impairment—her parents' by choice, it seems, and her own through habit—imply that veiled realities still exist for her.

The implications of the revision are that the journey is more urgent, an "emergency journey." Laurel awakes, rested, her vision clear: she fully "recognize[s]" a dream she has had—"a dream of something that had really happened." Together, she and Phil had crossed "a long bridge" (RH, p. 159). The still house, even more still than in Laurel's childhood memory, and the memory of parents who are "not yet ready to open their eyes" are not appropriate in the revision. The house is now described as "bright and still, like a ship that has tossed all night and come to harbor" (RH, p. 163). Further additions show that although Laurel has weathered the storm and is now at peace, she hasn't forgotten what awaits her today. She turns off "the panicky lights of last night," no longer needing artificial illumination, and without eyeglasses, she "saw the bird at once" (RH, p. 163). When the bird quivers, she is uncomfortable but calm. The revised sentence "She *sped* down the stairs and *closed* herself into the kitchen *while she planned and break-fasted*" (RH, p. 163, new words italicized) shows a maturity and self-assurance that are not evident in the original, in which "She *fled* down the stairs and *shut* herself into the kitchen" (NY, p. 119, emphasis mine). Laurel's self-awareness is evident. Part Three originally closed with Laurel weeping in grief and love, as she concluded her odyssey toward self-revelation—at least as far as we can tell. In the revised story, however, she is merely at the point of embarking on her journey (RH, p. 154).

In *One Writer's Beginnings*, Welty observes that "it is our inward journey that leads us through time. . . . Each of us is moving, changing, with respect to others. As we discover, we remember; remembering, we discover; and most intensely do we experience this when our separate journeys converge. Our living experience at those meeting points is one of the charged dramatic fields of fiction" (*OWB*, p. 102). With these words Welty begins to discuss *The Optimist's Daughter* and "the wonderful word *confluence*," which indeed is a wonderful word as she uses it in this novel. It is *the* word which enriches and expands a good story into a superb novel, a word "which of itself exists as a reality and a symbol in one. It is the only kind of symbol," Welty says, "that for me as a writer has any weight, testifying to the pattern, one of the chief patterns, of human experience" (*OWB*, p. 102).

The rich symbolism of that word as it is used in Laurel's remembering *is* the reality of her experience during the night of harsh illumination. In a confluence of vision, memory, and experience, she awakens to focus on the word, a summation of her experience—past and present—and the many images of *The Optimist's Daughter* flow together in their own confluence: journey motif—water, river, bridge—bird, bare trees, illumination. The pattern that they form is the "pattern . . . of human experience"; it finds meaning and expression in Laurel's consciousness, just as clearly as the pattern that the child Laurel made with scraps of cloth on the floor of this same room—for her creativity has been tested in this room this night. Now, in the stark light of day, she relives the memory of herself and Phil on their journey to Mississippi to be married. "All they could see was sky, water, birds, light, and confluence. It was the whole morning world" (RH, p. 160). Laurel and Phil saw the confluence together, they saw clearly, and Laurel who had "always taken the sleeper . . . saw it for the first time" (RH, p. 159), with Phil to point it out. It was the beginning of their marriage, their morning world, and they saw, together, "pale light widening." The water reflected the sun, which was "low, early" (RH, p. 159). In every way this was the beginning for them; watching the confluence, "they were riding as one with it, right up front" (RH, p. 160). But in another year, water—and light the intensity of fire—had become Phil's grave.

The "bare trees" that Laurel sees on this earlier journey with Phil are contrasted with the one that she sees from the train as it departs from New Orleans with her dead, coffined father—a beech tree, holding onto last year's leaves, and significantly reflecting her own face in the window. The growing awareness of self and of relations that Welty suggests by this contrast is now fully realized by Laurel—the Laurel who will jet back over the same confluence of the Ohio and the Mississippi on her return trip to Chicago. The intensity of her vision, too long arrested in "low, early" light, now enables her to see even that which is *not* visible to the eye. No longer shrouded in the dark of a sleeper or dependent upon Phil to point out the confluence, the mature Laurel knows that, although the confluence will be "out of sight" on this trip, there is "nothing in between except thin air" (RH, p. 160).

Welty concludes *One Writer's Beginnings* with comments as pertinent to *The Optimist's Daughter* as to her own life:

> Of course the greatest confluence of all is that which makes up the human memory—the individual human memory. My own is the treasure most dearly regarded by me, in my life and in my work as a writer. Here time, also, is subject to confluence. The memory is a living thing—it too is in transit. But during its moment, all that is remembered joins, and lives—the old and the young, the past and the present, the living and the dead. (*OWB*, p. 104)

Welty's personal philosophy is voiced similarly by Laurel who, reflecting upon her dream, recognizes that Phil is still capable of teaching her through memory—"a living thing"—and that the essence of one's life is "the *continuity* of its love" (RH, p. 160, emphasis mine). "She believed it just as she believed that the confluence of the waters was still happening at Cairo" (RH, p. 160). The confluence of these rivers is as emblematic of Welty's memory as of Laurel's. Philip, the "Ohio country boy" ("the Ohio was his river"), and Laurel, the girl from Mississippi, were on the journey to their wedding, the symbolic uniting of their lives, when they watched in awe the merging of those two rivers. Laurel, noting that West Virginia (Becky's home state) was just across the river from Ohio, speculated that she and Phil might have "common memories" (RH, p. 161). Indeed, one might even see Becky coming down river to Mississippi to join her life with Clint McKelva's. The several levels of common memory suggested here also remind the reader that Welty's own mother and father were from West Virginia and Ohio, respectively, and that the confluence of their lives in the waters of the Ohio melded into the great Mississippi, the river for which Welty's native state is named. Welty seems to be pondering the confluence of memory of all peoples, which is as far reaching and as alive as one's capacity to stretch the mind—in whatever direction it chooses.

Thus it is that Laurel is able to confront Fay with the breadboard on the morning of her departure. She found it that morning in the "dark interior" of a forgotten cabinet, *"waiting for her to find,"* and she "drew it out into the light of the *curtainless* day" (NY, p. 127; RH, pp. 171–172, new words italicized). It was the gift of Phil's hands, a "labor of love" (RH, p. 175), and now as Laurel raises it above her head it becomes a life-supporting raft—like the raft that carried Becky over treacherous waters to Baltimore. "Baltimore was as far a place as you could go with those you loved," Laurel's mother had said, "and it was where they left you" (NY, pp. 117–118; RH, p. 151). Laurel has gone as far as she can go when she hears the clock whirr. The board was heavy, as Welty first described it, and Laurel's arms trembled while holding it before her like a shield. But when she revised, the author created a new Laurel, one with a new beginning ahead of her, as perhaps the rewriting of the novel was this writer's beginning too. Laurel understands, finally, that "memory lived not in initial possession but in the freed hands, pardoned and freed, and in the heart that can empty but fill again, in the patterns restored by dreams" (RH, p. 179). She puts down the breadboard and leaves.

1. Page references to *The Optimist's Daughter* (New York: Random House, 1972) and to "The Optimist's Daughter" (*New Yorker*, 15 March 1969) appear in parentheses following quotations, with the published novel identified by RH and the story version by NY. Bibliographical documents pertaining to *The Optimist's Daughter* (story and novel) have heretofore been unavailable for study. Restriction has recently been lifted, however, and at this printing the documents are being prepared for scholarly use at the Department of Archives and History in Jackson.

2. Introduction, *The Optimist's Daughter* (Franklin Center, PA: The Franklin Library, 1980). Further quotations from this source will be indicated in parentheses: (FM).

3. Reynolds Price, "The Onlooker, Smiling: An Early Reading of 'The Optimist's Daughter,'" *Shenandoah*, 20 (Spring 1969), 62.

4. Price, p. 59.

5. Price, p. 62.

6. Ruth Vande Kieft, "The Vision of Eudora Welty," *Mississippi Quarterly*, 26 (Fall 1973), 537.

7. Michael Kreyling, *Eudora Welty's Achievement of Order* (Baton Rouge & London: Louisiana State University Press, 1980), p. 173.

8. Kreyling, pp. 172–173.

9. Martha van Noppen, "A Conversation with Eudora Welty" (1978), in *Conversations with Eudora Welty*, ed. Peggy W. Prenshaw (Jackson: University Press of Mississippi, 1984), p. 242.

10. Eudora Welty, *One Writer's Beginnings* (Cambridge and London: Harvard University Press, 1984), p. 83. Subsequent page references to *OWB* will be noted parenthetically in the text.

11. Welty recalls in *OWB* that "control came imperfectly to all of us:

we reached it at different times of life, frustrated, shot into indignation, by different things—some that are grown out of, and others not."

" 'I don't understand where you children *get* it,' said my mother. 'I never lose my temper. I just get hurt.' (But that was it.)" See pp. 38–39.

12. Albert J. Devlin, *Eudora Welty's Chronicle* (Jackson: University Press of Mississippi, 1983), p. 180.

13. Peggy W. Prenshaw, "An Introduction to Eudora Welty's *The Optimist's Daughter*" (Jackson: Mississippi Library Commission, 1977), p. 9.

Subject and Object
in *One Writer's Beginnings*

Several reviewers have tried to name the appeal of *One Writer's Beginnings*. William Maxwell can speak for most of them: "Many children have loved to be read to who didn't become writers. There has to be something else, a kind of fermentation."[1] Writers, like the rich, are different from you and me, and not simply for the accident of being read to— although that obviously helps. *One Writer's Beginnings* makes us startlingly aware that the difference is substantial and has to do with the basic relationship of the self to experience. If writers are made, not born, then the difference happens so early in living-in-the-world as to seem one with birth itself. We are rightly skeptical of the critic who studies the matured difference and reconstructs the "growth of the poet's mind," but we welcome the memoir of the writer herself, especially if the writer has always shown a sensitive and significant use of memory in her fiction.

Something else again makes the beginnings of the woman writer a doubly different story. Welty's memoir makes us uniquely aware that writers come to writerly terms with the foundations of identity and culture earlier than we suspect. Difference begins in the genesis of the consciousness that writes. Becoming a writer is not a stage in becoming a person; it is simultaneous with personhood. The genesis of the woman writer, moreover, suggests an additional, or at least a more intricately willed, stage in the growth of the writing consciousness.

Harry Mark Petrakis, in his review of *One Writer's Beginnings* for the *Chicago Tribune*, is careful to note that women writers have, historically and culturally, borne a heavier burden than men in the same vocation. Women who choose to write, Petrakis says, encounter barriers in "marital and family pressures and the hostility they incur for an endeavor outside the bedroom or kitchen."[2] Such pressures as these, however, occur well into the maturity of the woman writer. Margaret Wimsatt's review suggests that complications appear much earlier in the life of the writing woman. For a woman to write, Wimsatt claims, she must see herself as "subject and object," an act of imagination and self-making that takes place well before the public issues of marriage and family materialize.[3] Welty the author has explored this territory often, with the help of her intrepid "wanderers": Laura McRaven and India Fairchild, Jenny Lockhart, Virgie Rainey, Cassie Morrison, Nina Carmichael, and Jinny Love Stark. Each of these girls, in her own stage of adolescence, faces a future limited to roles that do not seem to call for the full measure of her imagination and art. In their respective stories they pause to gather themselves for the vault into adulthood. Wimsatt's critical view, and Welty's fictional practice, seem complementary; the crucial moment is pushed backward from full maturity. The path is already taken before "bedroom or kitchen" loom as real fates. *One Writer's Beginnings* is eloquent evidence that the moment occurs earlier in the growth of the writer. To achieve a greater focus on this moment of beginning, though, we have to make a brief excursion.

We, the audience for works of art, are much more accustomed—from reading literature and looking at paintings and sculpture—to the portrait of the lady. We are less familiar with the figure of the woman writing as, for example, she appears in Vermeer's painting, comfortably holding the quill, symbol of the power to name and compose, and gazing confidently at us instead of being rigidly and passively posed. Vermeer's lady writing is both a subject beholding us and an object for us to behold. This simultaneity cannot so easily be affirmed of Leonardo's lady with an ermine, or Pound's woman of the Sargasso Sea. James's Isabel Archer moves toward her subjectivity, but only after pain. Several of Welty's female wanderers move beyond the frame where they are to sit poised and familiar. Virgie, of course, immediately springs to mind. Nina languishes at the moment of decision, paralyzed by the Medusa.

The central issue, then, is not merely one of traditions in portraiture or the coincidence of titles in literature. For a woman to choose writing as her work is to disturb a set of relationships, a frame of reference, and, in the process, to expose the bases of several of our assumptions about identity that are too automatic, too close to seeming to be "natural," for easy expression. Simone de Beauvior, in *The Second Sex*, removes some of the "naturalness" from these assumptions about gender and the identities appropriate to each. Her work gives us a vocabulary for translating the elusive nature of beginnings in *One Writer's Beginnings*, and deepens our sense of the story we are reading.

De Beauvoir's model of the rearing of boys and girls, perhaps too rigidly schematic for some, nevertheless echoes what reviewers of *One Writer's Beginnings* have sensed and helps us to see Welty's memoir as more than an insider's report on the sources of her own fiction in her life. De Beauvoir segregates the roles of transcendent subject and passive object, reserving, in the "formative years" of pre-adolescence, the former for boys and the latter for girls. She writes:

> In woman, on the contrary, there is from the beginning a conflict between her autonomous existence and her objective self, her "being-the-other"; she is taught that to please she must try to please, she must make herself object; she should therefore renounce her autonomy . . . for the less she exercises her freedom to understand, to grasp and discover the world about her, the less [sic] resources will she find within herself, the less will she dare to affirm herself as subject.[4]

We more readily accept this proposal applied to standards of feminine beauty and decorum. Let us apply it to writing as well. Writing is one way to "grasp and discover the world about" the self, but this activity has been privileged as a male preserve: the Word made flesh in our culture's great book is God's son; the implements of writing, pens and pencils, are etymologically linked with male anatomy. De Beauvoir can find other barriers as well, but none confront the boy: "The great advantage enjoyed by the boy is that his mode of existence in relation to others leads him to assert his subjective freedom. His apprenticeship for life consists in free movement toward the outside world . . ." (p. 315).

Adolescent girls, de Beauvoir writes, face a potentially ruinous moment in early adolescence when they discover that, knowing themselves as fit as boys for the "free movement toward the outside world," they are held back by a sort of cultural inertia. "At just this conquering age, woman learns that for her there is to be no conquest, that she must disown herself, that her future depends upon a man's good pleasure" (p. 402). Welty has dramatized this moment more than once in her fiction. In *The Golden Apples*, for example, Jinny and Nina, spying on the conquering, and naked, Loch Morrison, seem to sense a sudden denial of subjective freedom in simple sexual difference, and they respond with a denial of their own: they quixotically reject "man's good pleasure" by resolving never to marry.

For de Beauvoir woman is a "free and autonomous being like all human creatures—[who] nevertheless finds herself living in a world where men compel her to assume the status of the Other" (p. xxxiii). The Other does not write or paint, but sits for her portrait; she is an object dependent on another, a subject, for the rendering of her self in oil or marble or words. The habit of passivity, de Beauvoir argues, is imposed, falsely, on grounds that it is "natural" to the feminine. Indeed, it settles so early in life that it seems to be so.

One of de Beauvoir's countrywomen, Nathalie Sarraute,

provides a clear example of how a woman becomes a subject and a writer in spite of conventional and "natural" obstructions. Her memoir is all the more pertinent for the coincidence that it was published, under its French title, *Enfance*, in 1983, the year Welty delivered the William C. Massey, Sr., Lectures at Harvard University. *One Writer's Beginnings*, the published version of those lectures, appeared in 1984, as did Sarraute's memoir in its English translation, *Childhood*.[5]

For Sarraute, and as we shall see for Welty too, the instruments for "grasp[ing] and discover[ing] the world about her" are words, hers first to hear in the voices of her parents, and eventually hers to use in reading and writing. Making letters on paper, for example, is a milestone in her childhood (Sarraute, p. 118), and writing her name on book labels, fascinated by the elaborate T of her Russian surname (Tcherniak), is a memory as vivid as the present moment (p. 144). The simple manual operation of making letters on paper is the writer's initiation into the intersecting state of self, word, and world. The cultural consensus considers it more "natural" for the male to inhabit this space. Writing, therefore, is potentially "unsuitable" work for a woman; to become a writer she must break a "natural" frontier.

Sarraute gives the story of her infiltration a tangible heft. With words, Sarraute tells us, comes the power to judge the consensus and its makers. Her mother wrote books for children, and from childhood Sarraute never forgot the act and the result of writing that she witnessed so closely. Even though the writing of words to substitute for the actuality of sound and hue seemed to her "a little bit prefabricated" (p. 12), she was still enthralled with the operation. Early in her life she saw that the world is unknown and unknowable without words. We have no way out of passivity and into action (read: existence) without words.

Moments of time from childhood, for Sarraute, are banked up with words. Her parents' house at Ivanovo, where she spent summers as a child, triggers such a moment: "I want to touch, to caress this immutable image, to cover it with words, but not too thickly, I'm so afraid of spoiling it . . . I want the words to come here too, to alight . . . in the interior of the house" (p. 33). Words are autonomous, possessing identity and history; one cannot arbitrarily shift them around and expect the image to remain "immutable." Words, then, have power over time and death. Sarraute realizes that they are holy: "Why try to bring this back to life, without the words that might manage to capture, to retain, if only a few more instants, what happened to me . . ." (p. 56).

While the writer, merging the roles of Lazarus and Christ, can raise the past from oblivion with words, just the right words, she can also drive powerful wedges between herself and others. The power that words have given Sarraute also wounds. She remembers learning, through language, to recognize beauty. So far, a welcome acquisition. But seeing a hairdresser's mannequin, she compares its fashionable beauty with her mother's actual appearance and tells her mother that the block is more beautiful. The words hurt her mother; there is an estrangement between the two, and guilt for Sarraute, that neither overcomes (p. 85).

Sarraute continues to realize that becoming a writer is not a simple gravitation toward beauty and truth; it is also a move to establish the self as an autonomous subject and to extend its distance from others. Her move toward power is not, in her memoir, as swift and sure and deliberate as de Beauvoir's model predicts, but it does dramatize the denial of "conquest" by another that de Beauvoir proposed for girls in adolescence.

Sarraute's first formal act of authorship is a revealing moment in her education, as intense as her discovery of the letter but encompassing much more than naive joy: power, pain, distance. She remembers that she "must have seen nuggets sparkling in a far-off mist . . . the promise of treasures" in the first writing assignment at school (p. 183). Writing this piece, "My First Sorrow," gave her a feeling of "dignity," "of domination, of power" (p. 184), that reading had not yet supplied. Writing became the act of making herself autonomous and secret:

> I keep myself in the background, out of reach, I don't reveal anything that belongs only to me . . . but I prepare for other people something that I consider to be good for them. I choose what they like, what they might expect, one of those sorrows that suit them. . . . (p. 184)

Sarraute simply and boldly reverses the portrait of a lady; she prefers not to be the passive object. She is the author who conceals herself and the woman who becomes the pronouncing subject. She will prepare and present, and the beholders—who have been accustomed to gaze upon the displayed object—will be held instead in the subject's power and never know it. Welty also writes of her self-as-author in the blind of "hidden observer" (pp. 20–21), but adds that her material is her own feelings, her responses to real experience, to the relationships to which she has given most of herself (p. 100). Although she crosses the same frontier as Sarraute, her sense of the resistance is different.

Words, Sarraute discovers, not only make a still moment in the whirl of time; they can be instruments for making visions of the imagination real. Knowledge and control of words make one the person who originates the thing—one who begets—the author. De Beauvoir argues that the presumption of all such power to beget is the male's, upon the anatomical analogy. If so, then Sarraute's memoir of becoming a writer can be read as the memoir of the presumed object, the Other, who deflects "alterity" and seizes the privilege of the subject. Words, first in hearing and reading, but more importantly in writing, are the instruments of rebellion, the properties of self-creating acts. And there is a metaphorical violence associated with these acts. By design or accident, one of the first words Sarraute associates with her life as an author is the German "zerreissen" spoken by her governess when she, Sarraute, had grasped a forbidden pair of scissors (p. 5). Did Sarraute realize then, or later in memory, that one of the first words in her becoming self is a

variant on the German "reissen," to write? And that, farther
back in its history, it shares roots with the English "write"?
Is she preparing herself and us for the double power of
words to delight and to tear? For in Sarraute's memory the
word "zerreissen" is associated with a childhood tantrum, a
demand for attention, in which she plunged the scissors
into a settee, ripping it until the stuffing spilled out. Does
writing kill as it engenders? Does rendering experience also
rend it from its proper moment?

Welty's memoir begins less violently. By " listening" she
was introduced to the word, and for her the word, written
and spoken, has never yet been torn from the sound of the
human voice. Her memoir records the joy of learning the
alphabet and the sweet captivity to reading. It tells, more
importantly, of the physical objectivity of the word, something Sarraute also experienced and, in *Childhood*, made the
central motif of her memoir. For Welty, too, the physicality
of the word—a thing over which, within bounds, the writer
has power and responsibility—became a fact coeval with
personal consciousness:

> In my sensory education I include my physical awareness of
> the *word*. Of a certain word, that is; the connection it has with
> what it stands for. . . . Held in my mouth the moon became a
> word. (p. 10)

After the letter as physical object comes the word, with
mass and contour and even a taste. Welty's original word-as-
thing is not Sarraute's "zerreissen," carrying its severe associations and questions, but "moon," full of milder connotations.

In the beginnings of a writer the objectivity of the word
must be a common fact, the first object through which the
self discovers and begins to define itself as subject. Writing
of her father, a man of train schedules and survival techniques, the "optimist" who hauled hatchet and escape rope
to the family's hotel room each night on the road (p. 45),
Welty considers the other aspect of language—the word

used for the crisp and exact exchange of information, the word as catalyst rather than the thing that stays. Such information, if accurate, confers the illusion of control upon the holder. If a train is late, one can, with watch and schedule and memory of the road, picture its position and predict its arrival. Mr. Welty, his daughter remembers, "knew our way mile by mile; by day or by night, he knew where we were" (p. 73). Not only on the tracks but also in time, for Mr. Welty took charge of the present in the name of the future: "his face always deliberately turned toward the future" (p. 6). There would be irony in his future; he was to die early of a disease about which no one then knew enough. Journeys teach narrative; irony is one of the lessons.

Words as objects, however, continued to be the daughter's treasures: "Learning Latin (once I was free of Caesar) fed my love for words upon words, words in continuation and modification, and the beautiful, sober, accretion of a sentence" (p. 28). Words accumulated through reading and conversation, both forms of listening for this young writer, and they brought along stories inextricably as they clustered and took shape in time. "'Impressionable' was a new word" that brought along *Elsie Dinsmore* and her mother's cautionary tale (pp. 29–30). Movie captions and titles brought "jeopardy" and "somnambulist" along with visual images and stories of going to the Istrione theater (p. 36). And the Bible brought to Welty, as it has to many writers, its cadences and its guarantee: "'In the beginning was the Word'" (p. 34). Sarraute was also filled with words. Since her childhood echoed with French, German, English, and Russian words, the flood of sounds and images seems more cosmopolitan. She remembers "gniev" and "courroux," "zerreissen," "soleil" and "solntze," "podbrossili," and, toward the close of her memoir, the words of her half-sister's English governesses.

Like Sarraute, Welty began with words as physical objects that fused sight, sound, taste, bits of narrative, and marked the moments when her life intersected with otherness—the real beyond the frame. From beginnings in letters and words, the crucial confrontation with "alterity" and the first step toward the power and autonomy of the subject begin with the word. Sarraute's memoir leaves the impression that in seizing the scissors and the word "zerreissen" she seized authorship as all prometheans seize the forbidden. Welty's beginnings, as we shall see, only seem less hyperbolic; one of her more enigmatic and critiqued figures—Perseus slaying Medusa in *The Golden Apples*—is the image of a violent, rending act, an emblem of Virgie's willed and painfully won autonomy at the end of "The Wanderers."

"Learning to See" is learning to wait attentively upon "the continuous thread of revelation" (p. 69). The thread of revelation, missed by the impatient and preoccupied (those of us who turn out to be non-writers), is the fabric of narrative, of story, and it is the discovery of this, more than anything else, that constitutes the "something else" that makes story-writers different from the rest of us. Walter Clemons, in his *Newsweek* review, singles out this section of *One Writer's Beginnings* as the one in which Welty "makes a tale . . . as shapely as any of her fictions," telling the surface story of a summer trip and the more crucial story of "a young girl's discovery of her ability to perceive."[6] The ability to perceive means the power to cast one's own will into the flux of events and make "shapes"—stories—wholes of situation and implication and character. Sarraute had done it for a school assignment; for Welty it seems as natural as learning to see.

There are vivid examples in the second section of *One Writer's Beginnings*. Welty relates a visit that she and her mother made to her grandmother Andrews's home in West Virginia. She, her mother, her grandmother, and her uncles are out for a walk on the mountain when Eudora decides on impulse to strike out on a "superior track" and tumbles down a log chute, tearing her dress. Her grandmother seizes her, but not roughly, stares into her face, then into the face of her own daughter, Eudora's mother. "I learned on our trip," Welty writes, "what that look meant: it was matching family faces" (pp. 57–58). This is also a lesson in the sense of narrative, for that look confers shape on action (the child deserting kin for an independent track), resonance upon diction ("superior track"), and dimension to character (three generations of women see and accept their shared and diverging lives). Language becomes literary discourse; episode becomes story; a part of life that threatened to float away is now fixed to keep and return.

Endings can come in less overt ways too. The visit to her father's home in Ohio reveals another aspect of kin and another sense of the shaping of memory and experience into narrative. The silence at the Welty home disturbs the granddaughter. There are no family stories and the family organ stands mute and cold in memory of her father's long-dead mother. "To me," Welty remembers, "it [the silence] was a sound of unspeakable loneliness that I did not know how to run away from" (p. 67). Yet the writer-in-becoming can escape, for the habit of making narrative is becoming the habit of consciousness itself. Riding in her grandfather's buggy, holding the reins, Welty remembers that she could not see over the horse's hindquarters. "But standing up on the back seat, I could see, squinting through the peephole window at the back, where the narrow wheels on a rainy Sunday sliced the road to chocolate ribbons" (p. 66). In spite of the lonely silence, the chilling keys of the muted organ, there is sound leading out to the world: the sounds of words in "continuation and modification, and the beautiful, sober, accretion of a sentence." If seeing is blocked in one direction, it will find another.

This is a more subtle exercise of the power that Sarraute discovered and used when, as a schoolgirl, she tailored a story for teacher and classmates. But it is nevertheless an act of liberation, like the dash and tumble down the log chute, that both affirms the intimate others who confer name, alphabet, speech, identity, and establishes self separate from them. Becoming a writer, Sarraute and Welty tell us, is becoming free but not lost. "I am allowed [when writing]," Sarraute writes, "to frolic within its limits, on a well-prepared, well laid-out ground, just as I am in the school playground or even, since these frolics are accompanied by great efforts, in the gymnasium" (p. 188).

"Finding a Voice" brings Welty the emerging woman writer to self-consciousness of her power and responsibility. In college, first in Mississippi and then away from home, then behind a camera, and eventually behind a typewriter, she learns the difference between the frame and the real that will never be confined, the insistent actuality of the outer world and the tender visioning of the inner.

Once again her father emerges from the past with the banner of knowable fact: "my father put it all into the frame of regularity, predictability, that was his fatherly gift in the course of our journey" (p. 74). But there were soon irrefutable signs that there was always to be more world outside the frame of predictability. In art class at the University of Wisconsin: "As we sat at our easels, a model, a young woman, lightly dropped her robe and stood, before us and a little above us, holding herself perfectly contained, in her full self and naked" (p. 80). From that moment, the imperative of "wanting-to-know" (p. 84) introduced itself fully and candidly to the young writer's awareness and demanded its voice, just as the model insisted upon the tribute of attention. First came the camera, a way of holding transience in the still moment. Then words, as familiar as consciousness itself, eventually resumed their importance, perhaps never really interrupted: "And I felt the need to hold transient life in *words*—there's so much more of life that only words can convey—strongly enough to last me as long as I lived" (p. 85).

Re-reading her own work for a "dramatic counterpart" (p. 100) to the life of the artist, Welty finds two characters from *The Golden Apples*: Miss Eckhart, outcast and bereft, having given her gifts to exhaustion; and Virgie Rainey, the young girl to whom Miss Eckhart had given the last of herself. "Passionate, recalcitrant, stubbornly undefeated by failure or hurt or disgrace or bereavement, all the while heedlessly wasting of her gifts, she [Virgie] knows to the last that there is a world that remains out there, a world living and mysterious, and that she is of it" (p. 102). Sarraute, too, on the verge of writing her memoir senses "a world that remains out there": ". . . it's still vacillating, no written word, no word of any sort has yet touched it, I think it *is* still faintly quivering . . . outside words" (p. 3).

Two writers pay tribute to the world that remains beyond words, the world of which they and their works are a part, because in conjunction with that world they have made themselves. Becoming a writer for both women began with the discovery that words are the means of moving from passive object into the freedom of the subject. Both memoirs also suggest that, for the woman, to become a writer is to slip across the dividing line between object and subject, to take up with the materials of writing—words— the breaking of a "natural" condition. This is, of course, a remote target of Welty's image of Perseus slaying the Medusa. Perseus slays the universal beholder, the face that seals the self into eternal "alterity." Each act of the subject, then, is the stroke of Perseus—an "endless" rhythm. Perseus is the patron of all writers; perhaps the woman writer knows how deep is the debt.

1. William Maxwell, "The Charged Imagination," review of *One Writer's Beginnings*, by Eudora Welty, *New Yorker*, 20 February 1984, p. 133.

2. Harry Mark Petrakis, "Welty's Lyrical Remembrances of Things Past," review of *One Writer's Beginnings*, *Chicago Tribune*, 1 April 1984, sec. 14, p. 40.

3. Margaret Wimsatt, "Listening, Seeing, Finding a Voice," review of *One Writer's Beginnings*, *Commonweal*, 1 June 1984, p. 342.

4. Simone de Beauvoir, *The Second Sex*, trans. H. M. Parshley (New York: Random House, 1974). Hereafter cited in text.

5. Nathalie Sarraute, *Childhood*, trans. Barbara Wright (New York: George Braziller, 1984). All ellipses in quotations from Sarraute are the author's. Eudora Welty, *One Writer's Beginnings* (Cambridge and London: Harvard University Press, 1984). Both works hereafter cited in the text.

6. Walter Clemons, "Welty's Awakening," review of *One Writer's Beginnings*, *Newsweek*, 20 February 1984, p. 72.

The Antiphonies of
Eudora Welty's
One Writer's Beginnings
and Elizabeth Bowen's *Pictures*
and Conversations

Eudora Welty and Elizabeth Bowen first met in 1949, while Welty was traveling in Europe on a Guggenheim Fellowship. Bowen wrote to her friend, Charles Ritchie, about this first meeting in a letter that Victoria Glendinning quotes in her biography of Bowen. "You know my passion for her works," Bowen wrote. "She had apparently drifted over to Dublin on her own. She sent me a telegraph from there and I asked her to come down and stay." Bowen goes on to record the delight she took in Welty's visit to Bowen's Court, a visit which turned out to be extremely satisfying for both writers. "I take to her most immensely and I think you would. She's very un-writerish and *bien élevée*. A Southern girl from the State of Mississippi; quiet, self-contained, easy, outwardly old-fashioned, very funny indeed when she starts talking. . . . She's reserved (in itself, I think, a good point these days) so although we have chatted away a good deal, I really know little about her life, nor she about mine." Bowen found Welty's temperament, personal and aesthetic, entirely compatible with her own: "I think she's like me in preferring places to people. . . . No one would pick her out on sight as 'an interesting woman.' Actually I think she's a genius rather than an interesting woman, which I am glad of as I prefer the former."[1]

This meeting marks the beginning of a friendship that would last until Bowen's death in 1973. Welty visited Bowen at her family home in County Cork, Ireland, on this and later occasions, and Bowen returned the visits to Welty's home in Jackson, Mississippi. During Bowen's first visit in 1951, for example, Welty drove her on a day-long excursion to visit Elizabeth Spencer, who was then working on a new novel and living in Pass Christian on the Gulf Coast.[2] In 1960 Bowen saw Welty during a tour she made of the deep South while writing an article commissioned by *Holiday* magazine, and later, in 1969, she visited Welty in Jackson at Christmastime.

Much evidence exists of Welty's admiration of Bowen's fiction and of her personal affection for her. Welty's letters to Bowen during the time Welty was writing *The Bride of the Innisfallen* stories in the early fifties express her regard for Bowen's literary judgment, as well as her deep pleasure in having Bowen's encouragement and sympathetic support.[3] Bowen had earlier reviewed *Delta Wedding* and *The Golden Apples*, praising both, especially the later book. Of *The Golden Apples*, Bowen wrote that "Eudora Welty is an imaginative writer. With her, nothing comes out of stock, and it has been impossible for her to stand still. Her art is a matter of contemplation, susceptibility, and discovery: it has been necessary for her to evolve for herself a language, and to arrive, each time she writes, at a new form." In *The Golden Apples* Welty seemed to have found "the ideal form." "American, deliberately regional in her settings, she 'belongs,' in the narrow sense, to no particular nation or continent, having found a communication which spans oceans."[4]

Welty's admiration of Bowen's fiction has been equally spirited, both in essays and interviews. Speaking to Jean Todd Freeman in 1977 of contemporaries she particularly reads and admires, she praised Henry Green ("I've read everything that he's ever written, closely and with love") and then added: "I love E. M. Forster and Elizabeth Bowen very much. I revere Virginia Woolf but I don't want her preeminence now—everyone reading her and writing about her—accidentally to put Elizabeth Bowen in any kind of shadow because I think she was fully as good. And, in a rewarding way, more robust, human, and rounded. I'm not dreaming of trying to see them as competitors, which they *never were*. You can't look at writing like that. But Elizabeth died recently, and I don't want her books suddenly for that reason to drop behind, even briefly."[5] In a very recent interview, Welty has reiterated Bowen's significance for her in shaping the way she has thought and written about the craft of writing, noting that "Elizabeth was a marvelous writer about writing and very helpful to me."[6]

There is nothing particularly remarkable, of course, about two writers' admiring one another's work. What are remarkable and demand the attention of anyone interested in the literary achievement of these writers, however, are the deep affinities and correspondences that link their lives and art. Indeed, Welty scholars, no less than Welty herself, have consistently acknowledged the influence of Bowen's artistic theory and fictional style upon Eudora Welty. Writing the first book-length study of Welty in 1962, Ruth Vande Kieft devoted several pages of her concluding chapter to a discussion of parallels in the two writers' views of writing and in the lyrical, pictorial quality of their style. A further comparison of the form and technique of their short fiction was developed by Rebecca Smith Wild in a 1965 doctoral thesis on Bowen and Welty. Among others, Michael Kreyling and Elizabeth Evans have also noted, though briefly, the imprint of Bowen's example on Welty's writing.[7]

To understand fully the effect of the Bowen-Welty friendship upon their individual lives and work requires more detailed scholarly study than has been done, however, and certainly more detailed commentary than is possible in this discussion. Rather, what I should like to do here is point out and briefly trace a pattern of parallels in their autobiographical writings that may in some cases seem simply coincidental, but that in others suggests a striking similarity of experience and world view. Seeing the points of confluence of these works can deepen our understanding of the "design" that both writers seek to describe in their autobiographies—the design that connects childhood and girlhood with their lives as writers.

One might call Bowen and Welty "reluctant autobiographers." In 1939 Bowen began to write the history of her family, whose origins traced from the Welsh ap Owenses in the fifteenth century. During the growing confusion and outbreak of the World War, she completed *Bowen's Court*, writing in the afterword, "I have written (as though it were everlasting) about a home at a time when all homes are threatened and hundreds of thousands of them are being destroyed. I have taken the attachment of people to places as being generic to human life, at a time when the attachment is to be dreaded, as a possible source of too much pain." She acknowledges that the conditions of war time may have affected her view of her family, perhaps leading her to attribute too much importance to it; and yet she finds in her family a full embodiment of the larger world's experience. "I have tried to make it [the history of the Bowens] my means to approach a truth about life." To her, the isolation and self-centeredness of the Bowens add to their representativeness. "I have shown, if only in the family sphere, people's conflicting wishes for domination. That few Bowens looked beyond Bowen's Court makes the place a fair microcosm, a representative if miniature theatre."[8]

In a companion book that she wrote during the same period, a book of reminiscences about her early years when she spent winters in Dublin and summers at Bowen's Court, she wrote what she said would be as much of personal revelation as she would ever write. "*Seven Winters* could be called a fragment of autobiography. At the same time, I look on it as a self-contained work, for it is as much of my life story as I intend to write—that is, to write directly." Bowen then explains the cogency of her earliest reminiscences to an understanding of career as a writer of fiction: "Through most fiction is to be traced the thread of the author's own experiences, no doubt. But the early years of childhood contain most others: as we now know they are in part the cause of, in part the key to, what is to follow. No years, subsequently, are so acute. The happenings in *Seven Winters* are those that I shall remain certain of till I die. Here is the external world as I first saw it."[9]

Like Bowen, Eudora Welty has shied from personal revelation and autobiography. She has written a few memorable reminiscences, most of which are collected in *The Eye of the Story*—"A Sweet Devouring" (1957) and "The Little Store" (1975), most notably, in which she writes of her childhood love of books and of her neighborhood in Jackson, two blocks from the Mississippi State Capitol, where she spent her early years. For the most part, though, Welty has maintained a firm reticence about her private life. In a 1972 interview in the *Paris Review*, she told Linda Kuehl that she would feel "shy, and discouraged at the very thought" of a biography about herself, and she repeated her conviction that "a writer's work should be everything. A writer's whole feeling, the force of his whole life, can go into a story—but what he's worked for is to get an objective piece down on paper. That should be read instead of some account of his life." A little later she added, "Your private life should be kept private. My own I don't think would particularly interest anybody, for that matter. But I'd guard it; I feel strongly about that."[10]

Both Bowen and Welty later changed their minds about offering further revelations about themselves. Coincidentally, at about the same age each woman began writing her autobiography, Bowen in her seventy-third year, and Welty during the months preceding her seventy-fourth birthday in April 1983. Bowen's *Pictures and Conversations*, unfinished at the time of her death in 1973, was subsequently published in 1975, along with a chapter from an unfinished novel and some other short pieces, including her widely quoted "Notes on Writing a Novel," which had first appeared in *Orion* in 1945 and later in *Collected Impressions* (1950).

In the unfinished third chapter of *Pictures and Con-*

versations, Bowen describes her purpose and plan for the book: "The book is *not* to be an autobiography. It will differ from an autobiography (in the accepted sense) in two ways. (1) It will not follow a time sequence. (2) It will be anything but all-inclusive."[11] Interestingly, Bowen's sure sense of the traditionally accepted canon of autobiography compelled her to acknowledge her own different plan for her work and to disclaim any intent of writing a comprehensive chronicle of her private life. In this regard, *Pictures and Conversations*—and, indeed, Welty's *One Writer's Beginnings*—closely conforms to the patterns of women's autobiographies identified and discussed by Estelle C. Jelinek in her introduction to *Women's Autobiography*. Among other features, Jelinek notes the special propensity of women's autobiography toward "irregularity rather than orderliness. . . . The narratives of their lives are often not chronological and progressive but disconnected, fragmentary, or organized into self-sustained units rather than connecting chapters." Jelinek observes that women rarely emphasize the public aspects of their lives, nor do they engage in revelations about their private lives. Rather, they concentrate on what one might call the personal sphere—details of home, childhood, parents, friends, teachers, and others who influenced them in their youth. "This emphasis by women on the personal, especially on other people, rather than on their work life, their professional success, or their connectedness to current political or intellectual history clearly contradicts the established criterion about the content of autobiography," Jelinek writes. Finally, she notes that women typically employ a variety of forms of understatement in their autobiographies. "Women tend to write in a straightforward and objective manner about their girlhood and adult experiences. They also write obliquely, elliptically, or humorously in order to camouflage their feelings. . . . Even when they risk themselves by relating crises, usually in girlhood, it lacks that nostalgia men seem to experience. . . . Instead, the accounts of girlhood crises, while conveying their authors' awareness of their importance in shaping their later lives, are distanced by this understated treatment."[12] Readers will, of course, recognize many of these characteristics in the autobiographies of Bowen and Welty.

In the main, however, Bowen was extremely deliberate and precise about her plan for *Pictures and Conversations*, even though, as she reported, she did not find writing the synopsis of the projected book to be easy. "The underlying theme . . . will be the relationship (so far as that can be traceable, and perhaps it is most interesting when it is apparently not traceable) between living and writing. Dislike of pomposity inhibits me from saying, 'the relationship between life and art' (meaning my own)." She also commented that one reason prompting her to write the book was the spectacle of an ever-increasing body of critical study analyzing her and her work. "While appreciative of the honour done me and of the hard work involved, I have found some of them wildly off the mark. To the point of asking myself, if anybody *must* write a book about Elizabeth Bowen, why should not Elizabeth Bowen?" (pp. 61–62).

Doubtless something of the same reasoning persuaded Welty to turn to autobiography for the William E. Massey lectures that she gave at Harvard in April 1983, which she subsequently revised and published in 1984 as *One Writer's Beginnings*. She has also mentioned in the book's acknowledgments her gratitude to Daniel Aaron for suggesting "the direction and course the lectures might take."[13]

Welty's *One Writer's Beginnings* and Bowen's *Pictures and Conversations* elucidate one another in many suggestive and provocative ways. Like Bowen, Welty writes of her childhood and its strikingly visual, material world, which remains sharply etched in her memory. Also like Bowen, she seeks to locate the threads of attachment that link her early experiences within the family to the themes and landscapes that she would later create in fiction.

The chapter headings and titles of both books indicate the writers' preoccupation with the lessons of listening and seeing they learned as children. *Pictures and Conversations*, the title of which comes from *Alice in Wonderland*, is composed of the chapters "Origins," "Places," and the unfinished "People." Two projected chapters were to be titled "Genesis," to include remarks on the growth of one of Bowen's novels or longer stories, and "Witchcraft," to present some general conclusions about writing, with further references to her own work.

Welty's book, which is also an investigation of psychic and artistic origins, also comprises three chapters, "Listening," "Learning to See," and "Finding a Voice." Welty admired *Pictures and Conversations*, clearly indicating in the review she wrote for the *New York Times* her sympathy with Bowen's purpose and design: "Instead of the 'personal' (in the accepted sense), we were to be given the more revealing findings she herself could bring out of her life and her work, calling for the truer candor, the greater generosity—a work to do reader, as well as writer, honor."[14]

Structurally and thematically, both autobiographies are concentrated upon the people, especially the parents, and places of youth. What marks their sharpest similarity is the writers' emphasis upon the evolution in their childhood of a bifurcated vision of the world and of themselves, which they attribute partly to the differing personalities of their parents and partly to the division of their "home place."

Bowen writes in *Pictures and Conversations* of being always keenly aware of the contrasting natures of her parents' families. "My mother's family, the Colleys, had had misgivings as to her marriage to Henry Bowen, on the ground that the Bowens of Bowen's Court, County Cork, were rumoured to have an uncertain mental heredity. . . . To the Colleys, undeviatingly sane, ensconced, since their arrival in Ireland, in that central and civilised part of it known as The Pale, there could have seemed to be something fey and outlandish about those unpopulated stretches of County Cork with their unforgotten battlefields and abounding ruins" (p. 10).

Even more formative of her sense of doubleness was the recurrent experience of having two homes. As a child she had spent winters in Dublin, summers at Bowen's Court, with the result, she wrote in *Bowen's Court*, that by the time she began "to remember, life had divided itself into winter and summer halves" (p. 405). A further and more radical sense of division came after her father's breakdown, when at the age of seven she moved with her mother to England. "Possibly, it was England," she said in *Pictures and Conversations*, that "made me a novelist" (p. 23). She explains that the bravado of much of Irish writing—"all Anglo-Irish writing"—has inclined her countrymen toward drama, or, on occasion, to the short story, but definitely away from the novel, it being "too life-like, humdrum, to do us justice." Her description of the general perception of Ireland by non-natives, coincidentally, bears more than a passing similarity to popular and literary images of the southern United States current in both the nineteenth and twentieth centuries: "There is this about us: to most of the rest of the world we are semi-strangers, for whom existence has something of the trance-like quality of a spectacle. As beings, we are at once brilliant and limited . . ." (p. 23).

Leaving Ireland for England at the age of seven produced a "cleft" between her hereditary home and her environment that would ever after mark her sensibility. It made her self-consciously aware of a world quite separate from her. "It cannot be said that a child of seven was analytic," she wrote, "more, with a blend of characteristic guile and uncharacteristic patience I took note—which, though I had at that time no thought of my future art, is, after all, one of the main activities of the novelist" (p. 24).

One consequence of this early lesson in displacement was a precocious awareness of the outer world, the scenic world. As a seven-year-old, Bowen concentrated her gaze on "geographical setting." The same predilection for scene later came to be one of the most distinguishing features of her fiction, as she herself acknowledges. In the chapter "Places," she writes: "Am I not manifestly a writer for whom places loom large? As a reader, it is to the place-element that I react most strongly: for me, what gives fiction verisimilitude is its topography. No story gains absolute hold on me (which is to say, gains the required hold) if its background—the ambience of its happenings—be indefinite, abstract or generalised" (p. 34).

These words immediately remind one of Welty's discussion of place in two essays of the mid-fifties, "How I Write" and "Place in Fiction." They also reiterate Bowen's own earlier discussion of scene in "Notes on Writing a Novel." Like Bowen, Welty locates her dawning awareness of the outside world of appearance in the removals from home— for Welty, the dislocating, if beloved, summer journeys to Ohio and West Virginia, the visits to distant grandparents, her hereditary home. In the chapter "Learning to See," she describes the family's trips and her realization that her parents—and by extension she herself—belonged not only to Jackson, Mississippi, but to a land elsewhere. The journeys made her understand, she writes, how Ohio had her father "around the heart, as West Virginia had my mother" (p. 44).

For Welty, the trip to another, "earlier" home opened her eyes, taught her to see. Perhaps it was Ohio and West Virginia, Welty suggests, that nudged her toward writing. "The trips were wholes unto themselves," Welty says. "They were stories. Not only in form, but in their taking on direction, movement, development, change. They changed something in my life: each trip made its particular revelation, though I could not have found words for it" (p. 68).

In *One Writer's Beginnings*, Welty writes of having early formed an impression of her parents as embodying opposing, if complementary, personalities. Welty's relationship to her parents casts much light upon certain persistent themes in her fiction, particularly the existence of the mysterious otherness that lies below the surface of self. "All things are double," Clement Musgrove says in *The Robber Bridegroom*, and one finds in *One Writer's Beginnings* that Clement's creator traces her perception of doubleness from the example of Christian Webb and Chestina Andrews Welty. Mr. Welty was a believer in the future, in progress, a lover of clocks and maps and cameras, "instruments that would instruct and fascinate" (p. 3). In the family he was known as the "optimist," reminiscent of Judge McKelva in *The Optimist's Daughter*, whereas her mother claimed to be the "pessimist." Nonetheless, Welty notes that she was always aware that "he the optimist was the one who was prepared for the worst, and she the pessimist was the daredevil: he the one who on our trip carried chains and a coil of rope and an ax all upstairs to our hotel bedroom every night in case of fire, and she the one—before I was born—when there *was* a fire, had broken loose from all hands and run back—on crutches, too—into the burning house to rescue her set of Dickens which she flung, all twenty-four volumes, from the window before she jumped out after them" (pp. 45–46).

Welty's father read widely for information—there were books in the living room and encyclopedia tables and dictionary stand in the dining room—but her mother's first love was fiction: "she sank as a hedonist into novels," Welty writes. "She read Dickens in the spirit in which she would have eloped with him" (pp. 6–7). It was she who supported her daughter's ambition to be a writer, perhaps partly from a sense of relief, for she thought of writing, Welty says, as offering a "safe" career (p. 39). From the witness of the autobiography, one sees that the complementarities of her parents have provided Welty with a quite conscious design for patterning and formulating complementarities of great variety and scope in her fiction.

What emerges from reading *One Writer's Beginnings* and *Pictures and Conversations* side by side, proceeding antiphonally, is not the discovery that these writers led parallel lives—they did not—but rather the discovery that they locate the origins of their art, their literary creativity, in similar perceptions of childhood and youth. When as young women they began writing seriously—Bowen in the 1920s, Welty in the 1930s—they sought separation from youth, adult independence, largely through their work. Bowen wrote in the introduction to the 1951 edition of her *Early Stories* that the shiftings from Ireland to England had made her "diplomatic and imitative." "All through my youth," she continued, "I lived with a submerged fear that *I* might fail to establish grown-up status; and that fear had probably reached its peak when I started writing. A writer and a grown-up, it appeared to me, could not but be synonymous. . . . As far as I can see . . . I was anxious at once to approximate to the grownups and to demolish them" (p. x). Similarly, Welty locates the essential first act of writing at the outset of her career—and ever afterwards—as "getting her distance," in her words.

For Welty and Bowen the writing of fiction also turns out to be the chief way of maintaining the past, the family, one's youth. For both women, the means and meaning of writing have been the "welding together" of an "inner landscape," a connecting of the past, through memory, with the ever-changing, revealing outside world. "My work, in the terms in which I see it," writes Welty, "is as dearly matched to the world as its secret sharer" (p. 76). Bowen, too, stresses the same vital connections in *Pictures and Conversations*. "Since I started writing, I have been welding together an inner landscape, assembled anything but at random. But if not at random, under the influence of what? I suppose necessity, and what accompanies that" (p. 36).

Welty concludes *One Writer's Beginnings* with the comment that she has led a "sheltered life," but she does not hold her mother's view that the life of the writer is "safe." Rather, the sheltered life can be "daring indeed." Reading these two autobiographies, one sees that the daring, inward way was the necessary destination all along for both Elizabeth Bowen and Eudora Welty.

1. Victoria Glendinning, *Elizabeth Bowen* (1977; rpt. New York: Avon, 1979), pp. 238–239.

2. Peggy Whitman Prenshaw, *Elizabeth Spencer* (Boston: G. K. Hall, 1985), p. 10.

3. These letters from Eudora Welty to Elizabeth Bowen, dating mainly from the early 1950s, are in the Bowen collection at the Humanities Research Center, University of Texas at Austin.

4. Review of *The Golden Apples*, in *Books of Today*, Sept. 1950; rpt. in *Seven Winters and Afterthoughts* (New York: Alfred A. Knopf, 1962), pp. 215–218. See also the review of *Delta Wedding* in "EB Reviews," *Tatler and Bystander*, 6 Aug. 1947, pp. 182–183.

5. "An Interview with Eudora Welty," in *Conversations with Eudora Welty*, ed. Peggy Whitman Prenshaw (Jackson: University Press of Mississippi, 1984), pp. 195–196.

6. "The Color of the Air: A Conversation with Eudora Welty," *Saturday Review*, Nov./Dec. 1984, p. 33.

7. Ruth Vande Kieft, *Eudora Welty* (New York: Twayne, 1962), pp. 179–183; Rebecca Smith Wild, "Studies in the Shorter Fiction of Elizabeth Bowen and Eudora Welty," Diss. Univ. of Michigan, 1965; Michael Kreyling, *Eudora Welty's Achievement of Order* (Baton Rouge: Louisiana State University Press, 1980), pp. 119 ff.; Elizabeth Evans, *Eudora Welty* (New York: Frederick Ungar, 1981), pp. 113 ff.

8. *Bowen's Court* (New York: Alfred A. Knopf, 1942), p. 454. Subsequent references will be cited in the text.

9. *Seven Winters* (Dublin: Cuala Press, 1942); rpt. in *Seven Winters and Afterthoughts* (New York: Alfred A. Knopf, 1962), p. vii. Subsequent references will be cited in the text.

10. "The Art of Fiction XLVII: Eudora Welty," in *Conversations*, p. 81.

11. *Pictures and Conversations* (New York: Alfred A. Knopf, 1975), p. 61. Subsequent references will be cited in the text.

12. *Women's Autobiography: Essays in Criticism*, ed. Estelle C. Jelinek (Bloomington: Indiana University Press, 1980), pp. 7 ff.

13. *One Writer's Beginnings* (Cambridge and London: Harvard University Press, 1984). Subsequent references will be cited in the text.

14. Review of *Pictures and Conversations*, in *New York Times Book Review*, 5 Jan. 1975, pp. 4, 20; rpt. in *The Eye of the Story: Selected Essays and Reviews* (New York: Random House, 1978), p. 269.

A Eudora Welty Checklist, 1936–1972

The opportunity to reprint this Checklist, which originally appeared in the Fall 1973 Eudora Welty number of the *Mississippi Quarterly,* is a welcome one, and I am grateful to Al Devlin and Seetha Srinivasan for inviting me to do so. I have corrected a few errors of the original and brought up to date the publishing record of those volumes published before 1973; with Pearl McHaney's supplement, it should provide for readers of this volume a reasonably comprehensive record of Welty's works, and of the most significant commentary on that work.

This Checklist owes much to many people. To the roster of names accompanying the 1973 list, I would like to add those of Pearl McHaney, Thomas L. McHaney, Georges Pilard, Helen Hurt Tiegreen, and George Bixby, all of whom have contributed to the current and ongoing work on the full-scale descriptive bibliography. I owe a special word of gratitude to W. U. McDonald, Jr., editor of the *Eudora Welty Newsletter.* I also thank Thomas J. Richardson, James H. Sims, and Aubrey K. Lucas, of the University of Southern Mississippi, for their constant encouragement and support.

I. Primary

A. Separate Publications (Books and Pamphlets)

1941   *Eudora Welty: A Note on the Author and Her Work, by Katherine Anne Porter. Together with 'The Key,' One of Seventeen*

Stories from Miss Welty's Forthcoming 'A Curtain of Green'.
Garden City, N.Y.: Doubleday, Doran. [1]–7, 8–22 pp.

1941 *A Curtain of Green* (stories). Garden City, N.Y.: Double-
day, Doran. With an Introduction by Katherine Anne
Porter. [i]–xix, [1]–285 pp.
Contents: INTRODUCTION—LILY DAW AND THE THREE
LADIES—A PIECE OF NEWS—PETRIFIED MAN—THE KEY—
KEELA, THE OUTCAST INDIAN MAIDEN—WHY I LIVE AT THE
P. O.—THE WHISTLE—THE HITCH-HIKERS—A MEMORY—
CLYTIE—OLD MR MARBLEHALL—FLOWERS FOR MARJORIE—
A CURTAIN OF GREEN—A VISIT OF CHARITY—DEATH OF A
TRAVELING SALESMAN—POWERHOUSE—A WORN PATH.

London: John Lane the Bodley Head, 1943. With the
Porter Introduction. [1]–[14], 15–208 pp. Contents: as
above.

Stockholm/London: The Continental Book Company AB
(Zephyr Books, wrappers), 1947. Lacking the Porter
Introduction. [i–v], [1]–285 pp. Contents: as above.

Harmondsworth: Penguin Books (wrappers), 1947. With
the Porter Introduction. [1]–14, 15–207 pp. Contents: as
above.

New York: Harcourt, Brace, [1947]. With the Porter Introduction. [i]–xxiii, [1]–289 pp. Contents: as above.

Cf. *Selected Stories*.

New York and London: Harcourt Brace Jovanovich (A
Harvest/HBJ Book, wrappers), [1979]. With the Porter
Introduction. [i]–xxiii, [1]–289, [291] pp. Contents: as
above.

Cf. *Collected Stories*.

1942 *The Robber Bridegroom* (short novel). Garden City, N.Y.:
Doubleday, Doran. [i–v], [1]–185 pp.

London: John Lane the Bodley Head, 1944. With drawings by James Holland. [1–8], [9]–196 pp.

New York: Harcourt, Brace & World, [1948]. [i–v], [1]–
185 pp.

New York: Atheneum (wrappers), 1963. [i–ii], [1]–185,
[187–188] pp.

New York and London: Harcourt Brace Jovanovich (A
Harvest/HBJ Book, wrappers), [1978]. [i–v], [1]–185,
[186] pp.

London: Virago (wrappers), [1982]. With an Introduction
by Paul Binding. [i–iv], [v]–xiv, [1]–185, [186] pp.

Note: The Robber Bridegroom was adapted for the stage by
Alfred Uhry and Robert Waldman and published as a
book, New York: Drama Book Specialists, [1978]. [i–xi],
[1]–80 pp.

1943   *The Wide Net and Other Stories.* New York: Harcourt, Brace. [i–ix], [1]–214 pp.
    Contents: FIRST LOVE—THE WIDE NET—A STILL MOMENT—ASPHODEL—THE WINDS—THE PURPLE HAT—LIVVIE—AT THE LANDING.
    London: John Lane the Bodley Head, 1945. [1–6], 7–144 pp. Contents: as above.
    Cf. *Selected Stories.*
    New York and London: Harcourt Brace Jovanovich (A Harvest Book, wrappers), [1973]. [i–ix], [1]–214 pp. Contents: as above.
    Cf. *Collected Stories*

1946   *Delta Wedding* (novel). New York: Harcourt, Brace. [i–v], [1]–247 pp.
    London: The Bodley Head, 1947. [1–6], 7–271 pp.
    New York: New American Library (Signet, wrappers), 1963. [1–9], 11–287, [288] pp.
    New York and London: Harcourt Brace Jovanovich (A Harvest/HBJ Book, wrappers), [1979]. [i–v], [1]–247, [249] pp.
    London: Virago (wrappers), [1982]. With an Introduction by Paul Binding. [i–iv], [v]–ix, 3–247, [248] pp.

1948   *Music From Spain* (story). Greenville, Mississippi: The Levee Press. [i–iv], 1–62, [63] pp. Limited edition of 775 copies, signed by the author.

1949   *The Golden Apples* (related stories). New York: Harcourt, Brace. [i–ix], [1]–244 pp.
    Contents: SHOWER OF GOLD—JUNE RECITAL—SIR RABBIT—MOON LAKE—THE WHOLE WORLD KNOWS—MUSIC FROM SPAIN—THE WANDERERS.
    London: The Bodley Head, 1950. [i–vi], [1]–244, [245–246] pp. Contents: as above.
    New York: Harcourt, Brace & World (Harvest, wrappers), [1956]. [i–ix], [1]–277 pp. Contents: as above.
    Cf. *Collected Stories.*

1950   *Short Stories* (essay). New York: Harcourt, Brace. [i–iv], [1]–53, [55] pp. Limited edition of 1500 copies.
    Folcroft, Pa.: Folcroft Library Editions, 1971. [i–vi], [1]–53, [55] pp. Limited facsimile reissue of 150 copies.

1954   *Selected Stories of Eudora Welty.* New York: Modern Library. [i]–xxiii, [1]–289; [1]–214 pp. Contents: reprinted plates of Harcourt, Brace editions of *A Curtain of Green* (including the Porter Introduction) and *The Wide Net.*

1954   *The Ponder Heart* (short novel). New York: Harcourt, Brace. With drawings by Joe Krush. [i], [1–6], [7]–156 pp.

London: Hamish Hamilton, 1954. With the Krush drawings. [2–8], 9–140 pp.

New York: Dell Publishing Co. (wrappers), [1956]. With
the Krush drawings. [1–6], [7]–128.
Note: This is Dell No. 887. Reissued as Dell No. 7012 in
1962.

London: Hamish Hamilton, 1957. 144 pp. "Cheap Edition." [Information from CBI. I have not seen a copy.]

New York: Harcourt, Brace & World (Harbrace Paperback
Library, wrappers), [1967]. [i–v], [1]–117 pp.

New York and London: Harcourt Brace Jovanovich (A
Harvest/HBJ Book, wrappers), [1977]. With the Krush
drawings. [ii], [1–5], [6]–156, [157] pp.

London: Virago (wrappers), [1983]. With an Introduction
by Helen McNeil. [i–v], [vii–viii, 1–7], 9–132, [133–136]
pp.

Note: The Ponder Heart was adapted to the stage by Joseph
Fields and Jerome Chodorov, and published New York:
Random House, 1956. [i–ix], [1]–180 pp.

1955   *The Bride of the Innisfallen and Other Stories.* New York:
Harcourt, Brace. [i–vii], [1]–207 pp.
Contents: NO PLACE FOR YOU, MY LOVE—THE BURNING—
THE BRIDE OF THE INNISFALLEN—LADIES IN SPRING—
CIRCE—KIN—GOING TO NAPLES.

London: Hamish Hamilton, 1955. [1–7], 9–190 pp. Contents: as above.

New York: Harcourt Brace Jovanovich (Harvest, wrappers), [1972]. [i–vii], [1]–207, [209] pp. Contents: as
above.

Cf. *Collected Stories.*

1957   *Place in Fiction* (essay). New York: House of Books, Ltd.
[1–5, 7–37, 38] pp. Limited edition of 300 copies, signed
by the author.

1962   *Three Papers on Fiction* (essays). Northampton, Mas-
sachusetts: Smith College (wrappers). [i–ii], 1–46 pp.
Contents: PLACE IN FICTION—WORDS INTO FICTION—THE
SHORT STORY.

1964   *The Shoe Bird* (children's story). New York: Harcourt, Brace
& World. With Illustrations by Beth Krush. [1–6], 7–
[88] pp.

1965   *Thirteen Stories* selected, with an Introduction, by Ruth M.
Vande Kieft. Harcourt, Brace & World (Harvest, wrap-
pers). [i]–vi, [1]–243 pp.
Contents: INTRODUCTION—THE WIDE NET—OLD MR. MAR-
BLEHALL—KEELA, THE OUTCAST INDIAN MAIDEN—A
WORN PATH—PETRIFIED MAN—A STILL MOMENT—LILY

DAW AND THE THREE LADIES—THE HITCH-HIKERS—
POWERHOUSE—WHY I LIVE AT THE P. O.—LIVVIE—MOON
LAKE—THE BRIDE OF THE INNISFALLEN.

1969 *A Sweet Devouring* (autobiographical essay). New York: Albondocani Press (wrappers). [1–3, 5–16, 19–20] pp. Limited edition of 176 copies, signed by the author.

1970 *Losing Battles* (novel). New York: Random House. [ii–ix], [1]–436, [437] pp. *Note:* also published in a limited, separately printed, issue of 300 copies, signed by the author.

Greenwich, Conn.: Fawcett Publications (Crest, wrappers), 1971. [1–6], [7]–416 pp.

New York: Vintage, [1978] (wrappers). [1–8], 9–416 pp.

London: Virago, 1982 (wrappers). [iii–ix], 3–436, [438–39] pp.

1970 *A Flock of Guinea Hens Seen From A Car* (poem). New York: Albondocani Press (wrappers). [1–4] pp. Limited Edition of 300 copies.

1971 *One Time, One Place: Mississippi in the Depression, A Snapshot Album* (photographs). New York: Random House. With an introduction by Miss Welty. [i]–xiv, [1]–[113], [114] pp. *Note:* also published in a limited, separately printed, issue of 300 copies, signed by the author.

1972 *The Optimist's Daughter* (short novel). New York: Random House. [i–vii], [1]–180, [181] pp. *Note:* also published in a limited, separately printed, issue of 300 copies, signed by the author.

Greenwich, Conn.: Fawcett Publications (Crest, wrappers), 1973. [1–5], 7–208 pp.

London: André Deutsch, [1973]. [i–vii], [1]–180 pp.

New York: Vintage (wrappers). [1–7], 9–208 pp.

Franklin Center, Pennsylvania: The Franklin Library, 1978. Limited edition, with illustrations by Mitchell Hooks and an Introduction by the Franklin Library. [ii–xiii], [1]–190 pp.

Franklin Center, Pennsylvania: The Franklin Library, 1980. Limited edition, signed and with a "Special Message to Subscribers" by Eudora Welty; illustrated by Howard Rogers. [i–xix], [1]–194 pp.

London: Virago, 1984. With an Introduction by Helen McNeil. [i–iv], v–xi, 3–180 pp.

B. Contributions to Books and Periodicals

1. Fiction
a. Novels

THE ROBBER BRIDEGROOM *Philadelphia Inquirer,* 11 April 1943, pp. 2–19.

DELTA WEDDING *Atlantic Monthly,* 177 (January 1946), 113–132; (February 1946), 118–134; (March 1946), 121–134; (April 1946), 179–194.

THE PONDER HEART *New Yorker,* 29 (5 December 1953), 47–58, 60, 62, 64–65, 68–70, 72, 74–76, 78, 80–84, 86, 89–91, 94–96, 99–100, 102, 104–106, 109–110, 112, 114–116, 121–124, 126–128, 131–138.

THE OPTIMIST'S DAUGHTER *New Yorker,* 45 (15 March 1969), 37–46, 48, 50, 53–54, 56, 61–62, 64, 67–68, 70, 75–76, 78, 81–82, 84, 86, 88, 93–95, 98, 100, 103–106, 111–114, 117–120, 125–128.

b. Stories

DEATH OF A TRAVELING SALESMAN *Manuscript,* 3 (May–June 1936), 21–29. *CG*

THE DOLL *The Tanager* (Grinnell College, Grinnell, Iowa), 11 (June 1936), 11–14.

MAGIC *Manuscript,* 3 (September–October 1936), 3–7.

LILY DAW AND THE THREE LADIES *Prairie Schooner,* 11 (Winter 1937), 266–275. *CG*

RETREAT *River,* 1 (March 1937), 10–12.

A PIECE OF NEWS *Southern Review,* 3 (Summer 1937), 80–84. *CG*

FLOWERS FOR MARJORIE *Prairie Schooner,* 11 (Summer 1937), 111–120. *CG*

A MEMORY *Southern Review,* 3 (Autumn 1937), 317–322. *CG*

OLD MR. GRENADA *Southern Review,* 3 (Spring 1938), 707–713. *CG* as "Old Mr Marblehall"

A CURTAIN OF GREEN *Southern Review,* 4 (Autumn 1938), 292–298. *CG*

THE WHISTLE *Prairie Schooner,* 12 (Fall 1938), 210–215. *CG*

PETRIFIED MAN *Southern Review,* 4 (Spring 1939), 682–695. *CG*

THE HITCH-HIKERS *Southern Review,* 5 (Autumn 1939), 293–307. *CG*

KEELA THE OUTCAST INDIAN MAIDEN *New Directions in Prose & Poetry,* ed. James Laughlin. Norfolk, Conn.: New Directions Press, 1940, pp. 109–117. *CG*

A WORN PATH *Atlantic Monthly,* 167 (February 1941), 215–219. *CG*

WHY I LIVE AT THE P. O. *Atlantic Monthly,* 167 (April 1941), 443–450. *CG*

CLYTIE *Southern Review,* 7 (Summer 1941), 52–64. *CG*

A VISIT OF CHARITY *Decision,* 1 (June 1941), 17–21. *CG*

POWERHOUSE *Atlantic Monthly,* 167 (June 1941), 707–713. *CG*

THE KEY *Harper's Bazaar,* (August 1941), 71, 132–134. *CG*

THE PURPLE HAT   *Harper's Bazaar,* (November 1941), 68–69, 115. *WN*

FIRST LOVE   *Harper's Bazaar,* (February 1942), 52–53, 110, 112, 115–116, 118. *WN*

A STILL MOMENT   *American Prefaces,* 7 (Spring 1942), 226–240. *WN*

THE WIDE NET   *Harper's Magazine,* 184 (May 1942), 582–594. *WN*

THE WINDS   *Harper's Bazaar,* (August 1942), 92–93, 121–125. *WN*

ASPHODEL   *Yale Review,* 32 (September 1942), 146–157. *WN*

LIVVIE IS BACK   *Atlantic Monthly,* 170 (November 1942), 57–64. *WN* as "Livvie"

AT THE LANDING   *Tomorrow,* 2 (April 1943), 15–25. *WN*

A SKETCHING TRIP   *Atlantic Monthly,* 175 (June 1945), 62–70.

THE WHOLE WORLD KNOWS   *Harper's Bazaar,* (March 1947), 198–199, 332–338. *GA*

HELLO AND GOOD-BYE   *Atlantic Monthly,* 180 (July 1947), 37–40.

GOLDEN APPLES   *Harper's Bazaar,* (September 1947), 216–217, 286, 288–290, 295–302, 305–307, 311–320. *GA* as "June Recital"

SHOWER OF GOLD   *Atlantic,* 181 (May 1948), 37–42. *GA*

SIR RABBIT   *Hudson Review,* 2 (Spring 1949), 24–36. *GA*

THE HUMMINGBIRDS   *Harper's Bazaar,* (March 1949), 195–196, 227, 230–234, 246–247, 250–252. *GA* as "The Wanderers"

MOON LAKE   *Sewanee Review,* 57 (Summer 1949), 464–508. *GA*

PUT ME IN THE SKY!   *Accent,* 10 (Autumn 1949), 3–10. *BI* as "Circe"

THE BURNING   *Harper's Bazaar,* (March 1951), 184, 238, 241, 243, 244, 247. *BI*

THE BRIDE OF THE INNISFALLEN   *New Yorker,* 27 (1 December 1951), 53–56, 58, 60, 62, 64, 66, 68, 70–74, 77–84. *BI*

NO PLACE FOR YOU, MY LOVE   *New Yorker,* 28 (20 September 1952), 37–44. *BI*

KIN   *New Yorker,* 28 (15 November 1952), 39–48, 50, 52–54, 56, 58–60, 62, 64–67. *BI*

SPRING   *Sewanee Review,* 62 (Winter 1954), 101–116. *BI* as "Ladies in Spring"

GOING TO NAPLES   *Harper's Bazaar,* (July 1954), 54–58, 100–103, 108, 111–113. *BI*

WHERE IS THE VOICE COMING FROM?   *New Yorker,* 39 (6 July 1963), 24–25. An early version of this story, entitled FROM THE UNKNOWN is published in *Write and Rewrite: A Study of the Creative Process,* ed. John Kuehl. New York: Meredith Press, 1967, pp. 4–14.

THE DEMONSTRATORS   *New Yorker,* 42 (26 November 1966), 56–63.

2. Non-Fiction Prose: Essays, Sketches, Criticism

WOMEN!! MAKE TURBAN IN OWN HOME!   *Junior League Magazine,* 28

(November 1941), 20–21, 62.

IDA M'TOY *Accent*, 2 (Summer 1942), 214–222.

PAGEANT OF BIRDS *New Republic*, 99 (25 October 1943), 565–567.

SOME NOTES ON RIVER COUNTRY *Harper's Bazaar*, (February 1944), 86–87, 150–156.

JOSE DE CREEFT *Magazine of Art*, 37 (February 1944), 42–47.

LITERATURE AND THE LENS *Vogue*, 104 (1 August 1944), 102–103.

DEPARTMENT OF AMPLIFICATION [LETTER PROTESTING EDMUND WILSON'S REVIEW OF WILLIAM FAULKNER'S 'INTRUDER IN THE DUST'] *New Yorker*, 24 (1 January 1949), 50–51.

THE READING AND WRITING OF SHORT STORIES *Atlantic*, 183 (February 1949), 54–58; (March 1949), 46–49. In *3 Papers*, heavily revised, and in *Short Stories*.

THE TEACHING AND STUDY OF WRITING *Western Review*, 14 (Spring 1950), 165, 167–168.

GOOD INTENTIONS *New York Times Book Review*, 31 December 1950, p. 8.

THE CONCEPT IN REVIEW *Concept* (Converse College), 50 (May 1951), 4, 12.

THE ABODE OF SUMMER *Harper's Bazaar*, (June 1952), 50, 115.

HOW I WRITE *Virginia Quarterly Review*, 31 (Winter 1955), 240–251.

PLACE IN FICTION *The Archive* (Duke University), 67 (April 1955), 5–7, 9–11, 13–14. Also in *South Atlantic Quarterly*, 55 (January 1956), 57–72. Also published separately and in *3 Papers*.

IS THERE A READER IN THE HOUSE? *Mississippi Educational Advance*, 47 (November 1955), 12–13.

A SWEET DEVOURING *Mademoiselle*, 46 (December 1957), 49, 114–116. Also published separately.

THE RIGHT TO READ *Mississippi Magic*, 16 (May 1961), 15.

HENRY GREEN: A NOVELIST OF THE IMAGINATION *Texas Quarterly*, 4 (Autumn 1961), 246–256.

AUTHOR GAVE LIFE TO FICTIONAL COUNTY *Washington Post and Times-Herald*, 7 July 1962, p. 2-C.

AND THEY ALL LIVED HAPPILY EVER AFTER *New York Times Book Review*, Part II, 10 November 1963, p. 3.

[TRIBUTE TO FLANNERY O'CONNOR] *Esprit* (University of Scranton), 8 (Winter 1964), 49.

WORDS INTO FICTION *Southern Review*, 1 (July 1965), 543–553. Also in *3 Papers*.

MUST THE NOVELIST CRUSADE? *Atlantic*, 216 (October 1965), 104–108. Also *Writer's Digest*, 50 (February 1970), 32–35, 52–53, 55.

THE EYE OF THE STORY *Yale Review*, 55 (December 1965), 265–274. Also in *Katherine Anne Porter: A Critical Symposium*, ed. Lodwick Hartley and George Core. Athens: University of Georgia Press, 1969, pp. 103–112.

ENGLISH FROM THE INSIDE   *American Education*, 2 (February 1966), 18–19.

A NOTE ON JANE AUSTEN   *Shenandoah*, 20 (Spring 1969), 3–7. Also in *Atlantic Brief Lives*, ed. Louis Kronenberger. Boston: Little, Brown, 1971, pp. 23–25.

FROM WHERE I LIVE   *Delta Review*, 6 (November/December 1969), 69.

[COMMENT ON "A WORN PATH"]   In *This Is My Best*, ed. Whit Burnett. Garden City, N.Y.: Doubleday, 1970, p. 532.

EUDORA WELTY'S WORLD IN THE '30'S   *Mademoiselle*, 73 (September 1971), 162–165, 191. Reprints Introduction and some photographs from *One Time, One Place*.

SOME NOTES ON TIME IN FICTION   *Mississippi Quarterly*, 26 (Fall 1973), 483–492.

3. Book Reviews

THE LIFE OF A SOUTHERN TOWN   *Saturday Review*, 25 (19 September 1942), 22–23. Rev. Marguerite Steedman, *But You'll Be Back*.

PLANTATION COUNTRY   *New York Times Book Review*, 7 March 1943, p. 9. Rev. Bernice Kelly Harris, *Sweet Beulah Land*.

WOMEN AND CHILDREN   *NYTBR*, 2 May 1943, p. 8. Rev. Nancy Hale, *Between the Dark and the Daylight*.

EXOTIC, FROM ECUADOR   *NYTBR*, 18 July 1943, p. 6. Rev. Enrique Gil Gilbert, tr. Dudley Poore, *Our Daily Bread*.

A POWERFUL NOVEL OF THE PAMPAS   *NYTBR*, 15 August 1943, p. 4. Rev. Enrique Amorim, tr. Richard L. O'Connell and James Graham Lujan, *The Horse and His Shadow*.

THE GREAT BUDDHA   *NYTBR*, 29 August 1943, pp. 5, 16. Rev. Maurice Collis, *The Land of the Great Image*.

VICTORIAN HALF-BREED   *NYTBR*, 31 October 1943, pp. 6, 12. Rev. Margery Allingham Carter, *The Galantrys*.

ALABAMA FARM BOY   *NYTBR*, 26 March 1944, p. 4. Rev. Harry Harrison Kroll, *Waters Over the Dam*.

MIRRORS FOR REALITY   *NYTBR*, 16 April 1944, p. 3. Rev. Virginia Woolf, *A Haunted House, and Other Short Stories*.

STRICTLY PERELMAN   *NYTBR*, 2 July 1944, p. 6. Rev. of S. J. Perelman, *Crazy Like A Fox*.

TATTERS AND FRAGMENTS OF WAR   *NYTBR*, 16 July 1944, p. 3, 24. Rev. George Biddle, *Artist at War*. Signed "Michael Ravenna."

GERMAN HOME FRONT   *NYTBR*, 20 August 1944, p. 5. Rev. Franz Hoellering, *Furlough*. Signed "Michael Ravenna."

FAR NORTH   *NYTBR*, 27 August 1944, p. 5. Rev. Gilbert Gabriel, *I Got a Country*. Signed "Michael Ravenna."

ANIMAL, VEGETABLE, MINERAL GHOSTS   *NYTBR*, 3 September 1944, p. 5. Rev. H. F. Heard, *The Great Fog, and Other Weird Tales*.

GHOULIES, GHOSTIES AND JUMBEES *NYTBR*, 24 September 1944, pp. 5, 21. Rev. August Derleth, ed., *Sleep No More* and Henry S. Whitehead, *Jumbee and Other Uncanny Tales.*

FOR THE WINDOW-BOX FARMER *NYTBR*, 1 October 1944, p. 23. Rev. Dorothy H. Jenkins and Helen Van Pelt Wilson, *Enjoy Your House Plants.* Signed "E. W."

ONE-MAN SHOW *NYTBR*, 15 October 1944, p. 24. Rev. Richard Wilcox and David Fredenthal, *Of Men and Battle.* Signed "E. W."

DRAWN AT FIRST-HAND *NYTBR*, 29 October 1944, p. 20. Rev. Aimee Crane, ed., *G. I. Sketch Book.*

HAND-PICKED SPOOKS *NYTBR*, 10 December 1944, p. 6. Rev. Edward Wagenknecht, ed., *Six Novels of the Supernatural.*

SKIES WITHOUT A CLOUD *NYTBR*, 24 December 1944, p. 3. Rev. John Francis McDermott, ed., *The Western Journals of Washington Irving.*

FINE-SPUN FANTASIES *NYTBR*, 18 February 1945, pp. 4–5. Rev. Edita Morris, *Three Who Loved.*

SALEM AND ITS FOUNDING FATHER *NYTBR*, 25 February 1945, p. 4. Rev. Clifford K. Shipton, *Roger Conant, A Founder of Massachusetts.*

TOLD WITH SEVERITY AND IRONY *NYTBR*, 4 March 1945, pp. 1, 16, 18. Rev. Glenway Wescott, *Apartment in Athens.*

PLACE-NAMES AND OUR HISTORY *NYTBR*, 6 May 1945, pp. 1, 14, 15. Rev. George R. Stewart, *Names on the Land.*

FALL HARVEST FOR THE YOUNG READER *NYTBR*, 11 November 1945, p. 7. Rev. Sigrid Undset, *True and Untrue, and Other Norse Tales;* Norbert Guterman, *Russian Fairy Tales;* Charles Perrault, *French Fairy Tales.*

CREOLE GET-TOGETHER *NYTBR*, 30 January 1946, pp. 5, 14. Rev. Lyle Saxon, Edward Dreyer, and Robert Tallent, *Gumbo Ya-Ya, A Collection of Louisiana Folk Tales.*

HIGH JINKS TRAVELOGUE *NYTBR*, 8 August 1948, p. 5. Rev. S. J. Perelman, *Westward Ha! Around the World in 80 Cliches.*

SOMNOLENCE AND SUNLIGHT, SOUND OF BELLS, THE PACIFIC SURF *NYTBR*, 15 August 1948, p. 5. Rev. Dorothy Baker, *Our Gifted Son.*

INNOCENTS IN THE WOOD *NYTBR*, 19 September 1948, pp. 16, 18. Rev. Hollis Summers, *City Limit.*

IN YOKNAPATAWPHA *Hudson Review*, 1 (Winter 1949), 596–598. Rev. William Faulkner, *Intruder in the Dust.*

FIREWORKS IN ITALY *Saturday Review*, 33 (23 September 1950), 16–17. Rev. William Sansom, *South.*

A SEARCH, MADDENING AND INFECTIOUS *NYTBR*, 14 January 1951, p. 5. Rev. Jessamyn West, *The Witch Diggers.*

WHEN GOOD MEETS BAD *NYTBR*, 17 August 1952, p. 4. Rev.

Giovanni Guareschi, *Don Camillo and His Flock.*

THE SEEDS OF EVIL *NYTBR*, 5 October 1952, p. 5. Rev. Patrick Hamilton, *The West Pier.*

'LIFE IN THE BARN WAS VERY GOOD' *NYTBR*, 19 October 1952, p. 49. Rev. E. B. White, *Charlotte's Web.*

THREADS OF INNOCENCE *NYTBR*, 5 April 1953, p. 4. Rev. J. D. Salinger, *Nine Stories.*

THE THORNTONS SIT FOR A FAMILY PORTRAIT *NYTBR*, 27 May 1956, p. 5. Rev. E. M. Forster, *Marianne Thornton: A Domestic Biography.*

IRELAND WITH FIGURES *NYTBR*, 5 August 1956, pp. 4, 12. Rev. Walter Macken, *The Green Hills and Other Stories.*

A TOUCH THAT'S MAGIC *NYTBR*, 3 November 1957, p. 5. Rev. Isak Dinesen, *Last Tales.*

UNCOMMON READER *NYTBR*, 21 September 1958, p. 6. Rev. Virginia Woolf, *Granite and Rainbow.*

ALL IS GRIST FOR HIS MILL *NYTBR*, 12 October 1958, p. 4. Rev. S. J. Perelman, *The Most of S. J. Perelman.*

LIFE'S IMPACT IS OBLIQUE *NYTBR*, 2 April 1961, p. 5. Rev. John Russell, *Henry Green: Nine Novels and an Unpacked Bag.*

THE ACCEPTANCE OF LIFE IS A DEFENSE OF THE STORY *NYTBR*, 17 December 1961, p. 6. Rev. Eric O. Johannesson, *The World of Isak Dinesen.*

TIME AND PLACE—AND SUSPENSE *NYTBR*, 30 June 1963, pp. 5, 27. Rev. William Sansom, *The Stories of William Sansom.*

COOK, CARE FOR THE MAD, OR WRITE *NYTBR*, 7 February 1965, pp. 4, 44–45. Rev. Robert Langbaum, *The Gayety of Vision: A Study of Isak Dinesen's Art.*

MOVEMENT NEVER LIES *Sewanee Review*, 75 (July–September 1967), 529–533. Rev. LeRoy Leatherman, *Martha Graham: Portrait of the Lady as an Artist.*

FOUR REVIEWS BY EUDORA WELTY *NYTBR*, 24 May 1970, Part II, pp. 4–5, 45. Rev. Erich Kästner, *The Little Man and the Big Thief;* William Pène du Bois, *Otto and the Magic Potatoes;* and Natalie Babbit, *Knee-Knock Rise.* Note: only three books reviewed.

S. J. PERELMAN SHOULD BE DECLARED A LIVING NATIONAL TREASURE *NYTBR*, 30 August 1970, pp. 1, 25. Rev. S. J. Perelman, *Baby, It's Cold Inside.*

THE STUFF THAT NIGHTMARES ARE MADE OF *NYTBR*, 14 February 1971, pp. 1, 28–30. Rev. Ross Macdonald, *The Underground Man.*

THE SADDEST STORY *NYTBR*, 2 May 1971, pp. 1, 14, 16, 18. Rev. Arthur Mizener, *The Saddest Story: A Biography of Ford Madox Ford.*

A COLLECTION OF OLD NEW STORIES BY E. M. FORSTER *NYTBR*, 13

May 1973, pp. 27–28, 30. Rev. E. M. Forster, *The Life to Come and Other Short Stories*.

4. Miscellaneous: Introductions, etc.

WHAT STEVENSON STARTED   *New Republic*, 5 January 1953, pp. 8–9.

"WARMTH OF SPEECH . . . WITHOUT WORDS" WRITES EUDORA WELTY ABOUT HEIFETZ   *Words and Music: Comment by Famous Authors about the World's Greatest Artists*. RCA Victor Publicity Pamphlet, n.d. [ca. 1950?], p. 19. Also in an RCA advertisement in *New Yorker*, 26 (7 October 1950), 115.

A SALUTE FROM ONE OF THE FAMILY   *Lamar Life Insurance Company: A Tower of Strength in the Deep South, 50th Anniversary 1906–1956*. Montgomery, Alabama: Paragon Press, [1956?], pp. 3–5.

[TRIBUTE TO JOHN ROOD]   *October 7–25, 1958, Exhibition of Recent Sculpture: John Rood*. New York: The Contemporaries, 1958, pp. [2–3].

PRESENTATION TO WILLIAM FAULKNER OF THE GOLD MEDAL FOR FICTION   *Proceedings of the American Academy of Arts and Letters and the National Institute of Arts and Letters*. Second Series. Number 13. New York, 1963, pp. 225–226.

[TRIBUTE]   *Isak Dinesen: A Memorial*, ed. Clara Svendsen. New York: Random House, 1965, pp. 94–95.

INTRODUCTION   *Hanging By A Thread*, ed. Joan Kahn. Boston: Houghton Mifflin, 1969, pp. xv–xix.

THE FLAVOR OF JACKSON   *The Jackson Cookbook*. Jackson, Mississippi: Published by the Symphony League, 1971, pp. [ix–xii].

ACCEPTANCE BY MISS WELTY [OF THE GOLD MEDAL FOR THE NOVEL]   *Proceedings of the American Academy of Arts and Letters and the National Institute of Arts and Letters*. Second Series. Number 23. New York, 1973, p. 38.

5. Poetry

THERE   *Bozart-Westminster*, 2 (Autumn 1936), 10.

A FLOCK OF GUINEA HENS SEEN FROM A CAR   *New Yorker*, 33 (20 April 1957), 35. Also published separately.

6. Contributions to *St. Nicholas*

"A HEADING FOR AUGUST" (drawing) *St. Nicholas*, 47 (August 1920), 951.

ONCE UPON A TIME (poem)   *St. Nicholas*, 51 (November 1923), 108.

IN THE TWILIGHT (poem)   *St. Nicholas*, 52 (January 1925), 328.

7. Contributions to Mississippi State College for Women Student Publications

BURLESQUE BALLAD (poem)   *The Spectator*, 20 (26 September 1925), 3.

AUTUMN'S HERE (poem)   *The Spectator*, 20 (28 November 1925), 7.

DESIRE (poem)   *The Spectator*, 21 (16 October 1926), 3.

THE GNAT (play)   *The Spectator*, 21 (6 November 1926), 2.

"I" FOR IRIS—IRMA, IMOGENE (prose sketch)   *The Spectator*, 21 (27 November 1926), 6.

[POEM]   *The Spectator*, 21 (27 November 1926), 4. Signed 'E. W., '29'.

PANDORA REGRETS HAVING OPENED THE BOX (drawing)   *The Spectator*, 21 (12 February 1927), 3. Signed 'E. W.'

THE GARDEN OF EDEN—BY ONE WHO HAS NEVER BEEN THERE (drawing)   *Oh, Lady!*, 1 (April 1927), 17.

GENTLEMEN EATING PEANUTS (drawing and prose commentary)   *Oh, Lady!*, 1 (May 1927), 7. Only the drawing is signed, 'E. W.'

[DRAWING]   *Oh, Lady!*, 1 (May 1927), 12. Signed 'E. W.'

H. L. MENCKEN SINGING THE STAR SPANGLED BANNER IN HIS MORNING TUB (drawing and prose commentary)   *Oh, Lady!*, 1 (May 1927), 16. Only the drawing is signed, 'E. W.'

PHOPHECY (poem)   *The Spectator*, 21 (3 May 1927), 4.

INCIDENT (poem)   *The Spectator*, 21 (3 May 1927), 4.

FABLES & PARABLES (prose)   *The Spectator*, 21 (17 May 1927), 3. Signed '(Evidently, Eudora)'.

8. Photographs

Mississippi: A Guide to the Magnolia State, comp. Federal Writers' Project of the Works Progress Administration (New York: Hastings House, 1938).

Eudora Welty, "Literature and the Lens." *Vogue*, 104 (1 August 1944), 102–103.

"Welty Country." *New York Times Book Review*, 10 January 1954, p. 5.

Eudora Welty, "Place in Fiction." *The Archive* (Duke University), 67 (April 1955), 4, 8, 12.

Eudora Welty, *One Time, One Place*. New York: Random House, 1971.

9. Interviews

"New Writers: Eudora Welty." *Publishers' Weekly*, 6 December 1941, pp. 2099–2100.

"Eudora Welty." *Wilson Library Bulletin*, 16 (January 1942), 410.

Flavia Jo Russell, "Interview with Eudora Welty." *The Ephemera* (Mississippi State College for Women), (Winter 1942), 26–27.

Robert Van Gelder, "An Interview with Miss Eudora Welty." *New York Times Book Review*, 14 June 1942, p. 2.

Bernard Kalb, [Interview with Eudora Welty]. *Saturday Review*, 38 (9 April 1955), 18.

"Symposium: The Artist and the Critic." *Stylus* (Millsaps College), 9 (18 May 1960), 21–28.

Tony Klatzko, "Eudora Welty Tells Students About Writing." Jackson, Miss., *Clarion-Ledger*, 19 March 1962, p. 2.

Bill Ferris, "Quiet Eudora Welty Proclaims Her Craft." *The Davidsonian* (Davidson College, N.C.), 12 April 1963, p. 1.

"An Interview with Eudora Welty." *Comment* (University of Alabama), 4 (Winter 1965), 11–16.

B. O., "An Interview with Eudora Welty." *Senior Scholastic*, 89 (9 December 1966), 18.

Walter Clemons, "Meeting Miss Welty." *New York Times Book Review*, 12 April 1970, pp. 2, 46.

William Thomas, "Eudora Welty." *Mid-South* (Memphis *Commercial-Appeal* Sunday Magazine), 25 October 1970, pp. 7–8, 16–19.

Linda Keuhl, "The Art of Fiction XLVII: Eudora Welty." *Paris Review*, 55 (Fall 1972), 72–97.

Charles T. Bunting, " 'The Interior World': An Interview With Eudora Welty." *Southern Review*, 8 (October 1972), 711–735.

William F. Buckley, Jr., "The Southern Imagination" (Interview with Eudora Welty and Walker Percy). Columbia, S. C.: Firing Line, 1972. Published transcription of television broadcast of 24 December 1972. Also *Mississippi Quarterly*, 26 (Fall 1973), 493–516.

Alice Walker, "Eudora Welty: An Interview." *Harvard Advocate*, 106 (Winter 1973), 68–72.

Billy Skelton, "State Pays Eudora Welty Tribute." Jackson, Miss., *Clarion-Ledger*, 3 May 1973, pp. 1, 9.

II. Secondary

In the following selective checklist of secondary materials I have tried to include all full-length studies of aspects of Miss Welty's work, a sampling of contemporary reviews of her books as they were published, and only the most useful text-book explications of individual stories. For a more extensive listing of the former, see Seymour L. Gross's checklist listed below in Section B; for the latter, see Warren S.

Walker, comp., *Twentieth-Century Short Story Explication: Interpretations, 1900–1966* (Shoe String Press, 1967, Second Edition), and its supplement, covering 1967–1969 (1970). The most complete and useful on-going update of materials about Miss Welty appears in the annual checklist of scholarship on Southern literature in the Spring number of *Mississippi Quarterly.*

In general, articles are listed chronologically according to subject, and articles dealing significantly with more than one item are listed each time necessary. The multi-listing is by no means exhaustive, however, and is intended as a general, rather than as a comprehensive, guide to the material. I have annotated the entries only where it seems useful to do so.

A. Books and Pamphlets

Ruth M. Vande Kieft, *Eudora Welty.* New York: Twayne, 1962; revised New York: Twayne, 1987.

Alfred Appel, Jr., *A Season of Dreams: The Fiction of Eudora Welty.* Baton Rouge: Louisiana State University Press, 1965.

J. A. Bryant, Jr., *Eudora Welty.* Minneapolis: University of Minnesota Press, 1968. (Minnesota Pamphlet No. 66)

Niel D. Isaacs, *Eudora Welty.* Austin, Texas: Steck-Vaughn, 1969. (Steck-Vaughn Southern Writers Series, No. 8)

Marie-Antoinette Manz-Kunz, *Eudora Welty: Aspects of Reality in her Short Fiction.* Francke Verlag Bern, 1971.

Zelma Turner Howard, *The Rhetoric of Eudora Welty's Short Stories.* Jackson: University and College Press of Mississippi, 1973.

B. Bibliographies

Katherine Hinds Smythe, "Eudora Welty: A Checklist," *Bulletin of Bibliography,* 21 (January–April, 1956), 207–208.

Seymour L. Gross, "Eudora Welty: A Bibliography of Criticism and Comment." Secretary's News Sheet, Bibliographical Society, University of Virginia, No. 45, April 1960.

Leona Jordan, "Eudora Welty: Selected Criticism." *Bulletin of Bibliography,* 23 (January–April 1960), 14–15.

McKelva Cole, "Book Reviews by Eudora Welty: A Check-List." *Bulletin of Bibliography,* 23 (January–April 1963), 240.

W. U. McDonald, Jr., "Eudora Welty Manuscripts: An Annotated Finding List." *Bulletin of Bibliography*, 24 (September–December 1963), 44–46.

C. General Estimates, Thematic Studies

Martha Read, "Eudora Welty." *Prairie Schooner*, 18 (1944), 74–76.

Robert Penn Warren, "The Love and the Separateness in Miss Welty." *Kenyon Review*, 6 (Spring 1944), 246–259.

Eunice Glenn, "Fantasy in the Fiction of Eudora Welty." In *A Southern Vanguard*, ed. Allen Tate. New York: Prentice-Hall, 1947, pp. 78–91.

John W. Wilson, "Delta Revival." *English Journal*, 38 (March 1949), 117–124.

Granville Hicks, "Eudora Welty." *English Journal*, 41 (November 1952), 461–468. Also in *College English*, 14 (November 1952), 69–76.

Robert Daniel, "The World of Eudora Welty." *Hopkins Review*, 6 (Winter 1953), 49–58. Reprinted from same plates in *Southern Renascence: The Literature of the Modern South*, ed. Louis D. Rubin, Jr., and Robert D. Jacobs. Baltimore: The Johns Hopkins Press, 1953, pp. 306–315. Reprinted, with extensive revisions, as "Eudora Welty: The Sense of Place" in *South: Modern Southern Literature in Its Cultural Setting*, ed. Louis D. Rubin, Jr., and Robert D. Jacobs. New York: Doubleday Dolphin, 1961, pp. 276–286.

Harry C. Morris, "Eudora Welty's Use of Mythology." *Shenandoah*, 6 (Spring 1955), 34–40.

Tillman L. Martin, "Eudora Welty: Master of the American Short Story." *Southern Observer*, 3 (September 1955), 261–266.

Donald Heiney, "Eudora Welty." In his *Recent American Literature*. Great Neck, N.Y.: Barron's Educational Series, 1958, pp. 255–261.

William M. Jones, "Name and Symbol in the Prose of Eudora Welty." *Southern Folklore Quarterly*, 22 (December 1958), 173–185.

———, "Growth of a Symbol: The Sun in Lawrence and Eudora Welty." *University of Kansas City Review*, 26 (October 1959), 68–73.

Lorenza Galli. "La Narrativa Di Eudora Welty." *Studi Americani (Roma)*, 5 (1959), 281–300.

Ruth M. Vande Kieft, "The Mysteries of Eudora Welty." *Georgia Review*, 15 (Fall 1961), 343–357. Revised extensively, this appears as Chapter two of her *Eudora Welty*.

Mary Catherine Buswell, "The Love Relationships of Women in the Fiction of Eudora Welty." *West Virginia University Bulletin Philological Papers*, 13 (December 1961), 94–106.

254   Noel Polk

Alun R. Jones, "The World of Love: The Fiction of Eudora Welty." In *The Creative Present*, ed. Nona Balakian and Charles Simmons. New York: Doubleday, 1963, pp. 175–192.

Chester Eisinger, "Eudora Welty and the Triumph of the Imagination." In his *Fiction of the Forties*. Chicago: University of Chicago Press, 1963, pp. 258–283.

William Peden, [Commentary]. In his *The American Short Story*. Boston: Houghton Mifflin, 1964, pp. 164–168.

Marvin Felheim, "Eudora Welty and Carson McCullers." In *Contemporary American Novelists*, ed. Harry T. Moore. Carbondale: Southern Illinois University Press, 1964, pp. 41–53.

Ruth M. Vande Kieft, "Introduction." In *Thirteen Stories by Eudora Welty*, selected by Ruth M. Vande Kieft. New York: Harcourt, Brace & World (Harvest), 1965, pp. 3–14.

Louise Y. Gossett, "Violence as Revelation: Eudora Welty." In her *Violence in Recent Southern Fiction*. Durham: Duke University Press, 1965, pp. 98–117.

Frederick J. Hoffman, "Eudora Welty and Carson McCullers." In his *The Art of Southern Fiction: A Study of Some Modern Novelists*. Carbondale: Southern Illinois University Press, 1967, pp. 51–73.

Frank E. Smith and Aubrey Warren, "Eudora Welty." In their *Mississippians All*. New Orleans: Pelican Publishing House, 1968, pp. 27–34.

M. Thomas Inge, "Eudora Welty as Poet." *Southern Humanities Review*, 2 (Summer 1968), 310–311. Reprints Miss Welty's poem 'There.'

Nash K. Burger, "Eudora Welty's Jackson." *Shenandoah*, 20 (Spring 1969), 8–15.

Malcolm Cowley, [Tribute]. *Shenandoah*, 20 (Spring 1969), 36.

Martha Graham, [Tribute]. *Shenandoah*, 20 (Spring 1969), 36.

Joyce Carol Oates, "The Art of Eudora Welty." *Shenandoah*, 20 (Spring 1969), 54–57.

Walker Percy, "Eudora Welty in Jackson." *Shenandoah*, 20 (Spring 1969), 37–38.

Diarmuid Russell, "First Work." *Shenandoah*, 20 (Spring 1969), 16–19.

Allen Tate, [Tribute]. *Shenandoah*, 20 (Spring 1969), 39.

Robert Penn Warren, "Out of the Strong." *Shenandoah*, 20 (Spring 1969), 38–39.

Kenneth Graham, "La Double Vision d'Eudora Welty." *La Nouvelle Revue Française*, 17 (November 1969), 744–753.

Richard H. Rupp, "Eudora Welty: A Continual Feast." In his *Celebration in Postwar American Fiction 1945–1967*. Coral Gables, Fla.: University of Miami Press, 1970, pp. 59–75.

Anne M. Masserand, "Eudora Welty's Travellers: The Journey Theme in Her Short Stories." *Southern Literary Journal*, 3 (Spring 1971), 39–48.

Merrill Maguire Skaggs, *The Folk of Southern Fiction*. Athens: University of Georgia Press, 1972, pp. 234–248.

Elmo Howell, "Eudora Welty and the Use of Place in Southern Fiction." *Arizona Quarterly*, 28 (Autumn 1972), 248–256.

Jack D. Wages, "Names in Eudora Welty's Fiction: An Onomatological Prolegomenon." In *Love and Wrestling, Butch and O. K.*, ed. Fred Tarpley. Publication 2, South Central Names Institute. Commerce, Texas: Names Institute Press, 1973, pp. 65–72.

Charles East, "The Search for Eudora Welty." *Mississippi Quarterly*, 26 (Fall 1973), 477–482.

Ruth M. Vande Kieft, "The Vision of Eudora Welty." *Mississippi Quarterly*, 26 (Fall 1973), 517–542.

Thomas H. Landess, "The Function of Taste in the Fiction of Eudora Welty." *Mississippi Quarterly*, 26 (Fall 1973), 543–557.

Nell Ann Pickett, "Colloquialism as a Style in the First-Person-Narrator Fiction of Eudora Welty." *Mississippi Quarterly*, 26 (Fall 1973), 559–576.

Lewis P. Simpson, "An Introductory Note." *Mississippi Quarterly*, 26 (Fall 1973), 475–476.

D. Studies of Individual Works

1. *A Curtain of Green*

General

Katherine Anne Porter, "Introduction" to *A Curtain of Green*. Garden City, New York: Doubleday, Doran, 1941, pp. ix–xix.

"New Writer." *Time*, 38 (24 November 1941), 110–111.

Dale Mullen, "Some Notes on the Stories of Eudora Welty." *Mississippi Literary Review*, 1 (November 1941), 21–24.

Kay Boyle, "Full-Length Portrait." *New Republic*, 24 November 1941, p. 707.

Louise Bogan, "The Gothic South." *Nation*, 153 (6 December 1941), 572.

Frederick Brantley, "*A Curtain of Green*: Themes and Attitudes." *American Prefaces*, 7 (Spring 1942), 241–251.

Robert J. Griffin, "Eudora Welty's *A Curtain of Green*." In *The Forties: Fiction, Poetry, Drama*, ed. Warren French. Deland, Florida: Everett/Edwards, 1969, pp. 101–110.

Raymond Tarbox, "Eudora Welty's Fiction: The Salvation Theme." *American Imago*, 29 (Spring 1972), 70–91.

"Lily Daw and the Three Ladies"

Robert Y. Drake, Jr., "Comments on Two Eudora Welty Stories." *Mississippi Quarterly*, 13 (Summer 1960), 123–131.

"A Piece of News"

Cleanth Brooks and Robert Penn Warren, "Interpretation." In *Understanding Fiction*, ed. Cleanth Brooks and Robert Penn Warren. New York: Appleton-Century-Crofts, 1943, pp. 143–146. Revised somewhat extensively for republication in the Second Edition of *Understanding Fiction* (New York, 1959), pp. 128–133; revision also reprinted in Brooks and Warren, eds., *The Scope of Fiction*. New York: Appleton-Century-Crofts, 1960, pp. 108–113.

W. U. McDonald, Jr., "Eudora Welty's Revisions of 'A Piece of News'." *Studies in Short Fiction*, 7 (Spring 1970), 232–247.

"Petrified Man"

William M. Jones, "Welty's 'Petrified Man.'" *Explicator*, 15 (January 1957), item 21.

Donald A. Ringe, "Welty's 'Petrified Man.'" *Explicator*, 18 (February 1960), item 32.

Robert W. Cochran, "Welty's 'Petrified Man.'" *Explicator*, 27 (December 1968), item 25.

W. Keith Kraus, "Welty's 'Petrified Man.'" *Explicator*, 29 (April 1971), item 63.

Lee J. Richmond, "Symbol and Theme In Eudora Welty's 'Petrified Man.'" *English Journal*, 60 (December 1971), 1201–1203.

"The Key"

Wendell V. Harris, "Welty's 'The Key.'" *Explicator*, 17 (June 1959), item 61.

Kurt Opitz, "Eudora Welty: The Order of a Captive Soul." *Critique*, 7 (Winter 1964–65), 79–91.

"Keela, the Outcast Indian Maiden"

W. U. McDonald, Jr., "Welty's 'Keela': Irony, Ambiguity, and the Ancient Mariner." *Studies in Short Fiction*, 1 (Fall 1963), 59–61.

John Edward Hardy, "Eudora Welty's Negroes." In *Images of the Negro in American Literature*, ed. Seymour L. Gross and John Edward Hardy. Chicago: University of Chicago Press, 1966, pp. 221–232.

Ronald E. McFarland, "Vision and Perception in the Works of Eudora Welty." *Markham Review*, 2 (February 1971), 94–99.

Charles E. May, "*Le Roi Méhaigné* in Welty's 'Keela, The Outcast

Indian Maiden.'" *Modern Fiction Studies*, 18 (Winter 1972–73), 559–566.

"The Whistle"

W. U. McDonald, Jr., "Welty's 'Social Consciousness': Revisions of 'The Whistle.'" *Modern Fiction Studies*, 16 (Summer 1970), 193–198.

"The Hitch-Hikers"

John Edward Hardy, "The Achievement of Eudora Welty." *Southern Humanities Review*, 2 (Summer 1968), 269–278.

"A Memory"

Ruth Ann Lief, "A Progression of Answers." *Studies in Short Fiction*, 2 (Summer 1965), 343–350.

"Clytie"

Albert J. Griffith, "The Numinous Vision: Eudora Welty's 'Clytie.'" *Studies in Short Fiction*, 4 (Fall 1966), 80–82.

"Old Mr. Marblehall"

Cleanth Brooks and Robert Penn Warren, "Interpretation." In *Understanding Fiction*, ed. Cleanth Brooks and Robert Penn Warren. New York: Appleton-Century-Crofts, 1943, pp. 479–480.

Charles E. Davis, "Welty's 'Old Mr. Marblehall.'" *Explicator*, 30 (January 1972), item 40.

Robert Detweiler, "Eudora Welty's Blazing Butterfly: The Dynamics of Response." *Language and Style*, 6 (Winter 1973), 58–71.

"Flowers for Marjorie"

John Edward Hardy, "The Achievement of Eudora Welty." *Southern Humanities Review*, 2 (Summer 1968), 269–278.

"A Visit of Charity"

Lodwick Hartley, "Proserpina and the Old Ladies." *Modern Fiction Studies*, 3 (Spring 1957), 350–354.

Melvin Delmar Palmer, "Welty's 'A Visit of Charity.'" *Explicator*, 22 (May 1964), item 69.

Jo Allen Bradham, "'A Visit of Charity': Menippean Satire." *Studies in Short Fiction*, 1 (Summer 1964), 258–263.

William B. Toole, III, "The Texture of 'A Visit of Charity.'" *Mississippi Quarterly*, 20 (Winter 1966–67), 43–46.

Charles E. May, "The Difficulty of Loving in 'A Visit of Charity.'" *Studies in Short Fiction*, 6 (Spring 1969), 338–341.

"Death of a Traveling Salesman"

Eleanor Clark, "Old Glamour, New Gloom." *Partisan Review*, 16 (June 1949), 631–636.

Mark Schorer, "Comment." In *The Story: A Critical Anthology*, ed. Mark Schorer. Englewood Cliffs, N.J.: Prentice-Hall, 1950, pp. 354–357.

William M. Jones, "Eudora Welty's Use of Myth in 'Death of a Traveling Salesman.'" *Journal of American Folklore*, 73 (January–March 1960), 18–23.

John B. Vickery, "William Blake and Eudora Welty's 'Death of a Salesman.'" *Modern Language Notes*, 76 (November 1961), 625–632.

Albert J. Griffith, "Welty's 'Death of a Traveling Salesman.'" *Explicator*, 20 (January 1962), item 38.

Robert B. Heilman, "Salesmen's Deaths: Documentary and Myth." *Shenandoah*, 20 (Spring 1969), 20–28.

Ronald E. McFarland, "Vision and Perception in the Works of Eudora Welty." *Markham Review*, 2 (February 1971), 94–99.

"Powerhouse"

Ray B. West, Jr., and Robert Wooster Stallman, "Analysis: Form Through Theme." In *The Art of Modern Fiction*, ed. Ray B. West, Jr., and Robert Wooster Stallman. New York: Rinehart, 1949, pp. 403–408.

Ray B. West, Jr., "Three Methods of Modern Fiction: Ernest Hemingway, Thomas Mann, Eudora Welty." *College English*, 12 (January 1951), 193–203.

Alfred Appel, Jr., "Powerhouse's Blues." *Studies in Short Fiction*, 2 (Spring 1965), 221–234.

John Edward Hardy, "Eudora Welty's Negroes." In *Images of the Negro in American Literature*, ed. Seymour L. Gross and John Edward Hardy. Chicago: University of Chicago Press, 1966, pp. 221–232.

Benjamin W. Griffith, "'Powerhouse' As A Showcase of Eudora Welty's Methods and Themes." *Mississippi Quarterly*, 19 (Spring 1966), 79–84.

Smith Kirkpatrick, "The Anointed Powerhouse." *Sewanee Review*, 77 (January–March 1969), 94–108.

"A Worn Path"

William M. Jones, "Welty's 'A Worn Path.'" *Explicator*, 15 (June 1957), item 57.

Neil D. Isaacs, "Life for Phoenix." *Sewanee Review*, 71 (January–March 1963), 75–81.

Saralyn R. Daly, " 'A Worn Path' Retrod." *Studies in Short Fiction*, 1 (Winter 1964), 133–139.

Sara Trefman, "Welty's 'A Worn Path.' " *Explicator*, 24 (February 1966), item 56.

John E. Hardy, "Eudora Welty's Negroes." In *Images of the Negro in American Literature*, ed. Seymour L. Gross and John Edward Hardy. Chicago: University of Chicago Press, 1966, pp. 221–232.

Eudora Welty, ["Comment"]. In *This Is My Best*, ed. Whit Burnett. Garden City, N.Y.: Doubleday, 1970, p. 532.

Elmo Howell, "Eudora Welty's Negroes: A Note on 'A Worn Path.' " *Xavier University Studies*, 9 (Spring 1970), 28–32.

Grant Moss, Jr., " 'A Worn Path' Retrod." *College Language Association Journal* (Morgan State College), 15 (December 1971), 144–152.

2. *The Robber Bridegroom*

John Peale Bishop, "The Violent Country." In *The Collected Essays of John Peale Bishop*, ed. Edmund Wilson. New York: Charles Scribner's, 1948, pp. 257–259.

Ashley Brown, "Eudora Welty and the Mythos of Summer." *Shenandoah*, 20 (Spring 1969), 29–35.

Gordon E. Slethaug, "Initiation in Eudora Welty's *The Robber Bridegroom*." *Southern Humanities Review*, 7 (Winter 1973), 77–87.

Charles C. Clark, "*The Robber Bridegroom*: Realism and Fantasy on the Natchez Trace." *Mississippi Quarterly*, 26 (Fall 1973), 625–638.

3. *The Wide Net*

General

Diana Trilling, "Fiction in Review." *Nation*, 157 (2 October 1943), 386–387.

Isaac Rosenfeld, "Consolations of Poetry." *New Republic*, 109 (18 October 1943), 525–526.

"First Love"

Ronald E. McFarland, "Vision and Perception in the Works of Eudora Welty." *Markham Review*, 2 (February 1971), 94–99.

"A Still Moment"

Daniel Curley, "Eudora Welty and the Quondam Obstruction." *Studies in Short Fiction*, 5 (Spring 1968), 209–224.

"Asphodel"

Audrey Hodgins, "The Narrator as Ironic Device in a Short Story of Eudora Welty." *Twentieth Century Literature*, 1 (January 1956), 215–219.

"Livvie"

Elton F. Henley, "Confinement-Escape Symbolism in Eudora Welty's 'Livvie.'" *Iowa English Yearbook*, No. 10 (Fall 1965), 60–63.

Julian Smith, "'Livvie'—Eudora Welty's Song of Solomon." *Studies in Short Fiction*, 5 (Fall 1967), 73–74.

4. *Delta Wedding*

"Cloud-Cuckoo Symphony." *Time*, 47 (22 April 1946), 104, 106, 108.

Isaac Rosenfeld, "Double Standard." *New Republic*, 114 (29 April 1946), 633–634.

Diana Trilling, "Fiction in Review." *Nation*, 11 May 1946, p. 578.

John Crowe Ransom, "Delta Fiction." *Kenyon Review*, 8 (Summer 1946), 503–507.

John Edward Hardy, "*Delta Wedding* as Region and Symbol." *Sewanee Review*, 60 (July–September 1952), 397–417.

Neil D. Isaacs, "Four Notes on Eudora Welty." *Notes on Mississippi Writers*, 2 (Fall 1969), 42–54.

Peggy Prenshaw, "Cultural Patterns in Eudora Welty's *Delta Wedding* and 'The Demonstrators.'" *Notes on Mississippi Writers*, 3 (Fall 1970), 51–70.

Elmo Howell, "Eudora Welty's Comedy of Manners." *South Atlantic Quarterly*, 69 (Autumn 1970), 469–479.

———, "Eudora Welty and the Poetry of Names: A Note on *Delta Wedding*." In *Love and Wrestling, Butch and O.K.*, ed. Fred Tarpley. Publication 2, South Central Names Institute. Commerce, Texas: Names Institute Press, 1973, pp. 73–78.

5. *The Golden Apples*

Margaret Marshall, "Notes By the Way." *Nation*, 169 (10 September 1949), 256.

H. C. Morris, "Zeus and the Golden Apples: Eudora Welty." *Perspective*, 5 (Autumn 1952), 190–199.

Elizabeth Bowen, "The Golden Apples." In her *Seven Winters: Memories of a Dublin Childhood & Afterthoughts: Pieces on Writing*. New York: Alfred A. Knopf, 1962, pp. 215–218.

Wendell V. Harris, "The Thematic Unity of Welty's *The Golden*

Apples." *Texas Studies in Literature and Language*, 6 (Spring 1964), 92–95.

Louise Blackwell, "Eudora Welty: Proverbs and Proverbial Phrases in *The Golden Apples*." *Southern Folklore Quarterly*, 30 (December 1966), 332–341.

William M. Jones, "The Plot as Search." *Studies in Short Fiction*, 5 (Fall 1967), 37–43.

Neil D. Isaacs, "Four Notes on Eudora Welty." *Notes on Mississippi Writers*, 2 (Fall 1969), 42–54.

Robert S. Pawlowski, "The Process of Observation: *Winesburg, Ohio*, and *The Golden Apples*." *University Review*, 37 (June 1971), 292–298.

Franklin D. Carson, "'The Song of Wandering Aengus': Allusions in Eudora Welty's *The Golden Apples*." *Notes on Mississippi Writers*, 6 (Spring 1973), 14–17.

Thomas L. McHaney, "Eudora Welty and the Multitudinous Golden Apples." *Mississippi Quarterly*, 26 (Fall 1973), 589–624.

"Music From Spain"

Kurt Opitz, "Eudora Welty: The Order of a Captive Soul." *Critique*, 7 (Winter 1964–65), 79–91.

6. *The Ponder Heart*

V. S. Pritchett, "Bossy Edna Earle Had a Word for Everything." *New York Times Book Review*, 10 January 1954, p. 5.

"Southern Legend." *Newsweek*, 43 (11 January 1954), 82–83.

William Peden, "A Trial With No Verdict." *Saturday Review*, 37 (16 January 1954), 14.

Edwin Kennebeck, "People of Clay." *Commonweal*, 59 (22 January 1954), 410–411.

Warren French, "A Note on Eudora Welty's *The Ponder Heart*." *College English*, 15 (May 1954), 474.

Robert Y. Drake, Jr., "The Reasons of the Heart." *Georgia Review*, 11 (Winter 1957), 420–426.

Winifred Dusenbury, "*Baby Doll* and *The Ponder Heart*." *Modern Drama*, 3 (February 1961), 393–395.

Robert B. Holland, "Dialogue as a Reflection of Place in *The Ponder Heart*." *American Literature*, 35 (November 1963), 352–358.

Kurt Opitz, "Eudora Welty: The Order of a Captive Soul." *Critique*, 7 (Winter 1964–65), 79–91.

Louise Blackwell, "Eudora Welty and the Rubber Fence Family." *Kansas Magazine*, 30 (1965), 73–76.

Neil D. Isaacs, "Four Notes on Eudora Welty." *Notes on Mississippi Writers*, 2 (Fall 1969), 42–54.

7. *The Bride of the Innisfallen*

General

William Peden, "The Incomparable Welty." *Saturday Review*, 38 (9 April 1955), 18.

Walter Elder, "That Region." *Kenyon Review*, 17 (Autumn 1955), 661–670.

Louis D. Rubin, Jr., "Two Ladies of the South." *Sewanee Review*, 63 (Autumn 1955), 671–681.

Thomas H. Carter, "Rhetoric and Southern Landscapes." *Accent*, 15 (Autumn 1955), 293–297.

"No Place for You, My Love"

Eudora Welty, "How I Write." *Virginia Quarterly Review*, 31 (Winter 1955), 240–251.

Alun R. Jones, "A Frail Travelling Coincidence: Three Later Stories of Eudora Welty." *Shenandoah*, 20 (Spring 1969), 40–53.

"The Bride of the Innisfallen"
"Going to Naples"

Alun R. Jones, "A Frail Travelling Coincidence: Three Later Stories of Eudora Welty." *Shenandoah*, 20 (Spring 1969), 40–53.

"The Burning"

William H. McBurney, "Welty's 'The Burning.'" *Explicator*, 16 (November 1957), item 9.

Elmo Howell, "Eudora Welty's Civil War Story." *Notes on Mississippi Writers*, 2 (Spring 1969), 3–12.

"Kin"

Neil D. Isaacs, "Four Notes on Eudora Welty." *Notes on Mississippi Writers*, 2 (Fall 1969), 42–54.

8. *Losing Battles*

John W. Aldridge, "Eudora Welty: Metamorphosis of a Southern Lady Writer." *Saturday Review*, 11 April 1970, pp. 21–23, 35–36. Reprinted, unchanged, as "The Emergence of Eudora Welty" in his *The Devil in the Fire*. New York: A Harper's Magazine Press Book, 1972, pp. 249–256.

James Boatwright, "I Call This a Reunion to Remember, All!" *New York Times Book Review*, 12 April 1970, pp. 1, 32–34.

Joyce Carol Oates, "Eudora's Web." *Atlantic*, 225 (April 1970), 118–120, 122.

Jack Kroll, "The Lesson of the Master." *Newsweek*, 13 April 1970, pp. 90–91.

"Shangri-La South." *Time*, 4 May 1970, p. 100.

Jonathan Yardley, "The Last Good One?" *New Republic*, 162 (9 May 1970), 33–36.

Louis D. Rubin, Jr., "Everything Brought Out In The Open: Eudora Welty's *Losing Battles*." *Hollins Critic*, 7 (June 1970), 1–12.

Lewis Simpson, "The Chosen People." *Southern Review*, 6 (July 1970), xvii–xxii.

Louise Y. Gossett, "Eudora Welty's New Novel: The Comedy of Loss." *Southern Literary Journal*, 3 (Fall 1970), 122–137.

Thomas H. Landess, "More Trouble in Mississippi: Family Vs. Antifamily in Miss Welty's *Losing Battles*." *Sewanee Review*, 79 (October–December 1971), 626–634.

M. E. Bradford, "Looking Down From a High Place: The Serenity of Miss Welty's *Losing Battles*." *Recherches Anglaises et Américaines*, 4 (1971), 92–97.

Reynolds Price, "Frightening Gift." In his *Things Themselves: Essays and Scenes*. New York: Atheneum, 1972, pp. 139–142.

Raymond Tarbox, "Eudora Welty's Fiction: The Salvation Theme." *American Imago*, 29 (Spring 1972), 70–91.

Robert Griffin, "*Losing Battles* (Eudora Welty)." Deland, Florida: Everette/Edwards Cassette Tape Lecture No. 92.

Carol A. Moore, "The Insulation of Illusion and *Losing Battles*." *Mississippi Quarterly*, 26 (Fall 1973), 651–658.

Michael Kreyling, "Myth and History: The Foes of *Losing Battles*." *Mississippi Quarterly*, 26 (Fall 1973), 639–649.

9. *One Time, One Place*

Madison Jones, "One Time, One Place." *New York Times Book Review*, 21 November 1971, pp. 60, 62, 64.

Brendan Gill, "Books: The Inconstant Past." *New Yorker*, 47 (25 December 1971), 66–68.

Daniel Curley, "A Time Exposure." *Notes on Mississippi Writers*, 5 (Spring 1972), 11–14.

M. E. Bradford, "Miss Eudora's Picture Book." *Mississippi Quarterly*, 26 (Fall 1973), 659–662.

10. *The Optimist's Daughter*

Reynolds Price, "The Onlooker, Smiling: An Early Reading of *The Optimist's Daughter*." *Shenandoah*, 20 (Spring 1969), 58–73.

Reprinted, with added "Postscript" in his *Things Themselves: Essays and Scenes.* New York: Atheneum, 1972, pp. 114–138.

Howard Moss, "Eudora Welty's New Novel about Death and Class." *New York Times Book Review,* 21 May 1972, pp. 1, 18.

James Boatwright, "The Continuity of Love." *New Republic,* 166 (10 June 1972), 24–25.

Guy Davenport, "Primal Visions." *National Review,* 23 June 1972, p. 697.

Cleanth Brooks, "The Past Reexamined: *The Optimist's Daughter.*" *Mississippi Quarterly,* 26 (Fall 1973), 577–587.

11. Uncollected Stories

"The Demonstrators"

John Edward Hardy, "The Achievement of Eudora Welty." *Southern Humanities Review,* 2 (Summer 1968), 269–278.

Ruth M. Vande Kieft, "Demonstrators in a Stricken Land." In *The Process of Fiction,* ed. Barbara McKenzie. New York: Harcourt, Brace & World, 1969, pp. 342–349.

Peggy Prenshaw, "Cultural Patterns in Eudora Welty's *Delta Wedding* and 'The Demonstrators.'" *Notes on Mississippi Writers,* 3 (Fall 1970), 51–70.

"Where Is the Voice Coming From?"

John Kuehl, "Commentary." In *Write and Rewrite,* ed. John Kuehl. New York: Meredith Press, 1967, pp. 16–18.

E. Dissertations

Kurt Opitz, "Neoromantic Als Gestalterin der prosa Eudora Welty." University of Berlin—Freiburg, 1957.

Albert J. Griffith, "Eudora Welty's Fiction." University of Texas, 1959.

Gordon Raymond Folsom, "Form and Substance in Eudora Welty." University of Wisconsin, 1960.

Sarah Allman Rouse, "Place and People in Eudora Welty's Fiction: A Portrait of the Deep South." Florida State University, 1962.

Barbara McKenzie, "Region and World: The Achievement of American Women Writers of Fiction Since 1930." Florida State University, 1963.

Alfred Appel, Jr., "The Short Stories of Eudora Welty." Columbia University, 1963.

Rebecca Smith Wild, "Studies in the Shorter Fiction of Eudora Welty and Elizabeth Bowen." University of Michigan, 1965.

Mark Edward Blankenstein, "The Southern Tradition in Minor Mississippi Writers Since 1920." University of Illinois, 1965.

Robert Max Rechnitz, "Perception, Identity and the Grotesque: A Study of Three Southern Writers." University of Colorado, 1967.

Charles Edward Davis, "Eudora Welty's Art of Naming." Emory University, 1969.

Clyde Marshall Vinson, "Imagery in the Short Stories of Eudora Welty." Northwestern University, 1970.

Zelma Turner Howard, "Meaning Through Rhetoric In Eudora Welty's *A Curtain of Green*, *The Wide Net*, and *The Golden Apples*." University of Northern Colorado, 1970.

Peggy Joyce Whitman Prenshaw, "A Study of Setting in the Fiction of Eudora Welty." University of Texas, 1970.

Carol Porter Smith, "The Journey Motif in the Collected Works of Eudora Welty." University of Maryland, 1971.

Larry L. Finger, "Elements of the Grotesque in Selected Works of Welty, Capote, McCullers, and O'Connor." George Peabody College, 1972.

Victor H. Thompson, " 'Life's Impact is Oblique': A Study of Obscurantism in the Writings of Eudora Welty." Rutgers University, 1972.

William Porter King, "A Thematic Study of the Fiction of Eudora Welty." George Peabody College, 1972.

PEARL AMELIA MCHANEY

A Eudora Welty Checklist, 1973–1986

The following checklist is designed to supplement "A Eudora Welty Checklist" by Noel Polk published in the first special Welty issue of the *Mississippi Quarterly*, 26 (Fall 1973), 663–693. In the primary bibliography I have not included reprints or foreign editions of early novels, reprintings of Welty's essays or stories, or Welty's blurbs on other authors. In the secondary bibliography, I have attempted to list any item that seemed to make a significant contribution to Welty scholarship, but the checklist does not include mentions, brief analyses, newspaper clippings, or master's theses. The major sources of bibliographic information used to compile this checklist are the *Eudora Welty Newsletter (EuWN)*, the *Mississippi Quarterly* annual Checklist of Scholarship on Southern Literature, the *MLA* bibliographies, "Eudora Welty: A Bibliographical Checklist," by Noel Polk in *American Book Collector*, and "Eudora Welty," by Peggy Whitman Prenshaw in *American Women Writers: Bibliographical Essays* (the latter two are listed below). In all but a few entries (identified as "cited"), I have checked the information firsthand. It is my intention that Noel Polk's 1973 checklist and this supplement will provide a correct and useful bibliography for Welty scholars.

I wish to thank Helen Turt Tiegreen and Georges Pilard for their time and suggestions, and I am grateful for the guidance and assistance of Noel Polk, W. U. McDonald,

Jr., and Thomas McHaney. Their contributions to the fields of Welty scholarship and bibliographical studies are invaluable.

I. Primary

A. Separate Publications (Books and Pamphlets)

1974   *A Pageant of Birds.* New York: Albondocani Press. Limited, signed edition of 300 numbered and 26 lettered copies.

1975   *Fairy Tale of the Natchez Trace.* Jackson: Mississippi Historical Society. Limited edition of 1000 copies.

1977   *Welty: An Exhibition at the Mississippi State Historical Museum, Jackson, Mississippi. Photographs and Text by Eudora Welty.* Selected and edited by Patti Carr Black. Jackson: Mississippi Department of Archives and History.

1978   *The Eye of the Story: Selected Essays and Reviews.* New York: Random House. Also published in a limited edition of 300 signed copies.

CONTENTS: I. ON WRITERS: THE RADIANCE OF JANE AUSTEN—HENRY GREEN: NOVELIST OF THE IMAGINATION—KATHERINE ANNE PORTER: THE EYE OF THE STORY—THE HOUSE OF WILLA CATHER—REALITY IN CHEKHOV'S STORIES—II. ON WRITING: LOOKING AT SHORT STORIES—WRITING AND ANALYZING A STORY—PLACE IN FICTION—WORDS INTO FICTION—MUST THE NOVELIST CRUSADE?—"IS PHOENIX JACKSON'S GRANDSON REALLY DEAD?"—SOME NOTES ON TIME IN FICTION—III. REVIEWS: THE WESTERN JOURNALS OF WASHINGTON IRVING (ed. and annotated by John Francis McDermott)—NAMES ON THE LAND (George R. Stewart)—GRANITE AND RAINBOW (Virginia Woolf)—THE LETTERS OF VIRGINIA WOOLF, VOLUME II (ed. Nigel Nicolson and Joann Trautmann)—CHARLOTTE'S WEB (E. B. White)—INTRUDER IN THE DUST (William Faulkner)—SELECTED LETTERS OF WILLIAM FAULKNER (ed. Joseph Blotner)—MARIANNE THORNTON (E. M. Forster)—THE LIFE TO COME, AND OTHER STORIES (E. M. Forster)—THE MOST OF S. J. PERELMAN; BABY, IT'S COLD INSIDE (S. J. Perelman)—THE SADDEST STORY: A BIOGRAPHY OF FORD MADOX FORD (Arthur Mizener)—THE UNDERGROUND MAN (Ross Macdonald)—LAST TALES (Isak Dinesen)—THE COCKATOOS (Patrick White)—PICTURES AND CONVERSATIONS (Elizabeth Bowen)—IV. PERSONAL AND

OCCASIONAL PIECES: A SWEET DEVOURING—SOME NOTES
ON RIVER COUNTRY—FAIRY TALE OF THE NATCHEZ
TRACE—A PAGEANT OF BIRDS—THE FLAVOR OF JACKSON—
THE LITTLE STORE—IDA M'TOY—ONE TIME, ONE PLACE.
New York: Vintage, 1979.

1979 *Ida M'Toy.* Ed. with foreword by Charles Shattuck,
George Scouffas and Daniel Curley. Urbana: University
of Illinois Press. Limited, signed, numbered edition of
350 copies.

1979 *Women!! Make Turban in Own Home!* Winston-Salem, NC:
Palaemon Press Limited. A limited, signed, numbered
edition of 235 copies.

1980 *Acrobats in the Park.* Northridge, CA: Lord John Press.
Introduction by Eudora Welty. 300 numbered copies
signed by Welty. Deluxe edition of 100 copies specially
bound, signed by Welty. [See listing under B.1.]

1980 *Bye-Bye Brevoort.* Jackson: New Stage Theatre. First limited, signed edition of 400 copies. Also a first limited,
signed patron's issue of 50 numbered copies and a first
limited, signed, lettered issue of 26 copies.

1980 *Moon Lake and Other Stories.* Illustrated by Charles Reid,
drawing of Welty by Gordon Fisher. Franklin Center,
PA: The Franklin Library. Limited edition.
CONTENTS: MOON LAKE—OLD MR. MARBLEHALL—THE
WIDE NET—A WORN PATH—KEELA, THE OUTCAST INDIAN
MAIDEN—PETRIFIED MAN—A STILL MOMENT—LILY DAW
AND   THE   THREE   LADIES—THE   HITCH-HIKERS—
POWERHOUSE—WHY I LIVE AT THE P. O.—LIVVIE—THE
BRIDE OF THE INNISFALLEN.

1980 *The Collected Stories of Eudora Welty.* Franklin Center, PA:
The Franklin Library. First limited edition.
CONTENTS: ALL STORIES IN *A Curtain of Green and Other
Stories*—*The Wide Net and Other Stories*—*The Golden Ap-
ples*—*The Bride of the Innisfallen and Other Stories*—AND
UNCOLLECTED STORIES: WHERE IS THE VOICE COMING
FROM?—THE DEMONSTRATORS.
New York and London: Harcourt Brace Jovanovich, 1980.
Also published in a limited, signed edition of 500 cop-
ies. Contents: same as above.
London: Marion Boyars, 1981. Reprint of Harcourt Brace
Jovanovich edition.
Harmondsworth, Middlesex, England: Penguin Books,
Ltd., 1983. Reduced facsimile of Harcourt Brace
Jovanovich edition.
New York: Harcourt Brace Jovanovich (Harvest), 1982.

Reduced facsimile of Harcourt Brace Jovanovich edition.

1980 *Twenty Photographs.* Winston-Salem, NC: Palaemon Press Limited. With "A Word on the Photographs" by Welty. Limited to 90 copies. Oversized and boxed.

1980 *White Fruitcake.* New York: Albondocani Press. 175 copies with Albondocani Press/Ampersand Books on the first page and 275 copies for author's private use.

1981 *Retreat.* Winston-Salem, NC: Palaemon Press Limited. Limited edition of 240 signed copies.

1984 *Eudora.* [Photographs and text]. Selected and edited by Patti Carr Black. Jackson: Mississippi Department of Archives and History.

1984 *Four Photographs by Eudora Welty.* Northridge, CA: Lord John Press. Limited signed edition of 150 copies.

1984 *One Writer's Beginnings.* Cambridge, MA: Harvard University Press. Also in a limited, signed issue of 350 copies.
London/Boston: Faber and Faber, 1985. First English issue; typesetting derived from first American edition.
New York: Warner Books, 1985. Second American edition, first printing, October 1985.
Boston: G. K. Hall, 1985. Large Print Edition.

1985 *In Black and White: Photographs of the 30's and 40's:* Introduction by Anne Tyler. Northridge, CA: Lord John Press. 400 copies numbered and signed by Tyler and Welty. 100 deluxe copies boxed, signed by Tyler and Welty.

1985 *The Little Store.* Newton, IA: Tamazunchale Press. Limited, numbered edition of 250 copies.

B. Contributions to Books and Periodicals

1. Fiction—Stories

"Acrobats in a Park." *Delta,* 5 (November 1977), 3–11.

"Acrobats in a Park." *The South Carolina Review,* 11 (November 1978), 26–33. [A later version than the story published in *Delta.*]

2. Non-fiction Prose: Essays, Sketches, Criticism

"Is Phoenix Jackson's Grandson Really Dead?" *Critical Inquiry,* 1 (September 1974), 219–221. Rpt. as "The Point of the Story," *New York Times Book Review,* 5 March 1978, pp. 3, 32–33. Rpt. under original title in *The Eye of the Story,* pp. 159–162.

"The House of Willa Cather." In *The Art of Willa Cather,* ed. Bernice Slote and Virginia Faulkner. Lincoln: University of Nebraska Press, 1974, pp. 3–20. Rpt. in *The Eye of the Story,* pp. 41–60. Rpt. in *Miracles of Perception: The Art of Willa Cather.*

Charlottesville: Alderman Library, University of Virginia, 1980, pp. 8–30.

"The Physical World of Willa Cather." *New York Times Book Review,* 27 January 1974, pp. 19, [20], [22]. [From a speech delivered at the University of Nebraska's celebration of Willa Cather's birth.]

"The Corner Store." *Esquire,* 84 (December 1975), 161, 212, 215. Rpt. as "The Neighborhood Grocery Store" in *Mom, the Flag, and Apple Pie: Great American Writers on Great American Things,* compiled by the editors of *Esquire.* Garden City, NY: Doubleday, 1976, pp. 189–197. Rpt. as "The Little Store" in *The Eye of the Story,* pp. 326–335.

"Afterword." In *The Great Big Doorstep: A Delta Comedy,* by E. P. O'Donnell. Carbondale, IL: Southern Illinois University Press, 1979, pp. 355–366.

"Chodorov and Fields in Mississippi." *Eudora Welty Newsletter,* 3 (April 1979), 4–6.

"Looking Back at the First Story." *Georgia Review,* 33 (Winter 1979), 751–755.

"Weddings and Funerals." *Silhouette* [Virginia Tech Student Literary Magazine], 2 (Spring 1979), 2–4.

"Foreword." In *The Stories of Elizabeth Spencer.* Garden City, NY: Doubleday, 1981, pp. [xvii]–xix.

"Foreword." In *To the Lighthouse* by Virginia Woolf. New York and London: Harcourt Brace Jovanovich, 1981, pp. vii–xii.

"Foreword." In *The Capers Papers* by Charlotte Capers. Jackson: University Press of Mississippi, 1982, pp. 9–11.

"Afterword." In *Novel Writing in Apocalyptic Time* by Walker Percy. New Orleans: Faust, 1986, pp. 25–28.

3. Book Reviews

"Africa and Paris and Russia." *New York Times Book Review,* 1 December 1974, pp. 5, 22, 28. Rev. three photography books: Leni Riefenstahl, *The Last of the Nuba;* Andre Kertesz, *J'Aime Paris;* Henri Cartier-Bresson, *About Russia.*

"Meditation on Seeing." *New York Times Book Review,* 24 March 1974, pp. 4–5. Rev. Annie Dillard, *Pilgrim at Tinker Creek.*

"As if She Had Been Invited into the World." *New York Times Book Review,* 5 January 1975, pp. 4, 20. Rev. Elizabeth Bowen, *Pictures and Conversations.* Rpt. in *The Eye of the Story,* pp. 269–276.

"Life's Possibilities are Those Very Things Once Felt as Dangers." *New York Times Book Review,* 19 January 1975, pp. 4, 37. Rev. Patrick White, *The Cockatoos.* Rpt. in *The Eye of the Story,* pp. 264–268.

"The Letters of Virginia Woolf." *New York Times Book Review,* 14

November 1976, pp. 1, 10, 12, 14, 16, 18, 20. Rev. *The Letters of Virginia Woolf,* Volume II. Rpt. in *The Eye of the Story,* pp. 193–202.

"Dateless Virtues." *New York Times Book Review,* 25 September 1977, pp. 7, 43. Rev. *Essays of E. B. White.*

"Post Mortem." *New York Times Book Review,* 21 August 1977, pp. 9, 29. Rev. Katherine Anne Porter, *The Never-Ending Wrong.*

"Selected Letters of William Faulkner." *New York Times Book Review,* 6 February 1977, pp. 1, 28–30. Rev. Joseph Blotner, ed., *Selected Letters of William Faulkner.*

"A Family of Emotions." *New York Times Book Review,* 25 June 1978, pp. 1, 39–40. Rev. V. S. Pritchett, *Selected Stories.*

"Seventy-Nine Stories to Read Again." *New York Times Book Review,* 8 February 1981, pp. 3, 22. Rev. *The Collected Stories of Elizabeth Bowen.*

"Innocence, Sin and J. D. Salinger." *New York Times Book Review,* 19 August 1984, pp. 3, 17. Rev. *The Oxford Companion to Children's Literature.*

4. Miscellaneous: Introductions, etc.

"The Feast Itself." *New York Times,* 5 December 1974, p. C 47. Reprinted in *Cultural Post,* Newsletter for NEA, March 1975. [Adaptation of speech for the Governor's Conference on the Arts, Jackson, Mississippi.]

"In Memorium [sic]." *Jackson Clarion-Ledger,* 27 July 1975, p. 14H.

"'The Surface of Earth.'" *New York Times Book Review,* 20 July 1975, pp. 24–25. [Letter regarding Richard Gilman's review of Reynolds Price's *The Surface of Earth, NYTBR,* 29 June 1975, pp. 1–2.]

[Brief paragraph comments on *The Letters of Virginia Woolf,* Volume II, *Mrs. Dalloway's Party: A Short Story Sequence,* by Virginia Woolf, and *Brewer's Dictionary of Phrase and Fable*]. *New York Times Book Review,* 5 December 1976, p. 102.

"Preface[:] A Note on the Cook." In *The Southern Hospitality Cookbook* by Winifred Green Cheney. Birmingham: Oxmoor House, Inc., 1976, p. vii.

[For Allen Tate]. *Quarterly Journal of the Library of Congress,* 36 (Fall 1979), 354.

"Mississippi Has Joined the World." *Capital Reporter,* 24 January 1980, p. 5. [Welty's comments on the eve of William Winter's inauguration as governor of Mississippi.]

[Reminiscence about *The Southern Review*]. In *The Southern Review, Original Series, 1935–1942: A Commemoration,* ed. Lewis P. Simpson and others. Baton Rouge: Louisiana State University Press, 1980, pp. 19–20.

"That Bright Face is Laughing." *Kenyon Review*, n.s. 5 (Spring 1983), 120–121. [A birthday message to Robert W. Daniel.]

[Letter to Isabella Davis]. Included on p. [2] of a 6″ × 4-⅜″ card folded into a four-page advertisement for *Rye Times: A Recollection*, by Isabella Davis, privately printed in Chapel Hill, NC, 1984.

"Jackson Communique." *New Yorker*, 60 (18 February 1985), 33. [Transcription of a telephone conversation regarding cold weather in Mississippi.]

5. Interviews

Bill Ferris, "A Visit with Eudora Welty." In *Images of the South: Visits with Eudora Welty and Walker Evans, Southern Folklore Reports, No. 1*. Memphis, TN: Center for Southern Folklore, 1977, pp. [11]–26. Rpt. in *Conversations with Eudora Welty*, ed. Peggy Whitman Prenshaw. Jackson: University Press of Mississippi, 1984, pp. 154–171.

Betty Hodges, "Good Writing to Eudora Welty Is 'Just a Matter of Honesty.'" *Durham [NC] Morning Herald*, 22 March 1977, p. 30.

Jane Reid Petty, "The Town and the Writer." *Jackson Magazine*, 1 (September 1977), 28–31, 34–35. Rpt. in *Conversations with Eudora Welty*, ed. Peggy Whitman Prenshaw. Jackson: University Press of Mississippi, 1984, pp. 200–210.

Gayle White, "Eudora Welty: 'The Central Thing is a Sense of Belonging.'" *The Atlanta Journal and Constitution*, 15 May 1977, pp. 6, 42–45.

Jean Todd Freeman, "An Interview with Eudora Welty." In *Conversations with Writers II*, ed. Richard Layman. Detroit: Gale Research, 1978, pp. 284–316. Rpt. in *Conversations with Eudora Welty*, ed. Peggy Whitman Prenshaw. Jackson: University Press of Mississippi, 1984, pp. 172–199.

Reynolds Price, "Eudora Welty in Type and Person." *New York Times Book Review*, 7 May 1978, pp. 7, 42–43. Rpt. in *Conversations with Eudora Welty*, ed. Peggy Whitman Prenshaw. Jackson: University Press of Mississippi, 1984, pp. 230–235.

Jeanne Rolfe Nostrandt, "Fiction as Event: An Interview with Eudora Welty." *New Orleans Review*, 7, No. 1 (1979), 26–34.

Tom Royals and John Little, "A Conversation with Eudora Welty." *Bloodroot*, No. 6 (Spring 1979), 2–12. Rpt. in *Conversations with Eudora Welty*, ed. Peggy Whitman Prenshaw. Jackson: University Press of Mississippi, 1984, pp. 252–267.

Jan Nordby Gretlund, "An Interview with Eudora Welty." *Southern Humanities Review*, 14 (Summer 1980), 193–208. Rpt. in

Conversations with Eudora Welty, ed. Peggy Whitman Prenshaw. Jackson: University Press of Mississippi, 1984, pp. 211–229.

Anne Tyler, "A Visit with Eudora Welty." *New York Times Book Review*, 2 November 1980, pp. 33–34.

Jo Brans, "Struggling against the Plaid: An Interview with Eudora Welty." *Southwest Review*, 66 (Summer 1981), 255–266. Rpt. in *Conversations with Eudora Welty*, ed. Peggy Whitman Prenshaw. Jackson: University Press of Mississippi, 1984, pp. 296–307.

Scot Haller, "Creators on Creating: Eudora Welty." *Saturday Review*, June 1981, pp. 42–46. Rpt. in *Conversations with Eudora Welty*, ed. Peggy Whitman Prenshaw. Jackson: University Press of Mississippi, 1984, pp. 308–315.

John Griffin Jones, "Eudora Welty." In *Mississippi Writers Talking*, *I*. Jackson: University Press of Mississippi, 1982, pp. 3–35. Rpt. in *Conversations with Eudora Welty*, ed. Peggy Whitman Prenshaw. Jackson: University Press of Mississippi, 1984, pp. 316–341.

Joanna Maclay, "A Conversation with Eudora Welty." *Literature in Performance*, 1 (April 1982), 68–82. [Cited in *EuWN*, 6 (Summer 1982).] Rpt. in *Conversations with Eudora Welty*, ed. Peggy Whitman Prenshaw. Jackson: University Press of Mississippi, 1984, pp. 268–286.

Shari Schneider, assisted by Robby Williams and Roy Berry, "A Conversation with Eudora Welty." *Purple and White* [student newspaper at Millsaps College, Jackson, MS], 2 March 1982, pp. 6–7. [Cited in *EuWN*, 6 (Summer 1982).]

Martha van Noppen, "A Conversation with Eudora Welty." *Southern Quarterly*, 20 (Summer 1982), 7–23. Rpt. in *Conversations with Eudora Welty*, ed. Peggy Whitman Prenshaw. Jackson: University Press of Mississippi, 1984, pp. 236–251.

Barbara Lazear Ascher, "A Visit with Eudora Welty." *Yale Review*, n.s. 74 (Autumn 1984), 147–153. Rpt. with minor changes as "The Color of Air: A Conversation with Eudora Welty," *Saturday Review*, November/December 1984, pp. 31–35, and with original title in *Playing After Dark*. New York: Doubleday, 1986, pp. 133–147.

Peggy Whitman Prenshaw, ed., *Conversations with Eudora Welty*. Jackson: University Press of Mississippi, 1984. Reprints 26 interviews, 1942–1982. Second American edition, New York: Washington Square Press, 1985.

Charles Ruas, "Eudora Welty." In *Conversations with American Writers*. New York: Alfred A. Knopf, 1985, pp. 3–17.

Albert J. Devlin and Peggy W. Prenshaw, "A Conversation with

Eudora Welty, Jackson, 1986." *Mississippi Quarterly*, 39 (Fall 1986), [431]–454; rpt. this collection.

II. Secondary

In the following selective checklist of secondary materials, I have included any work that appears to contribute significantly to the field of Welty scholarship. In addition to Noel Polk's 1973 checklist in the *Mississippi Quarterly*, two bibliographic sources have aided Welty scholars: Victor Thompson's *Eudora Welty: A Reference Guide* (1976) and the *Eudora Welty Newsletter*, edited by W. U. McDonald, Jr. (biannually 1977-date). See entries under Bibliographies (II. B). This checklist supplements these works; it includes scholarship published from 1973 to summer 1986. Although newspaper clippings and brief references in short notices and in general thematic or genre studies are not included, it is my hope that along with Noel Polk's 1973 checklist, this compilation will provide a reliable and up-to-date bibliography of Welty scholarship.

Entries are listed chronologically by year according to subject classification. Where an article discusses more than one work, it is listed under each appropriate category. Essays in collections of criticism are listed individually. Cross-references and annotations are used to identify or clarify entries.

A. Books, Collections, and Pamphlets

Gayle Goodin, *An Introduction to Eudora Welty's LOSING BATTLES.* Jackson: Mississippi Library Commission, 1976.

Michael Kreyling, *Eudora Welty.* Jackson: Mississippi Library Commission, 1976. [Incorporated into his 1980 full-length study.]

Robert L. Phillips, Jr., *An Introduction to Eudora Welty's THE GOLDEN APPLES.* Jackson: Mississippi Library Commission, 1977.

Peggy Whitman Prenshaw, *An Introduction to Eudora Welty's THE OPTIMIST'S DAUGHTER.* Jackson: Mississippi Library Commission, 1977.

John F. Desmond, ed., *A Still Moment: Essays on the Art of Eudora Welty*. Metuchen, NJ, and London: The Scarecrow Press, 1978. Ten essays.

Louis Dollarhide and Ann J. Abadie, eds., *Eudora Welty: A Form of Thanks*. Jackson: University Press of Mississippi, 1979. Seven essays. Proceedings of the 1977 University of Mississippi Welty Conference.

Peggy Whitman Prenshaw, ed., *Eudora Welty: Critical Essays*. Jackson: University Press of Mississippi, 1979. Twenty-seven essays.

Michael Kreyling, *Eudora Welty's Achievement of Order*. Baton Rouge: Louisiana State University Press, 1980.

Elizabeth Evans, *Eudora Welty*. New York: Frederick Ungar, 1981.

Jennifer Lynn Randisi, *A Tissue of Lies: Eudora Welty and The Southern Romance*. Washington, DC: University Press of America, 1982.

Albert J. Devlin, *Eudora Welty's Chronicle: A Story of Mississippi Life*. Jackson: University Press of Mississippi, 1983.

W. U. McDonald, Jr., *The Short Stories of Eudora Welty: The Evolution of Printed Texts*. Toledo: William S. Carlson Library, 1983. [Catalogue of an exhibit at The Ward M. Canaday Center of Carlson Library, The University of Toledo, March–April 1983.]

Peggy Whitman Prenshaw, ed., *Eudora Welty: Thirteen Essays Selected from EUDORA WELTY: CRITICAL ESSAYS*. Jackson: University Press of Mississippi, 1983.

Carol S. Manning, *With Ears Opening Like Morning Glories: Eudora Welty and The Love of Storytelling*. Westport, CT/London: Greenwood Press, 1985.

Louise Hutchings Westling, *Sacred Groves and Ravaged Gardens: The Fiction of Eudora Welty, Carson McCullers, and Flannery O'Connor*. Athens: The University of Georgia Press, 1985.

B. Bibliographies

The Eudora Welty Newsletter is an invaluable bibliographic source. Since 1977 it has been published biannually (summer and winter) under the editorship of W. U. McDonald, Jr. Each number has a checklist of "Works by Welty" and a "Clipping File." Summer numbers have a "Checklist of Welty Scholarship." The "Clipping Files" are not included in this bibliography. For clarity and usefulness I have grouped corresponding checklists within the chronological listing, beginning with the earliest date of publication.

W. U. McDonald, Jr., "Eudora Welty Manuscripts: A Supplementary Annotated Finding List." *Bulletin of Bibliography*, 31 (July–September 1974), 95–98, 126, 132. "Eudora Welty Manuscripts: A Second Supplement." *Eudora Welty Newsletter*, 2 (Winter 1978), 4–5.

Victor H. Thompson, *Eudora Welty: A Reference Guide*. Boston: G. K. Hall, 1976. [See entries under van Noppen and Vande Kieft below.]

Alain Blayac, "The Eudora Welty Collection at the Humanities Research Center, The University of Texas at Austin." *Delta*, No. 5 (November 1977), 83–88. [In French.]

[Noel Polk and Ronald E. Tomlin], "Collections and Acquisitions." *Eudora Welty Newsletter*, 1 (Winter 1977), 5–6. [Checklist of manuscripts.]

W. U. McDonald, Jr., "Welty in British Periodicals: A Preliminary Checklist." *Eudora Welty Newsletter*, 1 (Summer 1977), 7–8. "Followup: Welty in British Periodicals." *Eudora Welty Newsletter*, 3 (Winter 1979), 9.

————, "Works by Welty: A Continuing Checklist." *Eudora Welty Newsletter*, 1 (Winter 1977), 6–7; 2 (Winter 1978), 7; 2 (Summer 1978), 7–8; 3 (Winter 1979), 9; (Summer 1972), 8–9; 3 (April 1979), 12; 3 (Summer 1979), 4; 4 (Winter 1980), 12; 4 (Summer 1980), 8; 5 (Winter 1981), 7–8; 5 (Summer 1981), 7; 6 (Winter 1982), 12; 6 (Summer 1982), 8–9; 7 (Winter 1983), 11–12; 7 (Summer 1983), 8; 8 (Winter 1984), 8–9; 8 (Summer 1984), 7–8; 9 (Winter 1985), 12; 9 (Summer 1985), 6; 10 (Winter 1986), 10–11; 10 (Summer 1986), 6–7.

Noel Polk, "A Checklist of Translations and Foreign-Language Editions of Eudora Welty's Works." *Eudora Welty Newsletter*, 1 (Summer 1977), 3–7.

Ruth M. Vande Kieft, Rev. of Victor H. Thompson, *Eudora Welty: A Reference Guide*. *Mississippi Quarterly*, 30 (Winter 1976–77), 169–178.

"Checklist of Welty Scholarship." *Eudora Welty Newsletter*, by Noel Polk, "1977–78," 2 (Summer 1978), 12–15; "1978–79," 3 (Summer 1979), 5–9; by V. H. Thompson, "1979–80," 4 (Summer 1980), 10–13; "1980–81," 5 (Summer 1981), 10–12; by W. U. McDonald, Jr., "1982–83", 7 (Summer 1983), 10–14; by O. B. Emerson, "1981–82," 6 (Summer 1982), 10–14; "1983–84," 8 (Summer 1984), 10–13; "1983–85," 9 (Summer 1985), 9–13; by Pearl A. McHaney, "1984–86," 10 (Summer 1986), 9–14.

Joan Givner, "The Eudora Welty Collection, Jackson, Mississippi." *Descant: The Texas Christian University Literary Journal*, 23 (Fall 1978), 38–48. [Cited in *MLA*, 1978.]

W. U. McDonald, Jr., "*The Eye of the Story*: Bibliographic Notes on the Contents." *Eudora Welty Newsletter*, 2 (Summer 1978), 1–5.

Martha van Noppen, "Eudora Welty Scholarship, 1959–1976: A Supplementary Checklist." *Eudora Welty Newsletter,* 2 (Summer 1978), 10–12. [Supplements Thompson, *Eudora Welty: A Reference Guide.*]

Ronald E. Tomlin, "The Eudora Welty Collection at the Mississippi Department of Archives and History." *Eudora Welty Newsletter,* 3 (April 1979), 10–12.

Noel Polk, "Eudora Welty: A Bibliographical Checklist." *American Book Collector,* n.s. 2 (January–February 1981), 25–37.

Mary Hughes Brookhart, "Welty's Current Reception in Britain: A Checklist of Reviews." *Eudora Welty Newsletter,* 7 (Summer 1983), 1–5.

O. B. Emerson, "Reviews of *Collected Stories:* A Preliminary Checklist." *Eudora Welty Newsletter,* 7 (Winter 1983), 4–6.

W. U. McDonald Jr., "A Checklist of Revisions in Collected Welty Stories: Phase I." *Eudora Welty Newsletter,* 7 (Winter 1983), 6–10.

Peggy Whitman Prenshaw, "Eudora Welty." In *American Women Writers: Bibliographical Essays,* ed. Maurice Duke, Jackson R. Bryer, and M. Thomas Inge. Westport, CT/London: Greenwood Press, 1983, pp. 233–267. [An essay surveying editions, manuscripts, and scholarship on Welty through 1980.]

Mary Hughes Brookhart, "Reviews of *One Writer's Beginnings:* A Preliminary Checklist." *Eudora Welty Newsletter,* 8 (Summer 1984), 1–4.

Bethany C. Swearingen, *Eudora Welty: A Critical Bibliography, 1936–1958.* Jackson: University Press of Mississippi, 1984. [See entry under Schmidt below.]

[Suzanne Marrs], "An Annotated Bibliography of the *Losing-Battles* Papers." *Southern Quarterly,* 23 (Winter 1985), 116–121.

[————], "Manuscript Acquisitions at Archives." *Eudora Welty Newsletter,* 10 (Winter 1986), 13–14, and 10 (Summer 1986), 15.

W. U. McDonald, Jr., "Eudora Welty." In *American Novelists,* ed. James J. Martine. Vol. I of *Contemporary Authors Bibliographical Series.* Detroit: Gale Research Co., 1986, pp. 383–421. [Checklist and bibliographical essay.]

Pearl A. Schmidt, Rev. of Bethany C. Swearingen, *Eudora Welty: A Critical Bibliography, 1936–1958. Notes on Mississippi Writers,* 18, No. 1 (1986), 73–75.

C. General Estimates, Thematic Studies

John R. Cooley, "Blacks and Primitives in Eudora Welty's Fiction." *Ball State University Forum,* 14 (Summer 1973), 20–28.

John F. Fleischauer, "The Focus of Mystery: Eudora Welty's Prose Style." *Southern Literary Journal,* 5 (Spring 1973), 64–79.

Seymour L. Gross, "Eudora Welty's Comic Imagination." In *The Comic Imagination in American Literature*, ed. Louis D. Rubin, Jr. New Brunswick, NJ: Rutgers University Press, 1973, pp. 319–328.

Clayton Robinson, "Faulkner and Welty and the Mississippi Baptists." *Interpretations: Studies in Language and Literature*, 5 (1973), 51–54.

Joan Givner, "Katherine Anne Porter, Eudora Welty, and Ethan Brand." *International Fiction Review*, 1 (July 1974), 32–37.

Franco La Polla, "La Tradizione dell'adolescenza, del sesso e della fuga in Eudora Welty e Erskine Caldwell." *Annali* [Feltre, Italy], 1974, pp. 299–307. [Cited in *MLA*, 1977.]

John A. Allen, "Eudora Welty: The Three Moments." *Virginia Quarterly Review*, 51 (Autumn 1975), 605–627; rpt. in *A Still Moment: Essays on the Art of Eudora Welty*, ed. John F. Desmond. Metuchen, NJ, and London: The Scarecrow Press, 1978, pp. 12–34.

Charles E. Davis, "The South in Eudora Welty's Fiction: A Changing World." *Studies in American Fiction*, 3 (Autumn 1975), 199–209.

Arnold Gingrich, "Goosing a Gander." *Esquire*, 84 (December 1975), 14, 161. [Concerning *Esquire's* rejection of an unidentified Welty story.]

Susan L. Meyers, "Dialogues in Eudora Welty's Short Stories." *Notes on Mississippi Writers*, 8 (Fall 1975), 51–57.

Michiko Yoshida, "Eudora Welty: The Meaning of Silence." In *American Literature in the 1940's*. Annual Report. Tokyo: Tokyo Chapter, American Literary Society of Japan, 1975, pp. 58–74.

Hunter M. Cole, "Welty on Faulkner." *Notes on Mississippi Writers*, 9 (Spring 1976), 28–49.

Louis Dollarhide, "Eudora Welty." In his *Mississippi Short Story Writers*. Jackson: Mississippi Library Commission, 1976, n.p.

Robert L. Phillips, Jr., ed., "III. A Time and A Place." In *Mississippi Writers in Context: Transcripts of "A Climate for Genius," A Television Series*. Jackson: Mississippi Library Commission, 1976, pp. 35–49.

Ruth M. Vande Kieft, Rev. of Victor H. Thompson, *Eudora Welty: A Reference Guide. Mississippi Quarterly*, 30 (Winter 1976–77), 169–178.

Margaret Bolsterli, "'Bound' Characters in Porter, Welty, McCullers: The Prerevolutionary Status of Women in American Fiction." *Bucknell Review*, 24 (1978), 95–105.

Patricia Chaffee, "Houses in the Short Fiction of Eudora Welty." *Studies in Short Fiction*, 15 (Winter 1978), 112–114.

Bessie Chronaki, "Eudora Welty's Theory of Place and Human Relationships." *South Atlantic Bulletin*, 43 (May 1978), 36–44.

Albert J. Griffith, "The Poetics of Prose: Eudora Welty's Literary Theory." In *A Still Moment: Essays on the Art of Eudora Welty*, ed. John F. Desmond. Metuchen, NJ, and London: The Scarecrow Press, 1978, pp. 51–62.

Jerry Harris, "The Real Thing: Eudora Welty's Essential Vision." In *A Still Moment: Essays on the Art of Eudora Welty*, ed. John F. Desmond. Metuchen, NJ, and London: The Scarecrow Press, 1978, pp. 1–11.

Lucinda H. MacKethan, "To See Things in Their Time: The Act of Focus in Eudora Welty's Fiction." *American Literature*, 50 (May 1978), 258–275; rpt. in *The Dream of Arcady*. Baton Rouge: Louisiana State University Press, 1980, pp. 181–206.

D. James Neault, "Time in the Fiction of Eudora Welty." In *A Still Moment: Essays on the Art of Eudora Welty*, ed. John F. Desmond. Metuchen, NJ, and London: The Scarecrow Press, 1978, pp. 35–50.

Lewis P. Simpson, "The Southern Aesthetic of Memory." *Tulane Studies in English*, 23 (1978), 207–227.

Ruth Vande Kieft, "Eudora Alice Welty." In *American Novelists Since World War II*, ed. Jeffrey Helterman and Richard Layman. *Dictionary of Literary Biography*, Vol. II. Detroit: Gale Research, 1978, pp. 524–537.

John Alexander Allen, "The Other Way to Live: Demigods in Eudora Welty's Fiction." In *Eudora Welty: Critical Essays*, ed. Peggy Whitman Prenshaw. Jackson: University Press of Mississippi, 1979, pp. 26–55; rpt. *Eudora Welty: Thirteen Essays Selected from EUDORA WELTY: CRITICAL ESSAYS*, ed. Peggy Whitman Prenshaw. Jackson: University Press of Mississippi, 1983, pp. 26–55.

Paul Binding, "Mississippi and Eudora Welty." In his *Separate Country: A Literary Journey Through the American South*. New York/London: Paddington Press, Ltd., 1979, pp. 131–148.

Cleanth Brooks, "Eudora Welty and the Southern Idiom." In *Eudora Welty: A Form of Thanks*, ed. Louis Dollarhide and Ann J. Abadie. Jackson: University Press of Mississippi, 1979, pp. 3–24.

Charlotte Capers, "Eudora Welty: A Friend's View." In *Eudora Welty: A Form of Thanks*, ed. Louis Dollarhide and Ann J. Abadie. Jackson: University Press of Mississippi, 1979, pp. 129–135.

———, "A Note on the Welty Papers." *Eudora Welty Newsletter*, 3 (April 1979), 9–10.

Albert J. Devlin, "Eudora Welty's Mississippi." In *Eudora Welty: Critical Essays*, ed. Peggy Whitman Prenshaw. Jackson: University Press of Mississippi, 1979, pp. 157–178; rpt. *Eudora Welty: Thirteen Essays Selected from EUDORA WELTY: CRITICAL ES-*

SAYS, ed. Peggy Whitman Prenshaw. Jackson: University Press of Mississippi, 1983, pp. 98–119.

Robert Drake, "Eudora Welty's Country—and My Own." *Modern Age*, 23 (Fall 1979), 403–409.

Chester E. Eisinger, "Traditionalism and Modernism in Eudora Welty." In *Eudora Welty: Critical Essays*, ed. Peggy Whitman Prenshaw. Jackson: University Press of Mississippi, 1979, pp. 3–25; rpt. *Eudora Welty: Thirteen Essays Selected from EUDORA WELTY: CRITICAL ESSAYS*, ed. Peggy Whitman Prenshaw. Jackson: University Press of Mississippi, 1983, pp. 3–25.

Warren French, "'All Things are Double': Eudora Welty as A Civilized Writer." In *Eudora Welty: Critical Essays*, ed. Peggy Whitman Prenshaw. Jackson: University Press of Mississippi, 1979, pp. 179–188; rpt. *Eudora Welty: Thirteen Essays Selected from EUDORA WELTY: CRITICAL ESSAYS*, ed. Peggy Whitman Prenshaw. Jackson: University Press of Mississippi, 1983, pp. 120–129.

Albert J. Griffith, "Henny Penny, Eudora Welty, and the Aggregation of Friends." In *Eudora Welty: Critical Essays*, ed. Peggy Whitman Prenshaw. Jackson: University Press of Mississippi, 1979, pp. 83–92.

John Edward Hardy, "Marrying Down in Eudora Welty's Novels." In *Eudora Welty: Critical Essays*, ed. Peggy Whitman Prenshaw. Jackson: University Press of Mississippi, 1979, pp. 93–119; rpt. *Eudora Welty: Thirteen Essays Selected from EUDORA WELTY: CRITICAL ESSAYS*, ed. Peggy Whitman Prenshaw. Jackson: University Press of Mississippi, 1983, pp. 71–97.

Elmo Howell, "Eudora Welty and the City of Man." *Georgia Review*, 33 (Winter 1979), 770–782.

Elizabeth M. Kerr, "The World of Eudora Welty's Women." In *Eudora Welty: Critical Essays*, ed. Peggy Whitman Prenshaw. Jackson: University Press of Mississippi, 1979, pp. 132–148.

Michael Kreyling, "Words into Criticism: Eudora Welty's Essays and Reviews." In *Eudora Welty: Critical Essays*, ed. Peggy Whitman Prenshaw. Jackson: University Press of Mississippi, 1979, pp. 411–422; rpt. *Eudora Welty: Thirteen Essays Selected from EUDORA WELTY: CRITICAL ESSAYS*, ed. Peggy Whitman Prenshaw. Jackson: University Press of Mississippi, 1983, pp. 224–235.

Elizabeth A. Meese, "Constructing Time and Place: Eudora Welty in the Thirties." In *Eudora Welty: Critical Essays*, ed. Peggy Whitman Prenshaw. Jackson: University Press of Mississippi, 1979, pp. 401–410.

Danièle Pitavy-Souques, "Eudora Welty in France: *Delta V.*" *Eudora Welty Newsletter*, 3 (Winter 1979), 3–5.

Noel Polk, "Water, Wanderers, and Weddings: Love in Eudora Welty." In *Eudora Welty: A Form of Thanks*, ed. Louis Dollarhide and Ann J. Abadie. Jackson: University Press of Mississippi, 1979, pp. 95–122.

Peggy W. Prenshaw, "Woman's World, Man's Place: The Fiction of Eudora Welty." In *Eudora Welty: A Form of Thanks*, ed. Louis Dollarhide and Ann J. Abadie. Jackson: University Press of Mississippi, 1979, pp. 46–77.

Reynolds Price, "A Form of Thanks." In *Eudora Welty: A Form of Thanks*, ed. Louis Dollarhide and Ann J. Abadie. Jackson: University Press of Mississippi, 1979, pp. 123–128.

William Jay Smith, "Precision and Reticence: Eudora Welty's Poetic Vision." In *Eudora Welty: A Form of Thanks*, ed. Louis Dollarhide and Ann J. Abadie. Jackson: University Press of Mississippi, 1979, pp. 78–94; rpt. *The Ontario Review*, No. 9 (Fall–Winter 1978–79), 59–70.

Elizabeth Spencer, "Eudora Welty: An Introduction." *Eudora Welty Newsletter*, 3 (April 1979), 2–3.

Ruth M. Vande Kieft, "Looking with Eudora Welty." In *Eudora Welty: Critical Essays*, ed. Peggy Whitman Prenshaw. Jackson: University Press of Mississippi, 1979, pp. 423–444; rpt. *Eudora Welty: Thirteen Essays Selected from EUDORA WELTY: CRITICAL ESSAYS*, ed. Peggy Whitman Prenshaw. Jackson: University Press of Mississippi, 1983, pp. 236–257.

Louis D. Rubin, Jr., "Growing Up in the Deep South: A Conversation with Eudora Welty, Shelby Foote, and Louis D. Rubin, Jr." In *The American South: Portrait of a Culture*, ed. Louis D. Rubin, Jr. Baton Rouge: Louisiana State University Press, 1980, pp. 59–85.

Robert Penn Warren, "Under the Spell of Eudora Welty." *New York Times Book Review*, 2 March 1980, pp. 1, 26–27. [Essay-review of *Eudora Welty: A Form of Thanks*, ed. Louis Dollarhide and Ann J. Abadie; *Eudora Welty: Critical Essays*, ed. Peggy Whitman Prenshaw; and *Eudora Welty's Achievement of Order*, Michael Kreyling.]

Noel Polk, "Welty, Eudora: 1909—." In *Lives of Mississippi Authors, 1817–1967*, ed. James B. Lloyd. Jackson: University Press of Mississippi, 1981, pp. 459–464.

William H. Slavick, "Up in Tishomingo County: Eudora Welty's Passion 'To Part a Curtain.'" *Southern Literary Journal*, 13 (Spring 1981), 105–115. [Essay-review of *A Still Moment: Essays on the Art of Eudora Welty*, ed. John F. Desmond; *Eudora Welty: A Form of Thanks*, ed. Louis Dollarhide and Ann J. Abadie; *Eudora Welty's Achievement of Order*, Michael Kreyling; *Eudora Welty: Critical Essays*, ed. Peggy Whitman Prenshaw.]

Albert J. Devlin, "Jackson's Welty." *Southern Quarterly*, 20 (Summer 1982), 54–91. [Includes Welty photographs of Jackson.]

Elizabeth Evans, "Eudora Welty: The Metaphor of Music." *Southern Quarterly*, 20 (Summer 1982), 92–100.

Jan Nordby Gretlund, "Out of Life into Fiction: Eudora Welty and the City." *Notes on Mississippi Writers*, 14 (1982), 45–62.

Sara McAlpin, "Family in Eudora Welty's Fiction." *Southern Review*, n.s. 18 (Summer 1982), 480–494.

W. U. McDonald, Jr., "An Unworn Path: Bibliographical and Textual Scholarship on Eudora Welty." *Southern Quarterly*, 20 (Summer 1982), 101–108.

Richard C. Moreland, "Community and Vision in Eudora Welty." *Southern Review*, n.s. 18 (Winter 1982), 84–99.

Ruth M. Vande Kieft, "Eudora Welty: The Question of Meaning." *Southern Quarterly*, 20 (Summer 1982), 24–39.

Barbara Harrell Carson, "Eudora Welty's Tangled Bank." *South Atlantic Review*, 48 (November 1983), 1–18.

Frederick R. Karl, *American Fictions 1940–1980*. New York: Harper and Row, 1983, pp. 6, 46, 71–74.

Noel Polk, "The Southern Literary Pieties." In *Southern Literature in Transition: Heritage and Promise*, ed. Philip Castille and William Osborne. Memphis: Memphis State University Press. 1983, pp. 29–41.

Waldemar Zacharasiewicz, "The Sense of Place in Southern Fiction by Eudora Welty and Flannery O'Connor." *Proceedings of the 2nd April Conference of University Teachers of English*. Cracow, 1981. Ed. Irena Kaluza. Cracow: 1984, pp. 123–142. [Cited in *EuWN*, 8 (Summer 1984).] Rpt. *Arbeiten aus Anglistik und Amerikanistik*, 10, Nos. 1 and 2 (1985), 189–206. [Cited in *MLA*, 1985.]

Anthony Bukoski, "Facts of Domesticity in Eudora Welty's Fiction." *Southern Studies*, 24 (Fall 1985), 326–342.

Charles E. Davis, "Eudora Welty's Blacks: Name and Cultural Identity." *Notes on Mississippi Writers*, 17, No. 1 (1985), 1–8.

Dean Flower, "Eudora Welty Come from Away." *Hudson Review*, 38 (Autumn 1985), 473–480.

Peggy Whitman Prenshaw, "Eudora Welty." In *The History of Southern Literature*, ed. Louis D. Rubin, Jr. Baton Rouge: Louisiana State University Press, 1985, pp. 470–475.

Barbara Wilkie Tedford, "West Virginia Touches in Eudora Welty's Fiction." *Southern Literary Journal*, 18 (Spring 1986), 40–52.

Danièle Pitavy-Souques, "A Blazing Butterfly: The Modernity of Eudora Welty." *Mississippi Quarterly*, 39 (Fall 1986), [537]–560; rpt. this collection.

Harriet Pollack, "Words Between Strangers: On Welty, Her

Style, and Her Audience." *Mississippi Quarterly*, 39 (Fall 1986), [481]–505; rpt. this collection.

Ruth M. Vande Kieft, "Eudora Welty: Visited and Revisited." *Mississippi Quarterly*, 39 (Fall 1986), [455]–479; rpt. this collection.

D. Studies of Individual Works

1.*A Curtain of Green*

General

Gary Carson, "The Romantic Tradition in Eudora Welty's *A Curtain of Green*." *Notes on Mississippi Writers*, 9 (Fall 1976), 97–100.

Noel Polk, "An Unknown Printing of *A Curtain of Green*." *Eudora Welty Newsletter*, 1 (Winter 1977), 2–3.

Gary Carson, "Versions of the Artist in *A Curtain of Green:* The Unifying Imagination in Eudora Welty's Early Fiction." *Studies in Short Fiction*, 15 (Fall 1978), 421–428.

Barbara Fialkowski, "Psychic Distances in *A Curtain of Green:* Artistic Successes and Personal Failures." In *A Still Moment: Essays on the Art of Eudora Welty*, ed. John F. Desmond. Metuchen, NJ, and London: The Scarecrow Press, 1978, pp. 63–70.

J. A. Bryant, Jr., "The Recovery of the Confident Narrator: *A Curtain of Green* to *Losing Battles*." In *Eudora Welty: Critical Essays*, ed. Peggy Whitman Prenshaw. Jackson: University Press of Mississippi, 1979, pp. 68–82; rpt. *Eudora Welty: Thirteen Essays Selected from EUDORA WELTY: CRITICAL ESSAYS*, ed. Peggy Whitman Prenshaw. Jackson: University Press of Mississippi, 1983, pp. 56–70.

Noel Polk, "The Text of the Modern Library *A Curtain of Green*." *Eudora Welty Newsletter*, 3 (Winter 1979), 6–9.

Ronald R. Butters, "Dialect at Work: Eudora Welty's Artistic Purposes." *Mississippi Folklore Register*, 16 (Fall 1982), 33–39.

John R. Cooley, "Eudora Welty." In his *Savages and Naturals: Black Portrayals by White Writers in Modern American Literature*. Newark: University of Delaware Press, 1982, pp. 124–137.

Michael Kreyling, "Modernism in Welty's *A Curtain of Green and Other Stories*." *Southern Quarterly*, 20 (Summer 1982), 40–53.

"Lily Daw and the Three Ladies"

W. U. McDonald, Jr., "Artistry and Irony: Welty's Revisions of 'Lily Daw and the Three Ladies.'" *Studies in American Fiction*, 9 (Spring 1981), 113–121.

"A Piece of News"

Carol Hollenbaugh, "Ruby Fisher and Her Demon-Lover." *Notes on Mississippi Writers*, 7 (Fall 1974), 63–68.

"Petrified Man"

Jeffrey Helterman, "Gorgons in Mississippi: Eudora Welty's 'Petrified Man.'" *Notes on Mississippi Writers*, 7 (Spring 1974), 12–20.

St. George Tucker Arnold, "Mythic Patterns and Satiric Effect in Eudora Welty's 'Petrified Man.'" *Studies in Contemporary Satire: A Creative and Critical Journal*, 4 (1977), 21–27.

Charlotte Capers, "The Narrow Escape of 'The [sic] Petrified Man': Early Eudora Welty Stories." *Journal of Mississippi History*, 41 (February 1979), 25–32.

Robert G. Walker, "Another Medusa Allusion in Welty's 'Petrified Man.'" *Notes on Contemporary Literature*, 9 (March 1979), 10.

W. U. McDonald, Jr., "The Caedmon Version of 'Petrified Man.'" *Eudora Welty Newsletter*, 4 (Winter 1980), 7–9.

————, "Published Texts of 'Petrified Man': A Brief History." *Notes on Mississippi Writers*, 13 (1981), 64–72.

Libby F. Jones, "The Stories of Welty's 'Petrified Man.'" *Notes on Mississippi Writers*, 18 (1986), 65–72.

"Keela, the Outcast Indian Maiden"

Robert W. Cochran, "Lost and Found Identities in Welty's 'Keela, the Outcast, Indian Maiden.'" *Notes on Modern American Literature*, 2 (Spring 1978), item 14.

John Irwin Fischer, "'Keela, the Outcast Indian Maiden': Studying It Out." *Studies in Short Fiction*, 15 (Spring 1978), 165–171.

A. R. Coulthard, "'Keela, the Outcast Indian Maiden': A Dissenting View." *Studies in Short Fiction*, 23 (Winter 1986), 35–41.

"Why I Live at the P.O."

Walter Herrscher, "Is Sister Really Insane? Another Look at 'Why I Live at the P.O.'" *Notes on Contemporary Literature*, 5 (January 1975), 5–7.

Nora Calhoun Graves, "Shirley-T. in Eudora Welty's 'Why I Live at the P.O.'" *Notes on Contemporary Literature*, 7 (March 1977), 6–7.

Charles E. May, "Why Sister Lives at the P.O." *Southern Humanities Review*, 12 (Summer 1978), 243–249.

Travis Du Priest, "'Why I Live at the P.O.': Eudora Welty's Epic Question." *Christianity and Literature*, 31, No. 4 (1982), 45–54. [Cited in *MLA*, 1982.]

"The Hitch-Hikers"

Nomi Tamir-Ghez, "Binary Oppositions and Thematic Decoding in E. E. Cummings and Eudora Welty." *PTL: A Journal for Descriptive Poetics and Theory*, 3 (April 1978), 235–248.

James Walter, "The Fate of the Story Teller in Eudora Welty's 'The Hitch-Hikers.'" *South Central Review*, 2 (Spring 1985), 57–70.

"A Memory"

Elaine Ginsberg, "The Female Initiation Theme in American Fiction." *Studies in American Fiction*, 3 (Spring 1975), 27–37.

Richard J. Gray, "Eudora Welty: A Dance to the Music of Order." *Canadian Review of American Studies*, 7 (Spring 1976), 57–65; rpt. in his *The Literature of Memory*. Baltimore/London: Johns Hopkins University Press, 1977, pp. 150–152, 174–185, 261.

Peggy W. Prenshaw, "Two Jackson Excursions." *Eudora Welty Newsletter*, 2 (Winter 1978), 3–4.

"Old Mr. Marblehall"

Robert Detweiler, "Eudora Welty's Blazing Butterfly: The Dynamics of Response." *Language and Style*, 6 (Winter 1973), 58–71.

Mildred K. Travis, "A Note on 'Wakefield' and 'Old Mr. Marblehall.'" *Notes on Contemporary Literature*, 4 (May 1974), 9–10.

A. R. Coulthard, "Point of View in Eudora Welty's 'Old Mr. Marblehall.'" *Notes on Mississippi Writers*, 8 (Spring 1975), 22–27.

Catherine H. Chengges, "Textual Variants in 'Old Mr. Grenada'/'Old Mr. Marblehall.'" *Eudora Welty Newsletter*, 10 (Summer 1986), 1–6.

"Flowers for Marjorie"

W. U. McDonald, Jr., "Eudora Welty, Reviser: Some Notes on 'Flowers for Marjorie.'" *Delta*, No. 5 (November 1977), 35–48.

Jan Nordby Gretlund, "Welty's Photos of New York in the Depression and 'Flowers for Marjorie,'" *Eudora Welty Newsletter*, 5 (Summer 1981), 4–5.

"A Curtain of Green"

St. George Tucker Arnold, "The Raincloud and the Garden: Psychic Regression as Tragedy in Welty's 'A Curtain of Green.'" *South Atlantic Bulletin*, 44 (January 1979), 53–60.

"A Visit of Charity"

Peggy W. Prenshaw, "Two Jackson Excursions." *Eudora Welty Newsletter*, 2 (Winter 1978), 3–4.

Edward E. Kelly, "Eudora Welty's Hollow Women." *Notes on Modern American Literature*, 6 (Autumn 1982), item 15. [Cited in *MLA*, 1983.]

"Death of a Traveling Salesman"

Wayne D. McGinnis, "Welty's 'Death of a Traveling Salesman' and William Blake Once Again." *Notes on Mississippi Writers*, 11 (Winter 1979), 52–54.

Ann Romines, "The Powers of the Lamp: Domestic Ritual in Two Stories by Eudora Welty." *Notes on Mississippi Writers*, 12 (Summer 1979), 1–16.

Nancy Sederberg, "Welty's 'Death of a Traveling Salesman.'" *Explicator*, 42 (Fall 1983), 52–54.

"Powerhouse"

William B. Stone, "Eudora Welty's Hydrodynamic 'Powerhouse.'" *Studies in Short Fiction*, 11 (Winter 1974), 93–96.

Timothy Dow Adams, "A Curtain of Black: White and Black Jazz Styles in 'Powerhouse.'" *Notes on Mississippi Writers*, 10 (Winter 1977), 57–61.

Whitney Balliett, "Jazz: Fats." *New Yorker*, 54 (10 April 1978), 110–112, 114–117.

Leroy Thomas, "Welty's 'Powerhouse.'" *Explicator*, 36 (Summer 1978), 15–17.

Loretta M. Lampkin, "Musical Movement and Harmony in Eudora Welty's 'Powerhouse.'" *CEA Critic*, 45 (November 1982), 24–28.

Thomas H. Getz, "Eudora Welty: Listening to 'Powerhouse.'" *The Kentucky Review*, 4 (Winter 1983), 40–48.

"A Worn Path"

Frances Seidl, "Eudora Welty's Phoenix." *Notes on Mississippi Writers*, 6 (Fall 1973), 53–55.

Frank R. Ardolino, "Life Out of Death: Ancient Myth and Ritual in Welty's 'A Worn Path.'" *Notes on Mississippi Writers*, 9 (Spring 1976), 1–9.

Jeanne R. Nostrandt, "Welty's 'A Worn Path.'" *Explicator*, 34 (January 1976), item 33.

Roland Bartel, "Life and Death in Eudora Welty's 'A Worn Path.'" *Studies in Short Fiction*, 14 (Summer 1977), 288–290.

Mary Ann Dazey, "Phoenix Jackson and the Nice Lady: A Note on Eudora Welty's 'A Worn Path.'" *American Notes and Queries*, 17 (February 1979), 92–93.

Marilynn Keys, "'A Worn Path': The Way of Dispossession." *Studies in Short Fiction*, 16 (Fall 1979), 354–356.

2. The Robber Bridegroom

Carol P. Smith, "The Journey Motif in Eudora Welty's *The Robber Bridegroom.*" *Shippensburg State College Review*, Shippensburg [PA] State College, 1973, pp. 18–32.

Merrill Maguire Skaggs, "The Uses of Enchantment in Frontier Humor and *The Robber Bridegroom.*" *Studies in American Humor*, 3 (October 1976), 96–102.

Marilyn Arnold, "Eudora Welty's Parody." *Notes on Mississippi Writers*, 11 (Spring 1978), 15–22.

Charles E. Davis, "Eudora Welty's *The Robber Bridegroom* and Old Southwest Humor: A Doubleness of Vision." In *A Still Moment: Essays on the Art of Eudora Welty*, ed. John F. Desmond. Metuchen, NJ, and London: The Scarecrow Press, 1978, pp. 71–81.

Michael Kreyling, "Clement and the Indians: Pastoral and History in *The Robber Bridegroom.*" In *Eudora Welty: A Form of Thanks*, ed. Louis Dollarhide and Ann J. Abadie. Jackson: University Press of Mississippi, 1979, pp. 25–45.

Warren Akin IV, "*The Robber Bridegroom:* An Oedipal Tale of the Natchez Trace." *Literature and Psychology*, 30, Nos. 3 and 4 (1980), 112–118.

Alan Holder, " 'It Happened in Extraordinary Times': Eudora Welty's Historical Fiction." In his *The Imagined Past: Portrayals of Our History in Modern American Literature.* Lewisburg, PA: Bucknell University Press, 1980, pp. 125–146.

Jennifer Randisi, "Eudora Welty's *The Robber Bridegroom* as American Romance." *Mid-Hudson Language Studies*, 3 (1980), 101–115.

Lisa K. Miller, "The Dark Side of Our Frontier Heritage: Eudora Welty's Use of the Turner Thesis in *The Robber Bridegroom.*" *Notes on Mississippi Writers*, 14 (1981), 18–26.

Peggy Whitman Prenshaw, "Two Mississippi Clippings." *Eudora Welty Newsletter*, 5 (Summer 1981), 1–3.

Melody Graulich, "Pioneering the Imagination: Eudora Welty's *The Robber Bridegroom.*" In *Women and Western American Literature*, ed. Helen Winter Stauffer and Susan J. Rosowski. Troy, NY: Whitston Publishing Co., 1982, pp. 283–296. [Cited in *MLA*, 1984.]

Bernard Cook, "Ritual Abduction in Early Mississippi." *Mississippi Quarterly*, 36 (Winter 1982–83), 72–73.

Bev Byrne, "A Return to the Source: *The Robber Bridegroom* and *The Optimist's Daughter.*" *Southern Quarterly*, 24 (Spring 1986), 74–85.

3. The Wide Net

General

F. Garvin Davenport, Jr., "Renewal and Historical Consciousness in *The Wide Net*." In *Eudora Welty: Critical Essays*, ed. Peggy Whitman Prenshaw. Jackson: University Press of Mississippi, 1979, pp. 189–200.

Noel Polk, "Sending Schedule for Stories in *The Wide Net*." *Eudora Welty Newsletter*, 9 (Summer 1985), 1–2.

W. U. McDonald, Jr., "Textual Variants in *The Collected Stories: The Wide Net* and *The Bride of the Innisfallen*." *Eudora Welty Newsletter*, 10 (Winter 1986), 7–10.

"First Love"

Victor H. Thompson, "Aaron Burr in Eudora Welty's 'First Love.'" *Notes on Mississippi Writers*, 8 (Winter 1976), 75–83.

John M. Warner, "Eudora Welty: The Artist in 'First Love.'" *Notes on Mississippi Writers*, 9 (Fall 1976), 77–87.

A. M. Bonifas-Masserand, "'First Love' ou la parole en creux." *Delta*, No. 5 (November 1977), 49–62.

Albert J. Devlin, "Eudora Welty's Historicism: Method and Vision." *Mississippi Quarterly*, 30 (Spring 1977), 213–234.

Alan Holder, "'It Happened in Extraordinary Times': Eudora Welty's Historical Fiction." In his *The Imagined Past: Portrayals of Our History in Modern American Literature*. Lewisburg, PA: Bucknell University Press, 1980, pp. 125–146.

St. George Tucker Arnold, "Eudora Welty's 'First Love' and the Personalizing of Southern Regional History." *Journal of Regional Cultures*, 1 (Fall–Winter 1981), 97–105.

Suzanne Marrs, "The Conclusion of Eudora Welty's 'First Love': Historical Backgrounds." *Notes on Mississippi Writers*, 13 (1981), 73–78.

"The Wide Net"

Margaret Bolsterli, "A Fertility Rite in Mississippi." *Notes on Mississippi Writers*, 8 (Fall 1975), 69–71.

St. George Tucker Arnold, "The Dragon in the Delta: The Hero-Archetype in Eudora Welty's 'The Wide Net.'" *Journal of Evolutionary Psychology*, 4 (August 1983), 133–144. [Cited in *MLA*, 1983.]

Nancy Anne Cluck, "*The Aeneid* of the Natchez Trace: Epic Structure in Eudora Welty's 'The Wide Net.'" *Southern Review*, n.s. 19 (Summer 1983), 510–518.

"A Still Moment"

Victor H. Thompson, "The Natchez Trace in Eudora Welty's 'A Still Moment.'" *Southern Literary Journal*, 6 (Fall 1973), 59–69.

Albert J. Devlin, "Eudora Welty's Historicism: Method and Vision." *Mississippi Quarterly*, 30 (Spring 1977), 213–234.

————, "From Horse to Heron: A Source for Eudora Welty." *Notes on Mississippi Writers*, 10 (Winter 1977), 62–68.

Peggy W. Prenshaw, "Coates' *The Outlaw Years* and Welty's 'A Still Moment.'" *Notes on Modern American Literature*, 2 (Spring 1978), item 17.

Alan Holder, "'It Happened in Extraordinary Times': Eudora Welty's Historical Fiction." In his *The Imagined Past: Portrayals of Our History in Modern American Literature*. Lewisburg, PA: Bucknell University Press, 1980, pp. 125–146.

Suzanne Marrs, "John James Audubon in Fiction and Poetry: Literary Portraits by Eudora Welty and Robert Penn Warren." *Southern Studies*, 20 (Winter 1981), 378–383.

————, "Eudora Welty's Snowy Heron." *American Literature*, 53 (January 1982), 723–725.

John Jolly, "The Schillerian Dialect and Eudora Welty's 'A Still Moment.'" *Notes on Mississippi Writers*, 15 (1983), 65–71.

Nancy Ann Cluck, "Audubon: Images of the Artist in Eudora Welty and Robert Penn Warren." *Southern Literary Journal*, 17 (Spring 1985), 41–53.

Pearl A. Schmidt, "Textual Variants of 'A Still Moment.'" *Eudora Welty Newsletter*, 9 (Winter 1985), 1–4.

"Asphodel"

Hunter M. Cole, "Windsor in Spencer and Welty: A Real and an Imaginary Landscape." *Notes on Mississippi Writers*, 7 (Spring 1974), 2–11

"The Winds"

Carol S. Manning, "Little Girls and Sidewalks: Glasgow and Welty on Childhood's Promise." *Southern Quarterly*, 21 (Spring 1983), 67–76.

Pearl A. Schmidt, "Textual Variants in 'The Winds.'" *Eudora Welty Newsletter*, 10 (Winter 1986), 3–7.

"Livvie"

Robert J. Kloss, "The Symbolic Structure of Eudora Welty's 'Livvie.'" *Notes on Mississippi Writers*, 7 (Winter 1975), 70–82.

Horst Oppel, "Eudora Welty, 'Livvie' (1942)." In *Die Amer-*

ikanische Short Story der Gegenwart: Interpretationen, ed. Peter Freese. Berlin: Schmidt, 1976, pp. 39–74. [Cited in *MLA*, 1976.]

Peggy Whitman Prenshaw, "Persephone in Eudora Welty's 'Livvie.'" *Studies in Short Fiction*, 17 (Spring 1980), 149–155.

"At The Landing"

Elaine Ginsberg, "The Female Initiation Theme in American Fiction." *Studies in American Fiction*, 3 (Spring 1975), 27–37.

Mary Hughes Brookhart and Suzanne Marrs, "More Notes on River Country." *Mississippi Quarterly*, 39 (Fall 1986), [507]–519; rpt. this collection.

4. Delta Wedding

Richard J. Gray, "Eudora Welty: A Dance to the Music of Order." *Canadian Review of American Studies*, 7 (Spring 1976), 57–65; rpt. in his *The Literature of Memory*. Baltimore/London: Johns Hopkins University Press, 1977, pp. 150–152, 174–185, 261.

Florence Phyfer Krause, "Emasculating Women in *Delta Wedding*." *Publications of the Missouri Philological Associaton*, 1 (1976), 48–57.

Douglas Messerli, "The Problem of Time in Welty's *Delta Wedding*." *Studies in American Fiction*, 5 (Autumn 1977), 227–240.

Margaret Jones Bolsterli, "Woman's Vision: The Worlds of Women in *Delta Wedding, Losing Battles* and *The Optimist's Daughter*." In *Eudora Welty: Critical Essays*, ed. Peggy Whitman Prenshaw. Jackson: University Press of Mississippi, 1979, pp. 149–156.

M. E. Bradford, "Fairchild as Composite Protagonist in *Delta Wedding*." In *Eudora Welty: Critical Essays*, ed. Peggy Whitman Prenshaw. Jackson: University Press of Mississippi, 1979, pp. 201–207.

Jane L. Hinton, "The Role of Family in *Delta Wedding, Losing Battles* and *The Optimist's Daughter*." In *Eudora Welty: Critical Essays*, ed. Peggy Whitman Prenshaw. Jackson: University Press of Mississippi, 1979, pp. 120–131.

Carol A. Moore, "Aunt Studney's Sack." *Southern Review*, n.s. 16 (Summer 1980), 591–596.

Allison Deming Goeller, "*Delta Wedding* as Pastoral." Interpretations: A Journal of Ideas, Analyses and Criticism, 13 (Fall 1981), 59–72.

W. U. McDonald, Jr., "The English Edition of *Delta Wedding*." *Eudora Welty Newsletter*, 6 (Winter 1982), 6–12. Concluded, *Eudora Welty Newsletter*, 6 (Summer 1982), 4–8.

Louise M. Harder, "How Eudora Welty Speaks to Us Through

Her Use of Names in *Delta Wedding*." *Literary Onomastics Studies*, 10 (1983), 133–146. [Cited in *MLA*, 1983.]

Louise Westling, "Demeter and Kore, Southern Style." *Pacific Coast Philology*, 19 (November 1984), 101–107. [Cited in *MLA*, 1985.]

Dan Fabricant, "Onions and Hyacinths: Unwrapping the Fairchilds in *Delta Wedding*." *Southern Literary Journal*, 18 (Fall 1985), 50–60.

Dorothy Griffin, "The House as Container: Architecture and Myth in Eudora Welty's *Delta Wedding*." *Mississippi Quarterly*, 39 (Fall 1986), [521]–535; rpt. this collection.

5. *The Golden Apples*

General

J. A. Bryant, Jr., "Seeing Double in *The Golden Apples*." *Sewanee Review*, 82 (Spring 1974), 300–315.

Franklin D. Carson, "Recurring Metaphors: An Aspect of Unity in *The Golden Apples*." *Notes on Contemporary Literature*, 5 (September 1975), 4–7.

Walter Sullivan, *A Requiem for the Renascence: The State of Fiction in the Modern South*. Mercer University Lamar Memorial Lectures No. 18. Athens: University of Georgia Press, 1976, pp. 41–49, 51–58.

Michael Kreyling, "The Reginald Birch Illustration in *The Golden Apples*." *Eudora Welty Newsletter*, 1 (Winter 1977), 3–5.

Robert L. Phillips, Jr., *An Introduction to Eudora Welty's THE GOLDEN APPLES*. Jackson: Mississippi Library Commission, 1977.

Douglas Messerli, "Metronome and Music: The Encounter between History and Myth in *The Golden Apples*." In *A Still Moment: Essays on the Art of Eudora Welty*, ed. John F. Desmond. Metuchen, NJ, and London: The Scarecrow Press, 1978, pp. 82–102.

Julia L. Demmin and Daniel Curley, "Golden Apples and Silver Apples." In *Eudora Welty: Critical Essays*, ed. Peggy Whitman Prenshaw. Jackson: University Press of Mississippi, 1979, pp. 242–257; rpt. *Eudora Welty: Thirteen Essays Selected from EUDORA WELTY: CRITICAL ESSAYS*, ed. Peggy Whitman Prenshaw. Jackson: University Press of Mississippi, 1983, pp. 130–145.

Danièle Pitavy-Souques, "Technique as Myth: The Structure of *The Golden Apples*." In *Eudora Welty: Critical Essays*, ed. Peggy Whitman Prenshaw. Jackson: University Press of Mississippi, 1979, pp. 258–268; rpt. *Eudora Welty: Thirteen Essays Selected from EUDORA WELTY: CRITICAL ESSAYS*, ed. Peggy Whit-man Prenshaw. Jackson: University Press of Mississippi, 1983, pp. 146–156.

Merrill Maguire Skaggs, "Morgana's Apples and Pears." In *Eudora Welty: Critical Essays*, ed. Peggy Whitman Prenshaw. Jackson: University Press of Mississippi, 1979, pp. 220–241.

Louis D. Rubin, Jr., "Art and Artistry in Morgana, Mississippi." *Missouri Review*, 4 (Summer 1981), 101–116; rpt. in his *A Gallery of Southerners*. Baton Rouge: Louisiana State University Press, 1982, pp. 49–66.

Lowry Pei, "Dreaming the Other in *The Golden Apples*." *Modern Fiction Studies*, 28 (Autumn 1982), 415–433.

Elaine Upton Pugh, "The Duality of Morgana: The Making of Virgie's Vision, The Vision of *The Golden Apples*." *Modern Fiction Studies*, 28 (Autumn 1982), 435–451.

Noel Polk, "Sending Schedule for the Stories in *The Golden Apples*." *Eudora Welty Newsletter*, 8 (Winter 1984), 1–3.

Patricia S. Yaeger, " 'Because a Fire Was in My Head': Eudora Welty and the Dialogic Imagination." *PMLA*, 99 (October 1984), 955–973; *Mississippi Quarterly*, 39 (Fall 1986), [561]–586, and rpt. in revised form, this collection.

Mary Jane Hurst, "Fire Imagery." *PMLA*, 100 (March 1985), 236–237. [Letter responding to Yaeger, "Dialogic Imagination," *PLMA*, 99 (October 1984).]

W. U. McDonald, Jr., "Textual Variants in *The Collected Stories: The Golden Apples*." *Eudora Welty Newsletter*, 9 (Summer 1985), 3–6.

Jill Fritz-Piggott, "The Sword and the Song: Moments of Intensity in *The Golden Apples*." *Southern Literary Journal*, 18 (Spring 1986), 27–39.

"Shower of Gold"

Danièle Pitavy, " 'Shower of Gold' ou les ambiguités de la narration." *Delta*, No. 5 (November 1977), 63–81.

"June Recital"

Neil Corcoran, "The Face that was in the Poem: Art and 'Human Truth' in 'June Recital.' " *Delta*, No. 5 (November 1977), 27–34.

Marilyn Arnold, "When Gratitude Is No More: Eudora Welty's 'June Recital.' " *South Carolina Review*, 13 (Spring 1981), 62–72.

Danièle Pitavy-Souques, "Watchers and Watching: Point of View in Eudora Welty's 'June Recital.' " Trans. Margaret Tomarchio. *Southern Review*, n.s. 19 (Summer 1983), 483–509.

"Sir Rabbit"

Franklin D. Carson, "The Passage of Time in Eudora Welty's 'Sir Rabbit.'" *Studies in Short Fiction*, 12 (Summer 1975), 284–286.

"Moon Lake"

Arline Garbarini, "'Moon Lake' and *The Re-Creation of Brian Kent.*" *Eudora Welty Newsletter*, 2 (Winter 1978), 1–3.

Carol S. Manning, "Male Initiation, Welty Style." *Regionalism and the Female Imagination*, 4, No. 2 (1978), 53–60.

Patricia S. Yaeger, "The Case of the Dangling Signifier: Phallic Imagery in Eudora Welty's 'Moon Lake.'" *Twentieth Century Literature*, 28 (Winter 1982), 431–452.

6. *The Ponder Heart*

Cleanth Brooks, "More on 'F.H.B.'" *Eudora Welty Newsletter*, 2 (Summer 1978), 7.

Tinkham Brooks, "'F.H.B.' in *The Ponder Heart.*" *Eudora Welty Newsletter*, 2 (Winter 1978), 5.

Brenda G. Cornell, "Ambiguous Necessity: A Study of *The Ponder Heart.*" In *Eudora Welty: Critical Essays*, ed. Peggy Whitman Prenshaw. Jackson: University Press of Mississippi, 1979, pp. 208–219.

Rachel V. Weiner, "Eudora Welty's *The Ponder Heart:* The Judgment of Art." *Southern Studies*, 19 (Fall 1980), 261–273.

John L. Idol, Jr., "Edna Earle Ponder's Good Country People." *Southern Quarterly*, 20 (Spring 1982), 66–75.

7. The Bride of the Innisfallen

General

W. N. Free, Jr., "Textual Variants in the American and British First Editions of *The Bride of the Innisfallen.*" *Eudora Welty Newsletter*, 9 (Winter 1985), 5–11.

W. U. McDonald, Jr., "Textual Variants in *The Collected Stories: The Wide Net* and *The Bride of the Innisfallen.*" *Eudora Welty Newsletter*, 10 (Winter 1986), 7–10.

"The Burning"

Edward Gallafent, "The Landscape of 'The Burning.'" *Delta*, No. 5 (November 1977), 19–26.

"The Bride of the Innisfallen"

Don Harrell, "Death in Eudora Welty's 'The Bride of the Innisfallen.'" *Notes on Contemporary Literature*, 3 (September 1973), 2–7.

Lorraine Liscio, "The Female Voice of Poetry in 'The Bride of the Innisfallen.'" *Studies in Short Fiction*, 21 (Fall 1984), 357–362.

Marshall Toman, "Welty's 'The Bride of the Innisfallen.'" *Explicator*, 43 (Winter 1985), 42–44.

"Ladies in Spring"

Margaret Bolsterli, "Mythic Elements in 'Ladies in Spring.'" *Notes on Mississippi Writers*, 6 (Winter 1974), 69–72.

"Circe"

Andrea Goudie, "Eudora Welty's Circe: A Goddess Who Strove with Men." *Studies in Short Fiction*, 13 (Fall 1976), 481–489.

8. *Losing Battles*

William E. McMillen, "Conflict and Resolution in Welty's *Losing Battles*." *Critique*, 15, No. 1 (1973), 110–124.

James Boatwright, "Speech and Silence in *Losing Battles*." *Shenandoah*, 25 (Spring 1974), 3–14.

Gayle Goodin, *An Introduction to Eudora Welty's LOSING BATTLES*. Jackson: Mississippi Library Commission, 1976.

Danièle Pitavy, "La Guerre du Temps dans *Losing Battles* et *The Optimist's Daughter*." *Recherches Anglaises et Américaines*, 9 (1976), 182–196.

M. E. Bradford, "Looking Down from a High Place: The Serenity of Miss Welty's *Losing Battles*." In *A Still Moment: Essays on the Art of Eudora Welty*, ed. John F. Desmond. Metuchen, NJ, and London: The Scarecrow Press, 1978, pp. 103–109. [Rpt. from *Ranam*, 4 (1971), 92–97.]

William McMillen, "Circling-In: The Concept of Home in Eudora Welty's *Losing Battles* and *The Optimist's Daughter*." In *A Still Moment: Essays on the Art of Eudora Welty*, ed. John F. Desmond. Metuchen, NJ, and London: The Scarecrow Press, 1978, pp. 110–117.

Larry J. Reynolds, "Enlightening Darkness: Theme and Structure in Eudora Welty's *Losing Battles*." *Journal of Narrative Technique*, 8 (Spring 1978), 133–140.

Margaret Jones Bolsterli, "Woman's Vision: The Worlds of Women in *Delta Wedding*, *Losing Battles* and *The Optimist's Daughter*." In *Eudora Welty: Critical Essays*, ed. Peggy Whitman Prenshaw. Jackson: University Press of Mississippi, 1979, pp. 149–156.

J. A. Bryant, Jr., "The Recovery of the Confident Narrator: *A Curtain of Green* to *Losing Battles*." In *Eudora Welty: Critical Essays*, ed. Peggy Whitman Prenshaw. Jackson: University Press of Mississippi, 1979, pp. 68–82; rpt. *Eudora Welty: Thirteen*

Essays Selected from EUDORA WELTY: CRITICAL ESSAYS, ed. Peggy Whitman Prenshaw. Jackson: University Press of Mississippi, 1983, pp. 56–70.

Mary Anne Ferguson, *"Losing Battles* as a Comic Epic in Prose." In *Eudora Welty: Critical Essays,* ed. Peggy Whitman Prenshaw. Jackson: University Press of Mississippi, 1979, pp. 305–324.

Louise Y. Gossett, *"Losing Battles:* Festival and Celebration." In *Eudora Welty: Critical Essays,* ed. Peggy Whitman Prenshaw. Jackson: University Press of Mississippi, 1979, pp. 341–350.

Seymour Gross, "A Long Day's Living: The Angelic Ingenuities of *Losing Battles."* In *Eudora Welty: Critical Essays,* ed. Peggy Whitman Prenshaw. Jackson: University Press of Mississippi, 1979, pp. 325–340; rpt. *Eudora Welty: Thirteen Essays Selected from EUDORA WELTY: CRITICAL ESSAYS,* ed. Peggy Whitman Prenshaw. Jackson: University Press of Mississippi, 1983, pp. 193–208.

Robert B. Heilman, *"Losing Battles* and Winning the War." In *Eudora Welty: Critical Essays,* ed. Peggy Whitman Prenshaw. Jackson: University Press of Mississippi, 1979, pp. 269–304; rpt. *Eudora Welty: Thirteen Essays Selected from EUDORA WELTY: CRITICAL ESSAYS,* ed. Peggy Whitman Prenshaw. Jackson: University Press of Mississippi, 1983, pp. 157–192.

Jane L. Hinton, "The Role of Family in *Delta Wedding, Losing Battles* and *The Optimist's Daughter."* In *Eudora Welty: Critical Essays,* ed. Peggy Whitman Prenshaw. Jackson: University Press of Mississippi, 1979, pp. 120–131.

Douglas Messerli, " 'A Battle with Both Sides Using the Same Tactics': The Language of Time in *Losing Battles."* In *Eudora Welty: Critical Essays,* ed. Peggy Whitman Prenshaw. Jackson: University Press of Mississippi, 1979, pp. 351–366.

Patricia Elder Dean, "Eudora Welty's Onomastic Art." In *Places, Pets and Charactonyms,* ed. Laurence E. Seits and Jean Divine. Sugar Grove, IL: Waubonsee Community College, 1982, pp. 90–96. [Papers of North Central Names Institute 3. Cited in *MLA,* 1982.]

Shelia Stroup, " 'We're All Part of It Together': Eudora Welty's Hopeful Vision in *Losing Battles." Southern Literary Journal,* 15 (Spring 1983), 42–58.

Roesmary M. Magee, "Eudora Welty's *Losing Battles:* A Patchwork Quilt of Stories." *South Atlantic Review,* 49 (May 1984), 67–79.

Suzanne Marrs, "The Making of *Losing Battles:* Jack Renfro's Evolution." *Mississippi Quarterly,* 37 (Fall 1984), 469–474.

———, "An Annotated Bibliography of the *Losing Battles* Papers." *Southern Quarterly,* 23 (Winter 1985), 116–121.

————, "The Making of *Losing Battles:* Judge Moody Transformed." *Notes on Mississippi Writers,* 17 (1985), 47–53.

————, "The Making of *Losing Battles:* Plot Revision." *Southern Literary Journal,* 18 (Fall 1985), 40–49.

Danièle Pitavy-Souques, "Le Sud: territoire des femmes?" *Revue Française d'Études Américaines,* 10 (Février 1985), 25–50.

9. *One Time, One Place*

Barbara McKenzie, "The Eye of Time: The Photographs of Eudora Welty." In *Eudora Welty: Critical Essays,* ed. Peggy Whitman Prenshaw. Jackson: University Press of Mississippi, 1979, pp. 386–400; rpt. *Eudora Welty: Thirteen Essays Selected from EUDORA WELTY: CRITICAL ESSAYS,* ed. Peggy Whitman Prenshaw. Jackson: University Press of Mississippi, 1983, pp. 209–223.

Charles Mann, "Eudora Welty, Photographer." *History of Photography: An International Quarterly,* 6 (April 1982), 145–149.

Louise Westling, "The Loving Observer of *One Time, One Place.*" *Mississippi Quarterly,* 39 (Fall 1986), [587]–604; rpt. this collection.

10. *The Optimist's Daughter*

Donald E. Stanford, "Eudora Welty and the Pulitzer Prize." *Southern Review,* n.s. 9 (Autumn 1973), xx–xxiii.

Allen Shepherd, "Delayed Exposition in Eudora Welty's *The Optimist's Daughter.*" *Notes on Contemporary Literature,* 4, No. 4 (1974), 10–13.

Patricia Meyer Spacks, *The Female Imagination.* New York: Alfred A. Knopf, 1975, pp. 261, 264–267, 269–271, 273, 275.

William J. Stuckey, "The Use of Marriage in Welty's *The Optimist's Daughter.*" *Critique,* 17, No. 2 (1975), 36–46.

Danièle Pitavy, "La Guerre du Temps dans *Losing Battles* et *The Optimist's Daughter.*" *Recherches Anglaises et Américaines,* 9 (1976), 182–196.

Walter Sullivan, *A Requiem for the Renascence: The State of Fiction in the Modern South.* Mercer University Lamar Memorial Lectures No. 18. Athens: University of Georgia Press, 1976, pp. 41–49, 51–58.

Michael Kreyling, "Life with People: Virginia Woolf, Eudora Welty and *The Optimist's Daughter.*" *Southern Review,* n.s. 13 (April 1977), 250–271.

John Markham, "The Very Limited Edition of *The Optimist's Daughter.*" *Eudora Welty Newsletter,* 1 (Winter 1977), 2.

Peggy Whitman Prenshaw, *An Introduction to Eudora Welty's THE*

OPTIMIST'S DAUGHTER. Jackson: Mississippi Library Commission, 1977.

John F. Desmond, "Pattern and Vision in *The Optimist's Daughter.*" In *A Still Moment: Essays on the Art of Eudora Welty,* ed. John F. Desmond. Metuchen, NJ, and London: The Scarecrow Press, 1978, pp. 118–138.

William McMillen, "Circling-In: The Concept of Home in Eudora Welty's *Losing Battles* and *The Optimist's Daughter.*" In *A Still Moment: Essays on the Art of Eudora Welty,* ed. John F. Desmond. Metuchen, NJ, and London: The Scarecrow Press, 1978, pp. 110–117.

Noel Polk, "Page Proofs of *The Optimist's Daughter.*" *Eudora Welty Newsletter,* 2 (Winter 1978), 6.

Margaret Jones Bolsterli, "Woman's Vision: The Worlds of Women in *Delta Wedding, Losing Battles* and *The Optimist's Daughter.*" In *Eudora Welty: Critical Essays,* ed. Peggy Whitman Prenshaw. Jackson: University Press of Mississippi, 1979, pp. 149–156.

Jane L. Hinton, "The Role of Family in *Delta Wedding, Losing Battles* and *The Optimist's Daughter.*" In *Eudora Welty: Critical Essays,* ed. Peggy Whitman Prenshaw. Jackson: University Press of Mississippi, 1979, pp. 120–131.

Thomas Daniel Young, "Social Form and Social Order: An Examination of *The Optimist's Daughter.*" In *Eudora Welty: Critical Essays,* ed. Peggy Whitman Prenshaw. Jackson: University Press of Mississippi, 1979, pp. 367–385; rpt. in his *The Past in the Present: A Thematic Study of Modern Southern Literature.* Baton Rouge: Louisiana State University Press, 1981, pp. 87–115.

Robert L. Phillips, "Patterns of Vision in Welty's *The Optimist's Daughter.*" *Southern Literary Journal,* 14 (Fall 1981), 10–23.

Noel Polk, "The Franklin Library Text of *The Optimist's Daughter.*" *Eudora Welty Newsletter,* 5 (Winter 1981), 3–6.

Marilyn Arnold, "Images of Memory in Eudora Welty's *The Optimist's Daughter.*" *Southern Literary Journal,* 14 (Spring 1982), 28–38.

Jasbir Chaudhary, "Patterns of Love and Isolation: Eudora Welty's *The Optimist's Daughter.*" *Panjab University Research Bulletin (Arts),* 2 (13 October 1982), 65–72. [Cited in *MLA, 1982.*]

Patricia Elder Dean, "Eudora Welty's Onomastic Art." In *Places, Pets and Charactonyms,* ed. Laurence E. Seits and Jean Divine. Sugar Grove, IL: Waubonsee Community College, 1982, pp. 90–96. [Papers of North Central Names Institute 3. Cited in *MLA,* 1982.]

Donna E. Landry, "Genre and Revision: The Example of Welty's

The Optimist's Daughter." *Postscript*, 1 (1983), 90–98. [Cited in *MLA*, 1985.]

Danièle Pitavy-Souques, "Le Sud: territoire des femmes?" *Revue Française d'Études Américaines*, 10 (Février 1985), 25–50.

Naoka Fuwa Thornton, "Medusa-Perseus Symbolism in Eudora Welty's *The Optimist's Daughter.*" *Southern Quarterly*, 23 (Summer 1985), 64–76.

Floyd C. Watkins, "The Journey to Baltimore in *The Optimist's Daughter.*" *Mississippi Quarterly*, 38 (Fall 1985), 435–439.

Bev Byrne, "A Return to the Source: *The Robber Bridegroom* and *The Optimist's Daughter.*" *Southern Quarterly*, 24 (Spring 1986), 74–85.

Helen H. Tiegreen, "Mothers, Daughters, and One Writer's Revisions." *Mississippi Quarterly*, 39 (Fall 1986), [605]–626; rpt. this collection.

11. *The Eye of the Story*

General

Carole Cook, "Critic, Friend, and Teacher." *Saturday Review*, 29 April 1978, pp. 37–38. [Review of *The Eye of the Story.*]

Victoria Glendinning, "Eudora Welty in Type and Person." *New York Times Book Review*, 7 May 1978, pp. 7, 43. [Review of *The Eye of the Story.*]

W. U. McDonald, Jr., "*The Eye of the Story:* Bibliographic Notes on the Contents." *Eudora Welty Newsletter*, 2 (Summer 1978), 1–5.

"Pageant of Birds"

Jeanne Rolfe Nostrandt, "Eudora Welty and the Children's Hour." *Mississippi Quarterly*, 29 (Winter 1975–76), 109–118.

W. U. McDonald, Jr., "Eudora Welty's Revisions of 'Pageant of Birds.'" *Notes on Mississippi Writers*, 10 (Spring 1977), 1–10.

"The Little Store"

Carol S. Manning, "Little Girls and Sidewalks: Glasgow and Welty on Childhood's Promise." *Southern Quarterly*, 21 (Spring 1983), 67–76.

12. *The Collected Stories*

General

Paul Gray, "Life With a Touch of the Comic." *Time*, 116 (3 November 1980), 110. [Review of *The Collected Stories.*]

Maureen Howard, "A Collection of Discoveries." *New York Times*

Book Review, 2 November 1980, pp. 1, 31–32. [Review of *The Collected Stories*.]

Reynolds Price, "The Collected Stories of Eudora Welty." *New Republic*, 183 (1 November 1980), 31–34. [Review of *The Collected Stories*.]

Robert Towers, "Mississippi Myths." *New York Times Book Review*, 4 December 1980, pp. 30–32. [Review of *The Collected Stories*.]

Jennifer Uglow, "Journeys out of Separateness." *Times Literary Supplement*, 110 (8 January 1982), 26. [Review of *The Collected Stories*.]

Robert Drake, "The Loving Vision." *Modern Age: A Quarterly Review*, 27 (Winter 1983), 96–98. [Review of *The Collected Stories*.]

O. B. Emerson, "Reviews of *The Collected Stories:* A Preliminary Checklist." *Eudora Welty Newsletter*, 7 (Winter 1983), 4–6.

W. U. McDonald, Jr., "A Checklist of Revisions in Collected Welty Stories: Phase I." *Eudora Welty Newsletter*, 7 (Winter 1983), 6–10.

————, *The Short Stories of Eudora Welty: The Evolution of Printed Texts*. Toledo: William S. Carlson Library, 1983. [Catalogue of an exhibit at the Ward M. Canaday Center of Carlson Library, University of Toledo, March–April 1983.

"The Demonstrators"

Ann Romines, "The Power of the Lamp: Domestic Ritual in Two Stories by Eudora Welty." *Notes on Mississippi Writers*, 12 (Summer 1979), 1–16.

13. *One Writer's Beginnings*

Mary Hughes Brookhart, "Reviews of *One Writer's Beginnings:* A Preliminary Checklist." *Eudora Welty Newsletter*, 8 (Summer 1984), 1–4.

George Core, "Poetically the Most Accurate Woman Alive." *Southern Review*, n.s. 20 (Autumn 1984), 951–957. [Review of *One Writer's Beginnings* and Delvin's *Eudora Welty's Chronicle*.]

Eric Hornberger, "Delta Details." *Times Literary Supplement*, 242 (20 July 1984), 806. [Review of *One Writer's Beginnings*.]

Danièle Pitavy-Souques, "Le Sud: territoire des femmes?" *Revue Française d'Études Américaines*, 10 (Février 1985), 25–50.

Lee Smith, "Eudora Welty's Beginnings." *Southern Literary Journal*, 17 (Spring 1985), 120–126. [Review of *One Writer's Beginnings*.]

Michael Kreyling, "Subject and Object in *One Writer's Beginnings*." *Mississippi Quarterly*, 39 (Fall 1986), [627]–638; rpt. this collection.

Peggy Whitman Prenshaw, "The Antiphonies of Eudora Welty's *One Writer's Beginnings* and Elizabeth Bowen's *Pictures and Conversations*." *Mississippi Quarterly*, 39 (Fall 1986), [639]–650; rpt. this collection.

14. Uncollected Monographs and Sketches

Acrobats in a Park

Kenneth Graham, "ACROBATS IN A PARK: Performance and Catastrophe." *Delta*, No. 5 (November 1977), 13–18.

Jan Nordby Gretlund, " 'Remember How It Was with the Acrobats.' " *South Carolina Review*, 11 (November 1978), 22–25.

"A Sketching Trip"

W. U. McDonald, Jr., " 'A Sketching Trip' in America and England [Part I]." *Eudora Welty Newsletter*, 8 (Winter 1984), 3–8.

———, " 'A Sketching Trip' in America and England [Conclusion]." *Eudora Welty Newsletter*, 8 (Summer 1984), 4–7.

E. Dissertations

Charles William Hembree, "Narrative Technique in the Fiction of Eudora Welty." University of Oklahoma, 1974, 389 pp. *DAI*, 35A (March 1975), 6139A–6140A.

Jane Lee Hinton, " 'Out of All Times of Trouble': The Family in the Fiction of Eudora Welty." Vanderbilt, 1974. 331 pp. *DAI*, 35A (June 1975), 7906A.

Phillip Allen Tapley, "The Portrayal of Women in Selected Short Stories by Eudora Welty." Louisiana State University and Agricultural and Mechanical College, 1974. 497 pp. *DAI*, 35A (February 1975), 5429A–5430A.

St. George Tucker Arnold, Jr., "Consciousness and the Unconscious in the Fiction of Eudora Welty." Stanford, 1975. 287 pp. *DAI*, 36A (March 1976), 6094A.

Carol Manning Fullwinder, "Eudora Welty's Fiction: Its Unconventional Relationship to the Southern Literary Tradition." SUNY at Albany, 1975. 331 pp. *DAI*, 36A (May 1976), 7420A–7421A.

Ruby P. Herlong, "A Study of Human Relationships in the Novels of Eudora Welty." University of South Carolina, 1975. 201 pp. *DAI*, 36A (May 1976), 7422A.

Michael P. Kreyling, "The Novels of Eudora Welty." Cornell, 1975. 240 pp. *DAI*, 36A (April 1976), 6685A.

Charles C. Nash, "The Theme of Human Isolation in the Works of Eudora Welty." University of Minnesota, 1975. 190 pp. *DAI*, 37A (July 1976), 314A–315A.

Jeanne R. Nostrandt, "Survival by Endurance: A Motif in the Short Fiction of Eudora Welty." University of North Carolina (Chapel Hill), 1975. 218 pp. *DAI*, 37A (September 1976), 1551A.

Bessie Chronaki, "Breaking the 'Quondam Obstruction': Place as an Aspect of Meaning in the Work of Eudora Welty." Duke, 1976. 361 pp. *DAI*, 37A (January 1977), 4351A.

Jerry L. Harris, "Eudora Welty: the Achieved Worlds of her Early Stories." Ohio University, 1976. 448 pp. *DAI*, 37A. (February 1977), 5122A.

Ellen McNutt Millsaps, "The Family in Four Novels of Eudora Welty." University of Tennessee, 1976. 180 pp. *DAI*, 37A (August 1976), 951A.

Margarette J. Sather, "Man in the Universe: the Cosmic View of Eudora Welty." University of Louisville, 1976. 266 pp. *DAI*, 37A (February 1977), 5127A.

Kathleen Callaway, "In Her Time, In Her Place: Caste and Class in the Fiction of Eudora Welty." University of Virginia, 1977. 281 pp. *DAI*, 39A (January 1979), 4253A–4254A.

Arline Garbarini, "'The Feast Itself': A Study of Narrative Technique in the Fiction of Eudora Welty." St. John's University, 1977. 259 pp. *DAI*, 38A (July 1977), 261A–262A.

Suzanne Story Karem, "Mythology in the Works of Eudora Welty." University of Kentucky, 1977. 181 pp. *DAI*, 39A (December 1978), 3581A.

Marcia Phillips McGowan, "Patterns of Female Experience in Eudora Welty's Fiction." Rutgers, 1977. 274 pp. *DAI*, 38A (August 1977), 788A.

Bernard Feld, "The Short Fiction of Eudora Welty." Columbia University, 1978. 251 pp. *DAI*, 39 (July 1978), 278A.

Allison Deming Goeller, "The Pastorals of Eudora Welty." Temple University, 1978. 153 pp. *DAI*, 39A (October 1978), 2272A.

Carol Lefever Turner, "Eudora Welty's Short Fiction: A Survey of Structural and Narrative Techniques." Georgia State University, 1978. 258 pp. *DAI*, 39A (February 1979), 4942A.

Rachel Victoria Weiner, "Reflections of the Artist in Eudora Welty's Fiction." University of North Carolina (Chapel Hill), 1978. 104 pp. *DAI*, 40A (July 1979), 253A.

Elizabeth Rose Lemieux, "Sexual Symbolism in the Short Stories of Eudora Welty." SUNY at Binghamton, 1979. 281 pp. *DAI*, 40A (February 1980), 4597A–4598A.

Jennifer Lynn Randisi, "Eudora Welty's Southern Romances: The Novels of Eudora Welty Viewed Within the Southern Romance Tradition." SUNY at Stony Brook, 1979. 276 pp. *DAI*, 40A (May 1980), 5867A.

Juanita Browning Laing, "The Southern Tradition in the Fiction of Eudora Welty." University of Kansas, 1980. 232 pp. *DAI*, 41A (November 1980), 2111A.

Phillip Lamar Owens, "Time in the Novels of Eudora Welty." University of North Carolina (Greensboro), 1980. 232 pp. *DAI*, 41A (October 1980), 1598A–1599A.

Mary Hughes Brookhart, "The Search for Lost Time in the Early Fiction of Eudora Welty." University of North Carolina (Chapel Hill), 1981. 242 pp. *DAI*, 42A (December 1981), 2667A–2668A.

Frances Beck Foreman, "Women's Choices: A Study of the Feminine Characters in the Novels of Eudora Welty." University of South Florida, 1981. 231 pp. *DAI*, 42A (October 1981), 1634A.

Dianne Cothran, "Myth and Eudora Welty's Mississippi: An Analysis of *The Golden Apples*." Florida State University, 1982. 134 pp. *DAI*, 46A (Nos. 1–2, 1985), 151A.

Anne Carman, "Eudora Welty's Aesthetic Principle: The Mind of the Artist." University of Missouri (Columbia), 1983. 190 pp. *DAI*, 45A (July 1984), 179A.

Mary Alice Fisher, "Eudora Welty's Oral Chorus." University of Nebraska-Lincoln, 1983. 115 pp. *DAI*, 44A (February 1984), 2472A.

Harriet Pollack, "Words Between Strangers: Reading Eudora Welty's Fiction." University of Virginia, 1983. 279 pp. *DAI*, 45A (Nos. 9–10, 1985), 3132A.

Sally Wolff, "Love in the Art of Eudora Welty." Emory University, 1983. 167 pp. *DAI*, 44A (November 1983), 1457A.

Contributors

Mary Hughes Brookhart is an assistant professor at North Carolina A & T State University. She is working on a study of artist figures in the fiction of selected Afro-American women writers.

ALBERT J. DEVLIN is a professor of English at the University of Missouri-Columbia. His publications include *Eudora Welty's Chronicle: A Story of Mississippi Life*, *Conversations with Tennessee Williams*, and essays on Faulkner, Welty, and D. H. Lawrence. He served as guest editor for the special Welty number of the *Mississippi Quarterly* (Fall 1986).

DOROTHY G. GRIFFIN is doing post-doctoral work at Georgia State University in Atlanta. Work-in-progress includes articles on William Henry Drayton and John Fowles.

MICHAEL KREYLING is a professor of English at Vanderbilt University. He is the author of *Eudora Welty's Achievement of Order*, *Figures of the Hero in Southern Narrative*, and several articles on Southern literature. He is at work on a study of Diarmuid Russell, Welty's friend and literary agent.

SUZANNE MARRS, an associate professor of English at the State University of New York-Oswego, has published most recently on Welty's fiction in *The Southern Review* and the *Southern Literary Journal*. She was Welty Scholar-in-Residence at the Mississippi Department of Archives and History during the 1985–86 academic year.

PEARL AMELIA MCHANEY is a doctoral candidate at Georgia

State University in Atlanta. She has published textual studies of three stories from *The Wide Net*, and is currently responsible for compiling the annual checklist of Welty scholarship for the *Eudora Welty Newsletter.*

DANIÈLE PITAVY-SOUQUES teaches at the University of Dijon, France. She has published on Southern American and Canadian writers, and is preparing books on Eudora Welty and Southern women writers.

NOEL POLK, a professor of English at the University of Southern Mississippi, has written and edited critical and bibliographical studies of Faulkner and Welty.

HELEN POLLACK is an assistant professor at Sweet Briar College in Virginia.

PEGGY WHITMAN PRENSHAW is a professor of English and dean of the Honors College at the University of Southern Mississippi. She has recently published *Elizabeth Spencer* for Twayne.

HELEN HURT TIEGREEN is a doctoral candidate at the University of Southern Mississippi. Her dissertation on Eudora Welty is in progress.

RUTH M. VANDE KIEFT is a professor of English at Queens College in New York City. She has recently published a revised second edition of *Eudora Welty* for Twayne.

LOUISE WESTLING teaches in the English department at the University of Oregon. She is the author of *Sacred Groves and Ravaged Gardens*, a study of the fiction of Welty, McCullers, and O'Connor. At present she is editing the oral autobiography of Sarah Webb Rice, a black contemporary of Eudora Welty.

PATRICIA S. YAEGER is an assistant professor of English and Head Tutor of the History and Literature Concentration at Harvard University. She has published essays on Coleridge, Derrida, Lacan, and Welty, and is the author of *Honey-Mad Women: Emancipatory Strategies in Women's Writing.*

Index